LONGMAN LINGUISTICS LIBRARY
Title no 27

SPOKEN DISCOURSE
A MODEL FOR ANALYSIS

LONGMAN LINGUISTICS LIBRARY

General editors
R. H. Robins, University of London
G. N. Leech, University of Lancaster

Spoken Discourse

A model for analysis

Willis Edmondson

LONGMAN
LONDON AND NEW YORK

Longman Group Limited
Longman House
Burnt Mill, Harlow, Essex, UK

*Published in the United States of America
by Longman Inc., New York*

© Longman Group Limited 1981

First published 1981

ISBN 0 582 29120 8 Cased
ISBN 0 582 29121 6 Paper

British Library Cataloguing in Publication Data

Edmondson, Willis
  Spoken discourse. – (Longman linguistics
  library; no. 27).
  1. Discourse analysis   2. Speech
  I. Title
  415   P302   80–41190

Printed in Singapore by
Huntsmen Offset Printing Pte Ltd

To my father
James Willis Edmondson

Contents

Foreword

This book is essentially identical in content to my Dr Phil dissertation, which was submitted to the Faculty for Philology of the Ruhr-Universität Bochum in the summer of 1979. I wish to thank Hans-Jürgen Diller and Jochen Rehbein for their trenchant and helpful comments on that text, and the former more particularly for nursing the writer and his text through what was at times a difficult pregnancy. I am also grateful for some solid criticisms from an anonymous reviewer. I have, however, restricted myself to minor changes in revising the manuscript originally submitted.

I am myself a person who cannot easily commit ideas to paper without first having discovered them in the process of talk: for tolerating, and indeed (initially!) encouraging such talk I am especially grateful to my colleagues Juliane House, Gabi Kasper, John McKeown and Brigitte Stemmer.

There must be a sense in which an attempt to provide an explicit model for the analysis of spoken discourse at this point in time is premature. It has seemed to me, however, to be an attempt worth making, whatever its shortcomings, for which I of course remain accountable.

Bochum, February 1981   WJE

We are indebted to the following for permission to reproduce copyright material:
Linguistic Society of America for extracts from the article by Sacks, Schegloff and Jefferson in *Language*, 50, 1974.

Introduction

Dissatisfaction with early versions of transformational-generative grammar has led to attempts to incorporate into such grammars aspects of language use.[1] However the insights gained into the nature of language through transformational theory were explicitly based on a distinction between language-system and language-use, such that attempts inside such a theory to bridge this distinction necessarily lead to a confusion of levels and categories of analysis.[2] The analysis of conversation is still in its infancy, and the main stimuli to the considerable amount of current research into discourse analysis in general, and the analysis of multi-source spoken discourse in particular have come from outside linguistics, specifically from language philosophers and sociologists interested in conversational behaviour. In arguing towards the model for the analysis of spoken discourse to be presented here, I shall attempt to relate these different approaches (philosophical, sociological) both to each other, and to the position adopted in this study.

The first brief chapter is preliminary, and introduces some basic terms and distinctions. The second chapter addresses the question as to how far textgrammars as currently conceived and expounded provide an analytic framework for the analysis of spoken discourse, and begins to explore the relationship between spoken and written discourse. In Chapter 3 the sense in which that which is done when something is said may be termed an illocutionary act is discussed, as is the relationship between the 'saying' and the 'doing'. The fourth chapter reviews some aspects of the social, interactional significance of language use, and discusses the work of the ethnomethodologists on the analysis of conversation. The position is then adopted that in spoken discourse a significant conversational unit – let us say an utterance – is *both* 'illocutionary' and 'interactional' in its significance, and that we therefore require a model in which the approaches evidenced in Chapters 3 and 4 are combined and reconciled. In Chapter 5 several familiar approaches to the analysis of discourse are reviewed in the light of this position, and found deficient. The model presented in Chapter 6 is an attempt to remedy these deficiencies, and the degree to which it may be said to do so is discussed in the seventh and final chapter.

Insofar as the analyses developed in Chapter 6 concentrate on the use of *language* in conversation, the study may be deemed linguistic in its orientation. Further, as in an investigation of conversational behaviour it is clearly necessary to view language in relation to its 'origins, uses, and effects' (Morris 1964, *p* 64), this study is 'pragmatic' in its linguistic orientation. I shall therefore pay only passing attention to the syntax of English in what follows, and while I shall attempt to distinguish sharply between semantic and pragmatic issues, I shall not present a semantic theory, nor shall I discuss alternative theories. An approach to the analysis of spoken discourse which claims to be linguistic makes an implicit claim about the nature of language. The model presented in this book may be interpreted as claiming that language is a means of doing things with words with people. I would suggest that beneath the slickness of such a phrase lies a powerful description. It is my purpose to substantiate this suggestion.

Notes

1 Relevant instances are for example Ross 1970, 1975; Sadock 1974; Katz 1977. Developments inside generative grammar which reflect a concern to extend existing theories in order to embrace pragmatic aspects of language use are documented in the Introduction to Bever, Katz and Langendoen 1976 (*pp* 1–9).

2 For a review of Sadock 1974 and of Cole and Morgan 1975 which establishes the point being made here, see Leech 1977b. *Cf* also Kempson 1973, in which the need to distinguish the entailments of a sentence (a semantic issue) from the presuppositions of a speaker using that sentence (a pragmatic issue) is ably argued. For a discussion of Katz 1977, see Edmondson 1979c.

Chapter 1:

Some preliminaries

1.1 Some terms and distinctions

I shall assume it is necessary and valid to distinguish between semantic and pragmatic meaning, and shall be at pains to sharpen this distinction in critical instances, particularly in the case of the overt performative utterance (see 3.1 following). Semantic meaning will be referred to as the LOGICAL SENSE of an utterance, determined crudely by the content of the proposition expressed in that utterance, and by its LOCUTIONARY FORCE derived from the grammatical mood of the sentence used in that utterance (the notion of locutionary force is expanded in 3.2 below).

A useful starting-point for getting at the sense in which the term DISCOURSE will be used is Widdowson's phrase 'the use of sentences in combination' (Widdowson 1973, *pp* 66 et seq.). Widdowson contrasts the 'discourse' approach, which concentrates on the 'use of sentences' (and illustrated for him in the work of Labov), with the 'textual' approach, concentrating on 'sentences in combination' (and illustrated by the work of Zellig Harris). I shall follow this distinction, but we may develop Widdowson's opposition between 'the use of sentences' and 'sentences in combination', in which a feature {±} use is the distinguishing factor, by considering also the distinction between a 'sentence' as a highest significant linguistic unit as opposed to some suprasentential unit ('sentences in combination') as a second distinguishing feature. If we characterise these two binary distinctions as {±} suprasentential and {±} use, we may set up the following simplistic matrix:

[− suprasentential],   [− use]= the sentence
[+ suprasentential],   [− use]= the text
[− suprasentential],   [+ use]= the utterance
[+ suprasentential],   [+ use]= the discourse

Despite the gross over-simplification involved, these distinctions will be taken to match differences between sentence grammars, textlinguistics, speech act theory, and discourse analysis respectively. Two qualifications are immediately necessary. Firstly, in speech act theory (and we shall be largely interested in Austin and Searle here), the perlocutionary act clearly extends the notion of the significance of the utterance beyond itself towards its consequences or effects. However, this means that the perlocutionary act is not part of the speech act in the way that the locutionary and illocutionary acts may be said to be. It is also noticeable how relatively little attention the notion of the perlocution has received since Austin introduced the term, relative to the notion of the illocution. The claimed equivalence above is then more strictly between the utterance and the *illocutionary* act. Secondly, it may with justification be claimed that textlinguistics was and is centrally concerned with the functional use of stretches of language.[1] Hence 'text' is simply an alternative term to 'discourse' (and indeed the two terms are often used interchangeably). However, it has to be remembered that the terms 'utterance' and 'sentence' are often used interchangeably also: this is not a reason for ignoring the distinction, but rather a reason for insisting upon it.

I propose to retain the text-discourse distinction, and shall argue that there is a 'textual' as opposed to a 'discourse' orientation in much of the work known as Textlinguistics, and associated with names such as Dressler, Rieser, Petöfi, and van Dijk (see Ch. 2). A TEXT is a structured sequence of linguistic expressions forming a unitary whole, and a DISCOURSE a structured event manifest in linguistic (and other) behaviour. There is no absolute opposition here; at issue are two different approaches to the analysis of suprasentential stretches of language. To some extent the position adopted here matches that of Sandulescu 1976. Sandulescu sees the text-discourse distinction as marking two different trends in current research which he characterises in terms of the following oppositions:

Textlinguistik	v.	Discourse Analysis
(*eg* Bielefeld	v.	Birmingham)
model-centred	v.	data-centred
theoretical	v.	descriptive

type data	v.	token data
competence data	v.	performance data
written language	v.	spoken language

We may observe here the concentration on the empirical differences noted – the *status* of data in the research, and the *type* of data considered relevant to that research.[2]

COHESION will be used to indicate those devices by means of which TEXTURE is evidenced in a suprasentential stretch of language (*cf* Halliday & Hasan 1976, *p* 2). Texture is taken to be the sum of those features of a text, *distinct from its structure*, which make it a text and not a random sequence of sentences. Thus we take the following two sequences to exhibit the same texture – *ie* the same devices of cohesion – but clearly their *structure* is different, specifically as regards the 'tie' between what the first speaker says, and what the second says:

[1.1] (i)   – John's a good bloke. Is he coming tomorrow?
        – Yes
(ii)   – John's a good bloke. He's coming tomorrow
        – Yes

Concerning the structure of a text or discourse, I shall with Widdowson (1973) use the term COHERENCE to refer to a 'well-formed' text or discourse, and this will be equated with its interpretability (see 2.1 below). Cohesion is, however, neither a necessary nor a sufficient condition for coherence. In terms of the structure of a suprasentential stretch of language, it is necessary to distinguish between 'thematic', 'semantic', or 'textual' structure and 'discourse' or 'interactional' structure.[3] This reflects the distinction between textual coherence and discourse coherence. However as the terms 'text' and discourse' should not be seen as mutually exclusive, it follows that a discourse has both a 'textual' and a 'discourse' coherence or structure. I shall wish to claim that the former is a reflection of the latter, *ie* that it is interactional structure which gives coherence to a text or discourse, and that thematic or semantic structure or coherence is a reflection of this (see 7.2). It is necessary here to distinguish two senses in which a written stretch of language may be viewed as a discourse as opposed to a text. Crudely, these two senses reflect the encoding and decoding processes respectively. The claim is simply that in producing a written text an author anticipates at each relevant point the response of his intended reader, and structures the written discourse following this anticipatory process. Then in the reading process, a reader in interpreting the written discourse both seeks to put himself into the role of the idealised or intended reader the writer was writing for, and at the same time reacts to that written discourse in the light of his own beliefs, state of knowledge, and so on. In terms of the interactional structure of a written text, it is the first ('encoding') sense that is meant here.

'CONVERSATION' is used loosely and non-technically to refer to any interactional stretch of talk involving at least two participants, and taking place in a non-formalised setting, such that no special rules or conventions may be said to operate. Thus a debate in the House of Commons is scarcely a conversation, while an interview conducted on television may approximate to conversation if interviewer and interviewee 'relax' so far as to forget their respective roles in front of the cameras. The interview may certainly be followed by conversation between the interview participants, and on substantially the same topic(s): it is the setting which will have changed. Conversation is then a particular type of multiple-source spoken discourse. In fact in this study we shall be almost exclusively concerned with two-party face-to-face conversations.

In seeking to identify units of spoken discourse, and in discussing conversational behaviour as a type of interaction, I shall have recourse to the terms INTERACTIONAL ACT, INTERACTIONAL MOVE, and speaking TURN, or turn at talk. As the first two terms can be defined adequately only inside the discourse analytic model presented in Chapter 6, the intended sense can only be suggested here. An interactional act is the smallest identifiable unit of conversational behaviour, but does not necessarily further the conversation in which it occurs in terms of approaching a conversational goal. For example, a nod of the head, or an utterance of the form 'hum', 'I see', or suchlike, if occurring during a narrative by an interlocutor, and if occurring alone – ie not preceded or followed by contiguous utterances by the same speaker – would be an interactional act, but not an interactional move. An interactional MOVE is the smallest significant element by means of which a conversation is developed. For example, if I ask you 'Is it five o'clock yet?', and you nod your head, your doing so will constitute an interactional move, just as will my 'question'. If, instead of nodding your head, you say 'Yes, I think so, it must be five o'clock by now', this also constitutes one interactional move, though one might well wish to claim that more than one utterance has been made. On the other hand if you reply by saying 'Yes, why?' two[4] moves have been made inside one turn at talk, in that you have both 'answered' my 'question', and posed one of your own. (*Cf* Goffman 1976, *pp* 270–2; Sinclair and Coulthard 1975, *pp* 19–24).

TURN will be used to refer to both the opportunity to assume the role of speaker at a particular point of time in a conversation, and to what is said or done during the time for which the speaker role is continuously held by one individual. (It may be possible to think of cases in which two or more individuals might share the same turn, but such issues will be ignored here.) A turn and an interactional act or move are not necessarily coextensive.

I shall also make use of the terms 'face', 'face-saving', and 'face-work' in the sense of Goffman, assuming that much of what goes on in conversational behaviour is so organised as to allow the preservation of face on both sides:

> 'The term *face* may be defined as the positive social value a person effectively claims for himself by the line others assume he has taken during a particular contact. Face is an image of self delineated in terms of approved social attributes'.... 'By *face-work* I mean to designate the actions taken by a person to make whatever he is doing consistent with face' (Goffman 1955, *pp* 319, 324 in Laver and Hutcheson 1972).[5]

Finally, I propose a distinction between conversational rules and conversational strategies, between that which conversationalists may be said to 'know' and that which they actually do, between their COMMUNICATIVE competence and their SOCIAL competence.[6] For it is a matter of common experience that proficiency in face-work is something one learns, and that different people differ markedly in the degree to which they can 'handle' other people. In other words social competence is a variable for any group of individual members. Communicative competence is a theoretical construct, and may be described in sets of rules or conventions which may be said to express what one can do in a conversation. This competence underpins all language use by native-speakers of a language. It is not necessarily the case however that every native-speaker is able in his own conversational behaviour to act in a way consistent with those rules we may term communicative for the language community of which he is a member. (See here Hymes 1971 on 'sociolinguistic interference' and 'cultural deprivation'). Social competence on the other hand is reflected in the use to which an individual puts his communicative competence in his conversational behaviour to achieve goals without endangering face – i.e. without offending socially-accepted notions of what is and what is not acceptable behaviour.[7] One can choose not to reply to a greeting, and in doing so, in a European culture at least, one is thereby choosing not to comply with a norm of expectancy, and thereby acting in accord with rules of conversation in that one expects the source of the greeting – one's addresser – to 'get the point', and register that one is angry with him, unwilling to be disturbed, or whatever. However, it could be pointed out that the person so behaving was not showing a great deal of social 'charm', 'tact', or 'sensitivity' – his social competence we might wish to say seems to be somewhat deficient, *as shown by the use to which his communicative competence has been put*. Again, reacting in an interpretable way to an instance of the left-hand part of a tied pair, say a 'Request', is something one cannot help doing as a mature, non-mentally disturbed, and physically unimpaired speaker of the language. However *how* one reacts, and for example in the case of reacting by refusing the request, how one does so without endangering one's own or one's interlocutor's face is another matter – to bring this off is to evidence particular social skills. The notion of face is pervasive, as our social competence is constantly being put to the test in everyday communication. When we refer to 'not knowing what to say', 'saying the wrong thing', or 'being put in an awkward situation' the implicit evaluations are social ones: the 'wrong thing' to say may well be perfectly 'right' on any measure one might wish to invoke concerning linguistic or communicative competence.

Some of these terms and distinctions, as has been said, are explored in much greater (and one hopes more adequate) detail in what follows. For a fuller treatment of the notions of locutionary and illocutionary force, see 3.2 following. Interactional acts and moves are defined inside a model in 6.1.1 and 6.1.2 below. The relationship between communicative and social competence underpins the relationship between what is expounded in 6.1 and 6.3 and what is expounded in 6.2 and 6.4. For a summary, see *pp* 114–15. Further technical terms will be introduced and defined in situ as necessary.

1.2 Some graphic conventions

Inevitably in the course of this study different types of data will be brought forward. Different presentation procedures will be followed as convenient. Data segments presented in a separate paragraph or unit in the text will be numbered sequentially throughout a chapter, the chapter number preceding the number assigned to the data. Thus the first piece of data cited in Chapter 4 will be designated [4.1]. Data incorporated in the text, and thus not accorded a new line or paragraph will not be so enumerated. Sentences or linguistic items extracted therefrom will be in italic: utterances or extracts therefrom will be enclosed in single inverted commas. Lexical items will be given in small capitals. A proposition may be given in Quine's corners to distinguish it from a sentence or utterance expressing that proposition. Whenever conversational data is presented which is fabricated, this will be indicated.

Further graphic conventions will be adopted as necessary. Where technical terms are borrowed from the literature for discussion purpose, they will be given in single inverted commas, unless the term is adopted for my purpose with an essentially similar or indeed identical sense. Where a technical term is identical to an everyday lexical item, it will be given initial capitalisation if misunderstanding seems possible. The problems here are particularly acute when discussing illocutions. It will be necessary for example to distinguish between the lexical item PROPOSE, 'propose' as occurring in an utterance, an illocutionary act of 'Proposing' discussed in the literature, and a category of illocution – the Propose – which I may choose to define for my own purposes. Such nonce conventions will be explicated in situ as they are adopted.

Some graphic conventions will nonetheless be multifunctional. Italics will be used as is usual to represent primary stress in the spoken language – ie to add emphasis, and capitals will be used at times to draw attention to technical terms as they are introduced.

The model for the analysis of conversational behaviour presented in Chapter 6 is based on empirical data. The data source is outlined at the beginning of Chapter 6, where the elicitation procedure employed is also discussed. At times conversational data from this corpus is cited in preceding chapters, and it is therefore appropriate to give here the transcription conventions followed: these conventions will also where relevant be used in giving other instances of conversational talk. Intonational features will be given throughout following the broad transcription given below. The relevant conventions are as follows:[8]

(i)   Where recognisable 'words' are uttered, the conventional spelling of the uttered items is followed, regardless of the pronunciation. A phonetic transcript is avoided where possible, even with word segments.

(ii) A certain degree of licence is taken in transcribing various noises conventionally transcribed as *uhm*, *uh*, *oh*, *ah*, *mm*, and so on. Occasionally (noise) appears in the transcriptions, in which case something that might have been transcribed as one of the above is denoted.

(iii) Non-verbal activities deemed of potential significance to the conversational structure and/or the interpretation of the trΛnscribed locutions – in the case of exophoric reference, for example – are described in everyday terms, the descriptions appearing within round brackets. Problems of sequencing in time are dealt with in the tense reference of the given description.

(iv) Intonation is marked selectively only, using the following broad transcription:

   ` fall
   ´ rise
   ᵛ fall-rise
   ˆ rise-fall

– primary stress will be indicated by underscoring the relevant syllable

Pauses, which are here treated non-technically as observable discontinuations in the flow of speech, are marked thus: ₍ , the number of repetitions signifying increasing duration. A noticeable silence which would require an inordinate number of the above arrow-heads is noted as non-verbal behaviour.

(v) When more than one speaker is speaking, the utterance segments which overlap – *ie* occur within the same time-span – are enclosed within one pair of square brackets, as follows:

Y: ... we'll just have to ₍ just have to see ₍ if you could let me know though [if ₍ if you
X: yes allright] I'll give you a ring early in the mo[rning
Y: yes if] you can find someone

                                                    (1B22.5)

Note that the new speaker-new line convention which is followed, coupled with the above, can give the visual illusion of discontinuity in the case that an interspersed utterance is completely masked:

Y: allright ₍ I'll just go and get your [tea then
X: okay]
Y: and I'll come back ...

                                                    (2A23.6)

There is no discontinuity between the end of line 1 and the beginning of line 3 here: one turn at speech is taken by Y in this brief extract, not two.

Notes

1 Witness Peter Hartmann (1971, p 17): 'Texte sind ja nicht Repräsentationen des Sprachsystems, sondern der Verwendung von Sprachsystem' ...*Cf eg* Kallmeyer et al 1974, p 45; Breuer 1974, p 25.

2 Kallmeyer and Schütze (1976, p 4) see the distinctiveness of American ethnolinguists' and sociologists' work with the analysis of discourse *(Konversations-analyse)* as lying not only in the nature of the data used, but also in that they are concerned 'nicht nur mit formalen Strukturen, sondern auch mit den Aktivitäten der beteiligten Interaktionspartner und den Prozessen der Bedeutungszuschreibung'.

3 On the analysis of narrative, whereby thematic structure is derived from the linguistic surface texture, see *eg* Hendricks 1973; Doležel 1971; Scheglov & Zholkovskii 1975. For a localist approach to narrative structure see the work of Ikegami (*eg* 1976). On the application of the Prague notion of 'functional sentence perspective' to text structure, see *eg* Daneš 1970a, 1970b; Enkvist 1973, pp 115–17. For an extension of Zellig Harris's (1952) syntactic analytic procedures to the notion of semantic textual structure, see the work of Walter Koch (*eg* 1965, 1971).

4 The assumption here is of course that the utterance 'yes' 'answers' the 'question'. With various different intonations (Brazil 1975, 1978 suggests that 'key' is critical here), the utterance 'yes' might not do this, but signal that the speaker has heard, is considering the question, or otherwise hesitating. In such a case, the utterance 'yes' would not itself constitute an interactional move, but it would be an interactional act. Coming alone at this point in the ongoing conversation, it would not further that interaction towards a possible outcome.

5 'Face' is clearly a term operating on a quite different theoretical level from terms such as 'cohesion' and 'discourse': my purpose here is not to set up categories which are explicitly related to each other, but rather to establish some common terms of reference for future discussion.

6 I cannot claim to be very happy with these terms, as the opposition seems to imply that communication and social behaviour may be distinguished, whereas in fact communicative competence must be part of a general 'social' competence. However the sense in which I use the term 'communicative competence' is closely related to that of Hymes (*eg* 1971, 1972), who distinguishes between 'knowledge' and 'availability for use'. The term is now over-exposed, but this does not seem a sufficient reason for avoiding it. I have made use of the distinction between social and communicative competence in Edmondson 1978b.

7 *Cf* Argyle and Kendon 1967, p 44:
' ... in many encounters, those taking part are aiming at fairly specific outcomes, the achievement of which depends on the participants' success in keeping the encounter going and steering it in appropriate directions. Some people are better at this than others; we say they have greater social competence, or better social skills.'

8 I adopt here a transcription which is adequate for my purposes. There is of course a sense in which any transcription is itself a falsification (See *eg* Sandulescu 1976, p 357; Cicourel 1974, p 60). I adopt the position that the less technical and more immediately comprehensible a transcription, the less its potential falsification. The main features of the conventions adopted here are those used in Leech and Svartvik 1975.

Chapter 2:

Text grammars and discourse analysis

I have proposed distinguishing discourse and text on a $\{\pm\}$ use parameter, and that this distinction shall roughly match that between utterance and sentence. The potential confusion over the two terms 'text' and 'discourse' is increased by the absence in German of a term which is equivalent to 'discourse' as opposed to 'text', given the large amount of work on 'Textlinguistik' which has appeared in German, and indeed in English written by linguists working within a theory whose terms were first developed in the German language.

The purposes of this chapter are two. Firstly, I wish to elaborate the text/discourse distinction made in 1.1 above, and ask how far it may justifiably be seen as reflecting a difference in orientation between work done inside textlinguists, and work done inside discourse analysis. Secondly, I wish to consider how far a textgrammar provides or suggests a framework inside which a model for the analysis of conversational behaviour might be developed.

2.1 Text v. non-text

On what grounds may we distinguish a text from a non-text? Dressler (1972) poses this as the first question for textlinguistics. It is in fact not easy to fabricate 'non-texts', save by using cohesive devices – eg deletion – when no tie can be established, ie the deleted material can nowhere be recovered.[1]

For example when van Dijk (1972, p 40) claims of the 'sequence':

> We will have guests for lunch.
> Calderón was a great Spanish writer.

that it is 'ungrammatical' (unless used and interpreted as an enumeration of sentences), that is, 'any native-speaker of English will consider this sequence, when presented in one utterance, as non-sense', he is seriously wrong. On the contrary, any native-speaker (this generalisation in fact requires all sorts of caveats concerning social and cultural background etc) will immediately see a causal relation between the two assertions,[2] and assume that for example the lunch will be held in memory of Calderón as a mark of respect. Hence, a possible contextualisation such as the following immediately suggests itself:

- Do you know Calderón died exactly 100 years ago today?
- Good heavens! I'd forgotten. The occasion shall not pass unnoticed. We will have guests for lunch. Calderón was a great Spanish writer. I shall invite Professor Wilson and Senor Castellano right away . . .[3]

To take a further instance, in van Dijk 1973, *p* 49, the claim is made that the following is 'ungrammatical':

Peter needs a secretary to type his letters.
She is graduated from the University.

If we improve the grammar of the second sentence somewhat, however, and note that Peter is not exclusively a masculine nomenclature in English (Witness Bertrand Russell's third wife), the sequence is perfectly unremarkable, assuming of course a contextually-given anaphoric or exophoric reference for the pronoun *his* — *eg*

- How's Bertie's manuscript getting on?
- Peter needs a secretary to type his letters. She's a graduate, so it's beneath her dignity to type them herself.[4]

Consider finally the question posed by Dressler in Dressler 1972, (*p* 3). The text reads as follows:

'Warum sind etwa die beiden folgenden Kurzdialoge keine erfolgreichen Texte?

- Wo warst du?
- Irgendwo

- Warum ißt du nicht?
- Du Idiot!'

How we may ask is it possible to have presumably 'successful'[5] short dialogues which when written out do not constitute 'successful' texts? Precisely because the text is coherent as discourse –*ie* the coherence of the text lies not in its texture or thematic structure, but in the interpretability of the behaviour the text represents.

What these three examples suggest is that the crucial issue is not that of distinguishing a 'text' from a 'non-text', but distinguishing between coherent and non-coherent suprasentential stretches of language, and further that the critical issue here is *interpretability as discourse*. Interpretability is a matter of possible contextualisation, and thus the notion of coherence with regard to a text is to be equated with its possible use as a discourse. For, as has often been pointed out,[6] if a hearer or reader has grounds for believing that a stretch of language he is exposed to is coherent, *ie* represents a discourse or a discourse segment, he will go to remarkable lengths to interpret it as such, reading as it were coherence into it. It would be quite wrong to assume however that this is some unusual or extraordinary capacity – we all use these interpretative procedures the whole time.

We may refer then to texts as 'ungrammatical' or 'non-successful' on some criteria other than interpretability as discourse only if we divorce the notion of text and that of discourse. A text then become an artefact, a theoretical construct, having in this respect the same status as a sentence.[7]

2.2 Pragmatics in a theory of text

The fact that a text may be a theoretical construct, deemed to 'underlie' any occurrent instance of language in use, does not necessarily invalidate the potential importance and relevance of textgrammars for a model for the analysis of spoken discourse. The critical issue is what a *text* grammar can provide of relevance to the analysis of discourse that a sentence grammar cannot.

Firstly we should note that the phenomenon of cohesion justifies a distinct level of text if and only if it can be established that cohesion across sentence boundaries is different in kind from cohesion phenomena inside a sentence. Halliday and Hasan however, in the course of the fullest treatment of cohesion in English I am aware of remark that 'cohesive relations have in principle nothing to do with sentence boundaries', and that 'cohesion within the sentence need not be regarded as essentially a distinct phenomenon' (Halliday & Hasan 1976, *pp* 6,9).

It is difficult also to resist the conclusion of Dascal and Margalit

(1974) that 'the grammatical arguments which allegedly support T-grammars v. S-grammars do not in fact offer any evidence whatsoever for this claim' (p 211) (The authors are specifically discussing the arguments of van Dijk in van Dijk 1972). It is difficult to resist this conclusion because the authors concretely demonstrate that van Dijk's analyses of the grammatical phenomena he treats are either simply inadequate, or in fact available within the framework of sentence grammars (as van Dijk himself concedes – van Dijk 1972, p 132).[8]

I would suggest that the strongest argument for an approach to language that takes as its units something larger than the sentence or speech act is the coherence of dialogue – the fact that some segments of language are only interpretable as rejoinders or replies to preceding speech events brought about in the most obvious cases by some other speaker.[9] Data of the following kind seem obvious examples:

[2.1] (i) – John's still here, you know
            – He's not still here
       (ii) – John's already finished
            – I haven't already finished
       (iii) – Who's coming at nine tonight?
            – Who's coming when?
       (iv) – When's Bardot coming?
            – When's who coming?

The interpretability, indeed the grammaticality, of the responses here is determined by their placing in a conversational sequence.

Cohesive notions of substitution or deletion will not account for the grammatical structure of the replies in [2.1] above. Note that intonation is significant: however a theme-rheme analysis will not work for such data on a sentential or utterance level, as what appear as themes in such utterances are preceding speech acts or interactional moves.[10] However, it is fair to say as a generalisation that textgrammars have been developed as formal theories independent of pragmatic concerns, and then later a pragmatic component has been added, roughly as has been seen to occur in transformational sentence-grammars.[11] What this though may be seen to imply in theory and practice is that a *textpragmatics has to be set up inside the formal and theoretical framework set up for textgrammars*. The objection is then simply, what if the empirical facts of language use and specifically the interactional coherence of spoken discourse cannot be handled inside the framework established for some other type of linguistic data? In fact, the notion of interactional structure contradicts the notion of thematic structure – ie as Dressler points out (1972, p 83) it is impossible to treat a dialogic exchange as an extended sentence.

There is in fact some uncertainty as to whether a textgrammarian, faced with dialogic material, would wish to claim that each move or turn constitutes a 'text', or whether the dialogue itself is one text. Thus S. J. Schmidt's model (1973, p 165; 1975, p 35) essentially accounts for a 'Mitteilungsabsicht' and 'Wirkungsabsicht' made concrete in a 'textual deep structure', and then implemented *on the part of one speaker*. What we would appear to need is at least two such 'model-systems' interacting to produce one and the same 'text'. Similar remarks might be made of the model of Walter Koch (appearing in Koch 1971, p 218 for example). The model proceeds linearly from left to right from (roughly) morpheme to 'word' ('logeme') to sentence to text to 'bitext' to 'N-text', where 'bitext' is to be understood as dialogue, and 'N-text' as a text with N speakers participating. That a 'text' results from the interaction of two or more speakers cannot be derived from this model. Either we will view a dialogue as an intersection of two texts – contradicted by the fact that for example one end of a telephone conversation would not normally be considered coherent – or we will view each contribution to a dialogue by one speaker as a distinct text.

Van Dijk currently appears to take the position given above, namely that one contribution to a dialogue (whether move or turn is not clear) constitutes a 'text': 'just as sentences combine with sentences to form discourses, discourses combine with discourses to form DIALOGUES and CONVERSATIONS' (van Dijk 1977b, p 131). In order to interpret this claim, one must assume that 'discourse' is here used to refer to what van Dijk earlier called 'text'. This approach clearly weakens considerably the claims of textlinguistics, but seems to me to be essentially wrong apart from this fact. What it would suggest however is that in analysing spoken discourse we have one type of grammar – a textgrammar – in order to analyse the structure of an individual turn at talk, and then some other type of grammar – let us say an interactional grammar – in order to link these sequentially placed texts coherently. Clearly, if one system or model can do both tasks it is to be preferred.

The danger is however that as a concern with pragmatic issues has developed in textlinguistics as an *additional* or *additive* concern, conversational discourse is to be handled in a textgrammar inside a theoretical framework developed for linguistic data which is different in kind.

I wish to try to illustrate this danger briefly by discussing van Dijk 1977a. The paper is based on the assumption that as two sentences may be said to stand in a particular cohesive relation to each other by virtue of the occurrence of a sentence-connector which conjoins them 'semantically', so a sequence of 'speech-acts', whether performed by the same speaker or not, may be said to stand in a particular coherent relation to each other by virtue of the occurrence of a sentence-connector which joins then 'pragmatically'. Hence in [2.2] (i) below we have 'semantic BUT', while in [2.2] (ii) we have 'pragmatic BUT':

[2.2]   (i)   Henry was ill, but he came to the meeting
         (ii)   – Henry was ill
                – But I saw him at the meeting last night!

As I understand it, in order to interpret sequences of utterances in conversation, van Dijk proposes to set up 'pragmatic connectives' which make explicit the interactional links between sequenced utterances in dialogue: AND is provisionally characterised, for example, in terms such as 'ADDITION, CONTINUATION' (*p* 83), while BUT 'may be interpreted as a PROTEST against the speech act of the previous speaker' (*p* 85). Consider however the following:

[2.3]   (i)   – Let's all go to the pictures tomorrow night
         (ii)   – John won't want to go
         (iii) $\begin{Bmatrix} a \\ b \\ c \end{Bmatrix} - \begin{Bmatrix} \text{But} \\ \text{And} \\ - \end{Bmatrix}$ he won't want to stay here either!

(fabricated)

Let us assume three speakers producing the utterances (i), (ii), and (iii) [2.3] above respectively, and that the speaker of (iii) has three possible alternative utterances, *a*, *b*, *c*, distinguished solely by the occurrence of the connector BUT in *a*, the occurrence of AND in *b*, and the absence of any such connector in *c*. While the semantic meaning of AND or BUT guarantees that an element of 'addition' attaches to (iii)*b*, an element of 'protest' to (iii)*a*, we note that (iii)*c* may have either interpretation, and further that (ii) may itself be interpreted as a 'protest'. Further there are at least two senses in which (iii)*a* (and (iii)*c*) are to be interpreted as 'protests', according as the third speaker takes the second as presupposing that collective group activity is sacrosanct, or not: he may accordingly derive from (ii) the implicature ⌐John stay here⌐, or the implicature ⌐We all stay here⌐. In 'protesting', he is in the former case maintaining John's interests, and protesting against the implication that John may be abandoned, while in the latter case he is belittling (ii)'s concern with John's interest, and implying that John is a rather cheerless individual whose wishes do not merit consideration. This second interpretation is further available for the utterance (iii)*b* , as well as for (iii)*c*. It is conceded that such intuitive 'analyses' require some support, but they suffice to indicate that van Dijk's remarks have no empirical base. I would further claim that an attempt to interpret speech act sequences as a function of 'pragmatic connectives' is misguided in principle.[12]

The danger referred to above and illustrated by reference to van Dijk's paper on 'pragmatic connectives' is that in 'extending' a textgrammar in order to attempt to interpret conversational data, one may seek to reduce, transform, or otherwise transmute the conversational data such that it takes on the character of text – *ie* can be interpreted as exhibited semantic or thematic structure. An approach to the analysis of spoken discourse which proceeds from the generalisation of some form of sentence-grammar to a text,[13] and then some further extension of the textgrammar to dialogic data is both inefficient and psychologically implausible. I shall seek to show that the relationship between textual or thematic coherence and discourse or interactional coherence is more insightfully seen as one of discourse ──→ text, rather the opposite. This position will be argued more fully in 7.2 below.

Notes

1 Compare here Krzeszowski's demonstration (1975) that 'any two sentences representing the same grammatical type, for example any two declarative sentences . . . could be connected by any of the sentence connectives and result in a well-formed sequence' (*p* 41).

2 *Cf* Fillmore's observations about the two 'texts'

I had troube with the car yesterday. The carburetor was dirty.
I had trouble with the car yesterday. The ash-tray was dirty.
(Fillmore 1977, *p* 75)

3 Widdowson (1977, *p* 250) makes a similar observation about van Dijk's claim concerning this data.

4 *Cf* Allen's sentence *She slapped him in the face and then she hit the man* (Allen 1977, *p* 21). Consider also the following, taken from a review by Anthony Burgess appearing in the *Observer* of 29/10/78: 'That I am 20 years and Lord David 35 years older than she was when she died represents no advantage to either of us'.

5 *Cf* Andy Capp – SHE: Where are you going'?
                HE: Out
               SHE: When'll you be back?
                HE: Later (exits)
               SHE: As long as I know.

6 See *eg* Dixon 1963, *p* 73; Halliday & Hasan 1976, *p* 54.

7 In Petöfi 1973, texts are claimed to be 'abstract objects', generated by the grammar, which should indirectly 'provide the basis for the description of ordinary language activity' (*p* 206). In Petöfi 1976, the claim is made that the 'analysis of different examples' is 'useless', except in a certain stage of developing the theory (*pp* 109–10). In van Dijk 1977b, a text is said to be 'the abstract theoretical construct underlying what is usually called a discourse' (*p* 3).

8 See also here Kiefer 1977, *p* 190.

9 This is conceded by Dascal & Margalit 1973 (*p* 200, note 7), though their intention is in fact to argue *against* the necessity of abandoning sentence grammar in favour of text grammar.

10 Plausible theme-rheme structures here might be of the form for example:
Re [Your querying when X is coming] I query [X = who]
for [2.1] (iv) above. See Edmondson et al 1979.

11 Witness Petöfi 1973, *p* 271: '. . . However when outlining the broader context of a text grammar it has also been mentioned, that the text grammar is only one (co-textual) component of a text theory, and that it should be set up so as to allow various kinds of con-textual components to be attached to it'. *Cf* Rieser, (discussion in Gülich and Raible 1972, *p* 23): 'Mein primäres Interesse liegt jedoch darin, erst einmal eine Grammatik funktionsfähig zu machen. Es erscheint mir wenig sinnvoll, ein Pragmatikmodell diskutieren zu wollen, so lange man nicht weiß, welchen Umfang die Pragmatik haben soll und wie die Heuristik der Pragmatik beschaffen sein muß'. See also van Dijk 1972, *p* 342. 'The use of texts in interaction can be explained and described only when we have explicit insight into their structures, a task to be fulfilled by a basically different type of grammar, text grammar'. Kummer (1972) claims to provide a pragmatic base for a theory of texts, but concedes in the discussion of his paper that 'bei mir der Dialog noch gar nicht vorgesehen ist' (*p* 58 in Gülich and Raible 1972).

12 I have tried to show this in more detail in Edmondson 1978a. See also *pp* 132–3 below.

13 There is a paradox in the patently true observation of Petöfi and Rieser (in their prefatory 'Overview' to Petöfi and Rieser 1973) that the theoretical power of a text grammar depends 'to some extent (if not completely)' on the descriptive adequacy of the sentence-grammar which is 'generalised' (*p* 12), when the same authors claim that a sentence-grammar is by definition descriptively inadequate (*p* 1).

Chapter 3:

Re-interpreting speech-act theory

In re-interpreting some aspects of speech act theory as of direct relevance to the analysis of spoken discourse, I shall concentrate on the work of Austin, and particularly Searle. In Austin's theory, the notion of the perlocutionary act is an implicit recognition that a 'speech act' has an interactional component, but 'perlocutionary intent' and 'perlocutionary effect' are conflated or confused in Austin's account, such that it cannot be held that the perlocutionary act is part of a speech act in the way that the locutionary and illocutionary acts are claimed to be. For 'perlocutionary intent' is indistinguishable from illocutionary intent, while the 'perlocutionary effect' of an utterance cannot be said to be part of that utterance. In discussing some aspects of speech act theory I shall therefore be centrally concerned with the identification and characterisation of *illocutionary* acts (3.1), and also with the relationship between the locutionary and the illocutionary act (3.2). The no on of 'perlocutionary effect' is briefly discussed in 4.3 following.

The purpose of this investigation is to consider how far and in what ways speech-act theory (specifically that of Searle) gives us a framework inside which we may characterise insightfully what is being done when something is said by a speaker as a contribution to an ongoing spoken discourse. The central conclusion is that it is necessary to re-interpret the notion of an illocutionary act if this notion is to be relevantly applied in the analysis of discourse.

3.1 Identifying and characterising illocutionary acts

In characterising different illocutionary acts, Searle's procedure is to.

consider the 'paradigm cases', the 'simple and idealised case'. Thus in the case of 'Promising', the analysis is aimed at 'the center of the concept of Promising' (Searle 1969, *pp* 54–5). However in the empirical investigation of conversational behaviour we seldom come across the 'paradigm' cases (if indeed we ever do). A first question is then how far the 'necessary and sufficient conditions' for 'Promising' enable us to identify such illocutionary acts. Searle's evidence for his characterisation of 'Promising' is essentially native-speaker intuition. However, while it is true that we have intuitions about whether, for example, a promise to do P counts as an undertaking to do P, we do not have firm intuitions when we seek to ask of any specific contextualised utterance whether or not it constitutes a 'Promise'. Consider the following (fabricated) set of data, and let us assume that A and B are familiar social equals:

[3.1] (i)   A: I think I'll go and get a beer.
             B: Do that thing.
             A: <u>Okay.</u>
       (ii)   A: I think I'll go and get a beer. Do you want one too?
             B: Yeah. Good idea.
             A: <u>Okay.</u>
       (iii) A: I think I'll go and get a beer.
             B: Oh, get me one too, will you
             A: <u>Okay.</u>
       (iv)   A: If you write the introduction, I'll draft the report, okay?
             B: <u>Fine by me</u>
             A: <u>Okay.</u>

Accepting Searle's characterisation of what it is to perform a 'Promise', how far are we in a position to decide whether 'Promising' is going on in any or all of these sequences? What seems to be the critical utterance has been underscored in each case, two possible candidates appearing in [3.1] (iv). A first problem is the propositional content rule, *ie* determining whether and in what sense 'a proposition P is expressed in an utterance T'. The preparatory rule to the effect that S believe H would prefer S to do a predicated future act A to his not doing so suffers from the weakness that H's preferences and S's beliefs as to H's preferences are not open to inspection, except in so far as we may *deduce* these from the discourse itself. Similarly the sincerity condition clearly offers no identificational criterion, as following Gricean co-operative principles we *assume* sincerity.

Finally, the essential condition provides simply a dictionary definition of the notion of promising: if we know what it is to undertake a commitment, we presumably know what it is to make a 'Promise'. What makes us think that 'Promising' may be going on here is the sequencing of the utterances, and our awareness of what outcomes have been arrived at in these segments of talk. These intuitions have little to do with the characterisation of 'Promising' that Searle gives.

Despite this, we may ask a second question, namely: how far does Searle's classification of illocutionary acts (Searle 1976) provide an exhaustive framework for the classification of significant linguistic units encountered in spoken discourse? Searle's claim is: 'There are a rather limited number of basic things we can do with language: we tell people how things are, we try to get them to do things, we commit ourselves to doing things, we express our feelings and attitudes, and we bring about changes through our utterances.' (Searle 1976, pp 22–3)

The assumption is then that a classification of illocutionary acts is a classification of the (basic) things we can do with language. Consider however the case of the 'minimization' (the term is Goffman's – Goffman 1971, p 177). It most commonly follows an expression of thanks and possible locutions include

- not at all
- my pleasure
- don't mention it
- you're welcome

Is a distinctive illocutionary act being performed here? Presumably Searle would have to characterise 'not at all' (= 'don't thank me at all') and 'don't mention it' as directives, and 'my pleasure' and 'you're welcome' as 'representatives': there would be no distinctive illocutionary act being performed in these four cases – ie a 'minimization' is not a category of illocution. It is quite possible that Searle's five categories might be found to cover most if not all of the utterances occurring in spoken discourse, but the categories are so broad (particularly the representatives, expressives, and declarations) that their relevance for the analysis of spoken discourse is limited.

The reason is not hard to find. I have tried to show elsewhere (Edmondson 1979c) that what Searle characterises and classifies are not units of conversational behaviour, but concepts evoked by a set of lexical items in English – illocutionary verbs. The criterion for the existence of an illocutionary act of a specific kind is essentially the existence in English of a term which may be used in an explicit performative formula in the alleged performance of that act. Searle assumes the Austinian analysis of performative utterances whereby 'to utter the sentence (in of course the appropriate circumstances) is not to *describe* my doing of what I should be said in so uttering to be doing or to state that I am doing it: it is to do it' (Austin 1976, *p* 6). If this analysis is however not accepted, the whole rationale for positing the existence of illocutionary acts other than as concepts evoked by particular lexical items of English disappears. The 'descriptivist' interpretation of performative utterances does however offer a viable and preferable alternative to the Austinian 'performative' analysis.[1]

It may be appropriate here to summarize some arguments in favour of the descriptivist analysis of overt performatives. Three arguments against the 'performative' analysis are as follows;

(i) A first problem for the performative analysis is the interpretation of Austin's phrase 'making explicit'. The use of this phrase at the least implies that the illocutionary force made explicit in the performative formula is implicit elsewhere in the utterance event. If the utterance of the formula *I promise* makes explicit that *I'll go* is being used with the illocutionary force of a 'Promise', but does not *state* that *I'll go* has this illocutionary force, nor does it *describe* it as having such, how are we to interpret the sense in which it makes this notion explicit? The point here is that the Austinian analysis simply bypasses the problem of distinguishing semantic and pragmatic meaning: with the overt performative utterance, the issue of semantic interpretation 'does not arise' (Harris 1978, *p* 310).

(ii) Further, there would appear to be a cline operating between overt performatives and clear cases in which the relevant illocutionary verb is being used 'descriptively':

[3.2] (i)   I promise I'll be there
      (ii)   I'll be there, I promise
      (iii) I'll be there, that's a promise
      (iv)   I can definitely promise you that I'll be there
      (v)   I'll be there, I can promise you

(Data fabricated)

(iii) The case in which an 'explicit performative formula' is used 'non-literally' also poses problems for the performative analysis. Consider the following:

[3.3] (i)   I won't get killed, darling, I promise
       (ii) If you do that again you'll be sorry, I promise you
       (iii) I advise you not to move an inch buddy – it's loaded[2]
       (iv) I ask you, who the hell does he think he is?

These three problems for the performative analysis do not arise for the descriptivist analysis, which introduces symmetry into the notion of reporting events, in that the analysis views the use of performative verbs to describe the speaker's own speech activity as no different in kind from the reporting of any other form of activity.[3]

Consider the following:

Event/Act at t_0	Report at t_0	Report at t_1 ($t_1 > t_0$)
⌐his coming⌐	Here he comes	He came
⌐my going⌐	Here I go	I went
⌐His saying 'I'll come'⌐	He promises he'll come	He promised he'd come
⌐My saying 'I'll go'⌐	I promise I'll go	I promised I'd go

Note further that the descriptive analysis does not have to consider the case of Searle's declarations as distinctive, as we distinguish here between the semantic meaning of *You are fired* and the social significance of 'You are fired' uttered in particular circumstances, just as social convention determines that to say 'I promise to come' (in particular circumstances) is held to be to make a promise to come.[4]

   A possible counter-argument to the descriptive analysis is based on the fact that a simple tense appears in the performative formula and not a continuous tense. Thus it might be conceded that in 'I'm ordering you to go' ORDER is used descriptively, but not in 'I order you to go'. This argument does not hold water, however, as the present tense form may be used 'instantaneously' to refer to non-durative on-going events, often with a dramatic illocutionary force. The instantaneous use of the present tense presents events as coming into being at the moment of speaking. Examples are in demonstrations, sport commentaries, newspaper headlines, certain collocations involving locational or directional adverbials, and, of particular significance perhaps, with various verbs denoting the transmission and reception of verbal communications (See Edmondson et al 1977. *pp* 45–52; Leech 1971, *pp* 2–3).

   The descriptive analysis of performative utterance is therefore not at odds with the grammatical system of English; on the contrary, the grammatical facts lend weight to a descriptivist analysis.

If we accept then a descriptivist analysis of overt performative utterances, the question arises not as to whether terms which may appear in such performative utterances characterise all the basic things we can do with language, but as to *why* some utterances may be described appropriately by the use of such performative formulae, while others may not. We may assume that the existence of a distinctive illocutionary term as a means of describing some types of illocutionary act indicates the social significance of acts of that kind. An investigation matching illocutionary terms with systematically-distinguished categories of events which may be referred to in an utterance that may be characterised by that matching illocutionary term reveals which types of illocutionary act are conceptually distinguished in the lexis of English (Edmondson 1979c – *cf* Leech 1977a).

This distribution may then be interpreted as suggesting what I have called an 'H-Support' maxim which in part governs our perception of conversational events, and underlies our perception and evaluation of social behaviour in general. The H-Support maxim has three related formulations:

– Support your hearer's costs and benefits!
– Suppress your own!
– Give benefits when you receive them!
                                        (Edmondson 1979c).

There is a clear link between such maxims (to be collectively glossed as 'H-supportive') and the notion of politeness (See also Leech's 'tact maxim' – Leech 1977a, *pp* 19–21).

The conclusion to be drawn from this discussion is that illocutionary categories in Searle's theory are common-sense, not technical categories (*Cf* Schegloff 1977, *pp* 82–3). Searle is a philosopher, not a discourse analyst. For the characterisation of verbal behaviour in spoken discourse we require technical terms.

That illocutionary acts are in some sense an important aspect of what is said when something is done seems however indisputable. As suggested above, the set of terms existing in English for referring to categories of verbal behaviour is itself highly significant in revealing the social significance of particular contextualised kinds of speech activity.

We may begin to refine the notion of an illocutionary act by going back to Austin, and asking whether in fact it is the case that illocutionary acts are performed by an individual speaker via a specific locution uttered in appropriate circumstances. Classic instances in which this should be the case include the following:

[3.4] (i)   I bet you sixpence that P
       (ii)   I promise I'll come
       (iii) I do (said during the marriage service)

However, if you say 'I bet you sixpence that P', but I refuse to accept your bet, the sense in which you have bet me sixpence that P is rather limited. There is no wager resulting, no financial sum is at stake, in short, no bet has been made.[5] Similarly unless the 'appropriate circumstances' include a condition that the hearer not cancel or otherwise invalidate the 'Promise', we cannot say that the performative utterance *in itself* constitutes such an act. For example if I break a vase of yours and immediately say 'Sorry, I promise to buy you a new one tomorrow', you may well claim this is is unnecessary, extravagent, and so on. The conversation may then conclude without my having entered into any commitment to buy a new vase, although I have 'promised' to do so. The case of the marriage service is even more clearly a co-operative venture. If X says 'I do' in the appropriate circumstances he does not thereby take Y to be his lawfully wedded wife, unless, within a strictly determined time span, she also says 'I do', in appropriate circumstances. Neither party can bring off this venture alone. It is conceded here that the examples of performatives in [3.4] above are selected as conducive to the argumentation here, but the point is central to the discourse model developed later: with some performatives at least *'doing it' is a co-operative achievement*: it is not simply a case of the individual uttering a sentence in appropriate circumstances.

That a promise or a bet may be said to be co-operative achievements or conversational outcomes suggests either that the notion of an illocutionary act must be extended to include factors other than a proposition, a speaker and his intentional states, or that notions such as 'promising' or 'betting' be not considered illocutions in a technical sense we may wish to propose.

The case of the 'Promise' informally discussed above suggests further that the distinctiveness of some illocutionary categories (in a Searlean sense) derives at least in part from their sequential placing and relevance in a sequence of speech acts. Roulet (1977) suggests that what may distinguish an 'Offer' from a 'Promise' is that the former is eliciting, the latter elicited. Consider the fabricated sequences below:

[3.5] (i)   A: $\begin{cases} \text{Would you carry my bag?} \\ \text{Carry my bag please} \end{cases}$

              B: Okay

       (ii)   B: Shall I carry your bag for you

              A: $\begin{cases} \text{Yes please} \\ \text{Would you} \end{cases}$

We would probably not in every day usage refer to A's utterance in (ii) as a 'Request', though we would in (i), and would distinguish B's utterance in (i) from that in (ii) in terms such as 'Undertaking' as opposed to 'Offering'. Therefore either we have to expand the notion of an illocution to embrace such potential sequencing criteria, or, if we wish to claim that A and B perform essentially similar illocutionary acts in (i) and (ii) above, then we have to re-define the terms we use to denote categories of illocutionary activity, rather than rely on our everyday conception of what it is to make a promise or request. In other words, for the purposes of discourse analysis the notion of an illocutionary act will be a technical one, and not a common-sense notion derived from the concepts evoked by a range of lexical items in English we choose to refer to as illocutionary verbs.

If we wish to consider an illocutionary act as a locutionary act by means of which a speaker communicates his beliefs, attitudes or feelings vis à vis some event or state of affairs, terms such as *promise*, *offer*, *request*, *bet* in their everyday sense will prove misleading. The significance of such terms is a reflection of the social significance of the types of behaviour they may be used to describe.

3.2 On saying what you mean

The purpose of this section is to propose an alternative to Searle's theory of indirect speech acts, and thereby clarify the relationship between a locutionary and an illocutionary act. Some further claims as to the nature of spoken discourse will also be made, and supporting evidence will be brought forward for some of the claims made in 3.1 above.

According to Searle, 'the problem posed by indirect speech acts is the problem of how it is possible for the speaker to say one thing and mean that but also to mean something else' (Searle 1975, *p* 60). Note that in this formulation what is said is part of what is meant, such that 'primary' and 'secondary' illocutionary force need to be distinguished: 'one illocutionary act is performed indirectly by way of performing another' (1975, *p* 60). On this account then what distinguishes the 'simplest cases of meaning' is the *absence* of some additional speaker meaning.[6]

This is consistent with the otherwise puzzling and tantalising concluding remark in Searle 1976, where having established five categories of 'basic things we can do', Searle goes on to remark that we often do more than one of these five things in the same utterance (*p* 23). This would seem to imply that in one and the same utterance different illocutionary points might obtain, different world-word fits might somehow be co-present, and different types of proposition might somehow be simultaneously expressed. It is not easy to see how this could be.

Further we note what appears to be an inconsistency in Searle's account. On the one hand, Searle claims that the primary and secondary illocutionary force are somehow co-present in the utterance, such that the former is derived from the latter: on the other hand, a necessary stage in determining the primary (indirect) illocutionary force is the *rejection* of the expressed force. For example in Searle's analysis of *Can you pass the salt*, the hearer is taken to assume that the speaker is probably well aware of the fact that the hearer is capable of such action. If then we hold the sincerity condition for questions to be that S wishes to know if P, this condition is not met, and moreover we may assume that S knows that H will recognise that this is so. The utterance is therefore clearly not intended as a 'question'. On Searle's account the utterance appears then both to have and not to have this illocutionary force. The paradox in Searle's position here is reflected in the use to which Gricean co-operative principles are put in the argumentation. For the first stage in deriving the 'primary' illocutionary force is to recognise that a speaker is *not* being co-operative, in that the 'expressed' illocutionary force does not match the situation. On the other hand one then assumes the speaker *is* being co-operative, and on the basis of this assumption seeks a further illocutionary interpretation for the utterance. The paradox may now be phrased as that speakers are assumed to *break* conversational principles in order to *follow* conversational principles.

The difficulty may be solved if we take a line of argument similar to that we have pursued for the case of overt performatives, and distinguish more sharply between what is said and what is meant, between logical form and illocutionary force. The critical issue is that of mood, as it is tempting to assume that any declarative mood sentence will by that very fact be uttered with assertive force, interrogatives will be 'questions' in illocutionary force, and imperatives 'directive' speech acts. I wish to simply claim that the grammatical mood of a sentence is part of the meaning of the sentence, and as such belongs in a speech act analysis to the *locution*. Choice of mood therefore determines *locutionary force*.[7] We are handling here a system of choices determining how to *say* things with words, as it were, rather than how to *do* things with words. Without attempting to interpret grammatical mood markers semantically, I shall use the terms STATE, QUERY, and MAND to refer to the locutionary force of declaratives, interrogatives, and imperatives respectively.[8]

We shall now not distinguish between 'primary' and 'secondary' illocutionary force, though we may wish to claim that some illocutionary acts are performed more 'directly' than others, in that their illocutionary force is more directly derivable from their logical sense. Note that it is not the case that we shall claim in the case of an 'Assertion' (if we accept that it is meaningful to characterise an illocutionary act as such), or a straightforward 'Question' (again, assuming there is such a thing) that locutionary force and illocutionary point are *identical*, we shall rather claim that the illocutionary point is less 'indirectly' derivable from the sense.

We may now turn to the important question as to *why* speakers go to the trouble of expressing illocutionary point indirectly. I assume here that simply to state 'conventions' as to how locutionary force and illocutionary force may be matched (as in Searle 1975; Gordon and Lakoff 1975, for example) has little explanatory force unless some rationale for such procedures can be suggested. Further it is not merely the 'indirect' illocutions which need to be accounted for: we need also to account for the fact that some illocutionary acts cannot be performed indirectly, or at least seldom are. The expression of thanks would be a case in point. One cannot 'hint' here; on the contrary, *gushing* is normative, and gushing we may informally characterise as repetitive over-explicitness as to one's illocutionary point.

A first and critical point here is that 'indirectness' in speech behaviour is not motivated by a desire to communicate a *specific* illocutionary point I_1, by means of an utterance having some other locutionary point I_2. If this were so, the whole game would appear to have no point. Rather, the central significance of indirectness is that the actual illocutionary point is to some extent non-specific, it is essentially non-determinate, a matter of interpretation, of *negotiation*. Speech acts which we have been terming 'indirect' exhibit then what Leech in an important paper calls 'strategic indeterminacy' (Leech 1977a, *p* 5), and this is their point: they are not *meant* to be determinate, their significance is negotiable.[9]

Consider here the type of data brought forward in [3.1] and [3.2] above, and also the case of 'hinting'. An utterance of the kind 'It's cold in here' seems a clear case in which the illocutionary value of the utterance is a negotiable.

'Strategic indeterminacy' is of course motivated by a social concern with face: it is a matter of tact or politeness. An investigation of illocutionary terms and their potential performance 'indirectly' provides support for the H-supportive maxim suggested in 3.1 above (see Edmondson 1979c). 'Requests' are ripe candidates for indirectness, and there are also many verbs available in English for referring to this type of illocutionary act. The same holds for 'Complaining' illocutions, and for 'Offers'. In these three cases potential offense is involved – even if an 'Offer' is made as in the interests of the hearer, some invasion of privacy and some lessening of freedom of self-determination is implicit in such an act.

We may summarize the discussion of some aspects of speech act theory in this chapter as follows:

(i)   If an illocutionary act is viewed as an utterance by means of which a speaker communicates his feelings, attitudes, beliefs, or intentions with respect to some event or state of affairs, it is necessary to find appropriate technical terms to describe such acts, rather than relying on the denotations of existing lexical items of English. Searle essentially classifies and characterises illocutionary verbs, not segments of conversational behaviour.

(ii)   An H-Supportive maxim has been proposed as in part affecting our perception and evaluation of members' behaviour in spoken discourse.

(iii)   We need to distinguish between a locutionary and illocutionary act, and reject the notion of co-occurrent direct and indirect illocutionary acts. If the notion of illocutionary act is applicable to the analysis of spoken discourse, it is clearly necessary to suggest *one* value for any utterance assigned an illocutionary force, if possible. However, it would seem unlikely that in every instance specific illocutionary force is determinable, as we have also claimed that

(iv)   in many instances illocutionary force is 'strategically indeterminate'–ie a matter of negotiation.

Negotiation is an interactional process, and to this aspect of spoken discourse we may now turn.

Notes

1 See here Cohen 1964; Deveaux in discussion with Austin in Austin 1963, *p* 40; Wiggins 1971a, *pp* 21–2; Wiggins 1971b; Goffman 1976, note, *p* 303; Leech 1976; Edmondson 1979a.
2 This example is adapted from that of Meyer-Hermann (1976), *p* 3.
3 *Cf* Russell 1940, *p* 328 'Those who say that words falsify sensible facts forget that words *are* sensible facts'.
4 Habermas, while claiming universality for the categories of speech acts he sets up, specifically exempts institutionalised speech acts as culture-specific (Habermas 1972, *pp* 214–16). Further, there is some similarity between the oddness of the reply given in (i) below and that given in (ii)

(i) – I've got a headache
   – No you haven't

(ii) – I promise I'll come
   – No you don't

Note further that the reply becomes more normative if the speaker in (i) is a doctor, in (ii) a philosopher or linguist.
5 *Cf* Katz's remarks on BET, OFFER, and WAGER (Katz 1977, *pp* 217–18).
6 *Cf* the definitions of indirect speech acts offered in Ehrich and Saile, 1972, *p* 256; Franck, 1975, *p* 219, which rely on an observed difference between the expressed illocutionary force indicator, and the (primary) intended illocutionary point of the utterance.
7 This position is taken by Leech 1977a. *Cf* also Wunderlich 1976, *p* 471.
8 The terms are purely ad hoc. Downes (1977) presents some good arguments to suggest that the imperative is in fact a non-inflected verb form – *ie* in terms of the framework adopted above, an imperative sentence has a null locutionary force. I think he may be right, but not much hinges on this. The essential point is that if an utterance which is 'Requestive' in illocutionary force is also imperative in form, the illocutionary force is not a 'direct' consequence of the imperative form. On this point, Downes and I are in agreement.
9 *Cf* Downes 1977, *pp* 94–5: '. . . from the hearer's point of view, utterance meaning will be indeterminate between a small number of possibilities in any given context, that is, it is essentially indeterminate. . . What is "meant" then, except for ritualized exchanges, will have to be worked towards, explicated and negotiated by participants in ongoing conversations'. *Cf* also Garvey 1975, *p* 64.

Chapter 4:

Interactional aspects of spoken discourse

We finished the previous chapter by suggesting that the notion of what is done when something is said concerns more than the performance by the individual speaker of an illocutionary act of some kind: in a two-party conversation, both speakers contribute to the outcome of the conversation. Negotiation is a two-party process. Language is not merely a mode of action, but a means of interaction.[1]

In discussing some interactional aspects of spoken discourse in this chapter, our concern will be to begin exploring the nature of discourse *structure*. A first problem to be handled is that non-verbal acts may clearly be significant in terms of the development of a conversation: the relationship between verbal and non-verbal conversational behaviour is explored in 4.1. One obvious conclusion reached is that as non-verbal acts may be structurally significant, we shall need to look outside speech act theory in order to capture the notion of discourse structure. A second possibility is that turn-taking determines discourse structure. However in discussing turn-taking in 4.2 we are forced to conclude that to some extent at least turn-taking is independent of discourse structure. In 4.3 the notion of sequential relevance is explored, and the work of the ethnomethodologists on the analysis of conversation is discussed in some detail. A dilemma faced here is how far an initial interactional move determines what may relevantly follow it, and how far what follows determines the significance of what precedes that subsequent interactional move. The negotiable nature of conversational activity is stressed once more, but while it seems clear that the nature of discourse structure may be deemed interactional, no clear means of identifying such structures, or of relating them to what is actually said or done, are discovered.

4.1 Linguistic and non-linguistic behaviour in discourse

An important parameter to the interpretation of what is happening when a conversational interaction takes place is raised by the obvious observation that it is not only linguistic activity on the part of the interactants which is relevant to the structure of a conversation. There are several senses in which this is so. We may point out that while saying things, speakers are necessarily doing other things simultaneously. Again, we may say that what is sometimes done via a verbal act may on other occasions be achieved by a non-verbal act (thus a handshake may accompany an exchange of greetings, or may *constitute* an exchange of greetings, in that no verbalisations accompany this contact). Further, there are many occasions when to talk is not enough: a critical case to be considered is that of non-verbal behaviour forthcoming as a result of a request for that non-verbal behaviour.

A first relevant observation is that at times 'silence counts', *ie* saying nothing is doing something.[2] But clearly we are not in a position to say that silence in any sense constitutes a 'speech act' – *ie* we cannot assign an illocutionary value of the kinds discussed in 3.1 above to an instance in which nothing is said – or rather if we do so, we cannot argue the relevant illocutionary value is determined via negotiation and convention from the logical sense and force of the locutionary act, as there is none. The significance of the non-occurrence of a verbal act will have to be derived from elsewhere: speech act theory will not in itself suffice.

Secondly, in exemplifying 'elliptical coupling', Merritt (1976) contrasts two sequences as illustrated below:

[4.1] (i)   S1: John
              S2: yes
              S1: have you got a moment
              S2: sure
       (ii)   S1: John, have you got a moment
              S2: sure

Merritt interprets the non-occurrence in (ii) of S2's first response in (i) ('yes') as an instance of ellipsis. The point I want to make is simply that [4.1] (ii) might be transcribed as follows:

[4.2]   S1: John
            S2: (looks up)
            S1: have you got a moment
            S2: sure

Whatever the status of Merritt's notion of ellipsis (see 4.3 below for a brief discussion), it seems intuitively clear that [4.2] requires a different analysis from that which would be appropriate for [4.1] (ii) – probably the same analysis in fact as operates for [4.1] (i). In other words, the function of the summons 'John' might be informally termed attention-getting, and it is plausible to suggest that the establishment of eye-contact by S2 is as much an appropriate interactional response as the utterance 'yes' (the two are clearly not mutually exclusive).

The relationship between the establishment of eye-contact and the utterance 'yes' is worthy of investigation. For given that S2 responds to the summons by saying 'yes' (as in [4.1] (i)) *without* establishing eye-contact, it is quite possible, if not likely, that S1 will take further steps to ensure that he in fact has S2's attention. In other words it may be that if we have to choose between the linguistic response and the non-linguistic, it is the latter which is the more important in terms of the successful development of the conversation.[3]

As a further informal example, consider a Christmas party, at which guests arrive bearing gifts for their hosts. The following dialogue might conceivably occur:

S1: Hello John, I've bought a present for you!
S2: Oh have you! You shouldn't have bothered.
S1: Wait a minute. Here it is!
S2: Thank you.

(fabricated)

It is perfectly clear that in interpreting this dialogue we assume that the brought present changes hands. Unless this is the case the verbal activity transcribed above is probably uninterpretable. In this instance not only is the non-verbal activity clearly more central to the ongoing interaction than the verbal, but the latter only has point and purpose by reference to the former.

These three informal examples illustrate that extralinguistic activity may play differing functional roles in an ongoing conversation. In attempting to categorise these differing functional roles we need to consider the differing relations holding between what is done verbally, and what is done non-verbally.

Laver and Hutcheson in their introduction (1972, *pp* 11–14) distinguish linguistic, paralinguistic, and extralinguistic means of communicating information. Paralanguage (*cf* Abercrombie 1968) is purposeful, directed and adoptive (*ie* controllable) behaviour which may accompany or substitute for linguistic communication, and may therefore contribute to the development of a conversation. Paralanguage reliably elicits one of a narrow range of predictable responses from an interactant. Extralinguistic behaviour however is normally non-purposeful, non-directed, and non-controllable; I prefer to refer to *signalling*, as opposed to *communication* here, as otherwise one is obliged to refer to matters of dress and appearance, ways of walking and so on, as communications.[4]

Extralinguistic signalling may be verbal, in that one's voice may reveal one's sex, or one's age relative to one's hearer's (Benjamin 1977), and so on, or that one was born in Liverpool, that one is drunk or suffering from a heavy cold. Similarly a whole range of information may be unintentionally and indeed unwittingly signalled by one's somatic, kinetic, or vocal behaviour, and a psychologist, a social analyst, or a Sherlock Holmes may pick up and interpret such clues, possibly correctly. The information so transmitted will more often than not be indexical in character. Insofar as we can distinguish therefore between paralinguistic communication and extralinguistic signalling, we may wish to claim that the former may be relevant to the structural analysis of conversation in a way that the latter may not.

However, such a claim may be made true as a matter of definition only — *ie* as soon as an item of 'extralinguistic' behaviour is interpreted by a hearer as relevant and significant in terms of an ongoing conversation, it will have to be considered 'paralinguistic' as opposed to 'extralinguistic'. We face here an issue to be explored more fully in 4.3 following, namely that *alleged intentional states are only observable via their effects*.

Thus it would seem that practically any behaviour may be consciously and deliberately adopted by humans in the interests of achieving interactional goals. One would presumably take a cough under normal conditions to be a piece of extralinguistic behaviour, but an interactant might well use a cough as an attention-getting device (and thereby indirectly a floor-gaining strategy), or to communicate something like 'I think perhaps this drink is a little too strong – could I possibly have a little more ice?'. If the cough is so heard and interpreted (as shown in the response it evokes), then it has interactional significance: otherwise it would not 'count' in interactional terms.

Nor is the line between linguistic vocalisations and paralinguistic vocalisations in some sense given – this is evident as soon as one attempts to make a transcription of a given conversation using the conventional graphic resources of the language. For example is a given sound to be interpreted as the beginning of a 'word', and thus a false-start, or merely some hesitation-device, uptaker, or what have you, for which the graphic system has no conventional realisation? Are 'ers' and 'ums' and 'ahs' linguistic or paralinguistic behaviour?

What is being suggested here is that distinctions between linguistic, paralinguistic, and non-linguistic behavour are in no sense clear-cut. This means one cannot determine from the instance of behaviour itself whether or not it belongs to the one category or the other, or whether or not the behavioural token in question is 'relevant' to the structure of the interaction inside which it occurs.

We may follow up this observation by suggesting that the distinctions between linguistic, paralinguistic, and non-linguistic behaviour present an incomplete paradigm as concerns the relations between different modes of behaviour encountered in conversations. For while the notion of paralanguage suggests a 'substitution' relation between linguistic and non-linguistic acts[5], this substitution is in fact a reversible process.

We have implicitly raised the issue by discussing above the relative status of linguistic and non-linguistic responses to a summons, but shall consider another example here for expository purpose. Take the simple case in which a request is complied with:

[4.3] S1: could you close the window please – it's a bit draughty in here
S2: sure (closes window)

(fabricated)

What is the 'response' (in the neutral interactional sense) here? Does the response (the element tied to the request) consist of the verbal act of saying 'sure', or the non-verbal act of actually closing the window? Surely the latter: if S2 closes the window, but no verbal act precedes or accompanies this behaviour, he has clearly responded to the request, and appropriately. (We may find him somewhat surly or ill-mannered but this is a reflection of his social competence: thus given a particular social role relationship between S1 and S2 the absence of a verbal act is entirely appropriate.) However if S2 merely says 'sure' but makes no move within a roughly determinable time interval to close the window he has 'responded', *but only insofar as he has failed to close the window – ie* his non-activity is significant as an act of non-compliance, and that the non-compliance is accompanied (or more strictly speaking follows) a verbal assent to the request simply gives to his non-compliance a particular significance. I shall return to the question as to the relation between the verbal assent and the act of compliance shortly, but let us first extend the argument.

Consider then the case in which the request *cannot* be immediately[6] complied with, as in:

'Be here on time tomorrow, will you please' or
'Serve dinner at eight o'clock this evening, Jeeves'.

Clearly we shall not wish to say that such requests cannot be said to be 'responded to' until the time specified for the requested act comes into being. We shall expect some piece of linguistic behaviour on the part of S2 concerning his performance of the requested act, his willingness to comply with the request, his ability to do so, or suchlike. The verbal response in such cases is surely a token of or substitute for the performance or non-performance of the requested non-linguistic behaviour.

One may claim therefore, if these analyses are acceptable, that the two classes of paralanguage, namely paralinguistic behaviour which is dependent on, and may accompany linguistic behaviour, and paralinguistic behaviour which can itself independently function as would some functionally equivalent linguistic behaviour, find their parallels in some types of overtly *linguistic* behaviour. In other words, we may talk here of 'para-nonlinguistic' linguistic behaviour, and set up two classes to parallel the two claimed classes of paralanguage. Linguistic behaviour may be an optional accompaniment to a conversationally significant non-linguistic act (refinements of timing are left to one side here), or it may be a token or voucher for a future non-linguistic act. The relations between linguistic and non-linguistic behaviour are complex therefore: it seems unduly limiting when analysing conversation to seek to interpret relevant non-linguistic behaviour solely by reference to linguistic behaviour.

One way in which verbal and non-verbal acts may be linked in a conversational sequence is via the notion of performance or EXECUTION. Consider again the simple case in which a request is complied with as in [4.3] above. In saying 'sure' S2 may be held to have given an undertaking to close the window: his closing it therefore is simply the carrying out of that commitment. The structure here is highly simple, but is no different from the case in which my daughter requests I help with her homework, I agree to do so, and there follows a lengthy episode during which much verbal interaction takes place. In this instance the execution of the request is performed via verbal interaction: in the case of closing the window, the execution of a request involves simply one non-verbal act. The underlying structure may be held to be essentially similar however.

We face the fact once more then that in terms of the coherence of a conversational discourse there appears to be no essential difference between verbal and non-verbal acts. Any activity whatsoever may form a structural element in an ongoing conversation. Moreover it seems plausible that the contextual conditions which give to a particular *utterance* a specific significance in a conversation are essentially the same as those contextual conditions which give to *any* act a specific significance in a discourse. The central conclusion we draw is that it is in interactional terms that a discourse is structured,[7] and verbal behaviour is not the exclusive mode of performing an interactional move in a conversation. Elements of interactional structure may be realised by verbal or non-verbal acts, which may be related in complex ways, some of which have been characterised above.

4.2 On turn-taking

A conversation may be held to be such by virtue of the fact that speaker-hearer roles change during its occurrence, or in the case of two-party conversations (with which I shall be exclusively concerned), these roles alternate during the course of the conversation. That *alternation* occurs is itself of course significant: if two or more participants talk at the same time, the likelihood is that something other than a coherent conversation is in progress.[8] To refer to a room full of people conversing is normally to suggest that *several* conversations are simultaneously in progress: in that the room is *full* of people, we would prefer to refer to the 'meeting' or 'discussion' that is going on, rather than the 'conversation', in the case that one interactional event involving all those present is taking place.

This suggests a second point: in larger gatherings in which it is desired that purposeful talk take place, there are often special conventions which hold for organising turntaking. It is clear that different turn-taking conventions hold for different settings –*eg* in the classroom, the formal debate, the public lecture. Often in such formalised settings there is one participant who has a privileged role position whereby he controls turn-assignment at the conventionally determined transition points. He has for example authority as teacher, Speaker (in the House of Commons), judge (in a court of law), or chairperson. Such special conventions are relatively easily observed and described: our concern is rather with the conventions which regulate turn-taking in informal conversational settings for which no overt 'rules' may be said to exist such that participants need to be made aware of these rules. We wish to establish how far the structure of a spoken discourse is determined by the turn-taking procedures evidenced in it.

Sacks, Schegloff, and Jefferson (1974) (hence SS&J) propose a ('simplest') system for the organisation of turn-taking in conversation. For discussion purposes, the 'basic set of rules' needs to be cited in full:

(i)   For any turn, at the initial transition-relevance place of an initial turn-constructional unit:

    [a]   If the turn-so-far is so constructed as to involve the use of a 'current speaker selects next' technique, then the party so selected has the right and is obliged to take next turn to speak; no others have such rights or obligations, and transfer occurs at that place.

    [b]   If the turn-so-far is so constructed as not to involve the use of a 'current speaker selects next' technique, then self-selection for next speakership may, but need not, be instituted; first starter acquires rights to a turn, and transfer occurs at that place.

    [c]   If the turn-so-far is so constructed as not to involve the use of a 'current speaker selects next' technique, then current speaker may, but need not continue, unless another self-selects.

(ii)   If, at the initial transition-relevance place of an initial turn-constructional unit, neither i[a] nor i[b] has operated, and, following the provision of i[c], current speaker has continued, then the rule-set [a]–[c] re-applies at the next transition-relevance place, until transfer is effected.

(SS&J, p 704)

These rules have immediate intuitive appeal, but for the analysis of actual conversations, the critical issues are begged. Namely, how does one identify the 'initial transition-relevance place of an initial turn-constructional unit'? What is the range of options glossed as 'current speaker selects next' techniques? Until we can attempt to answer these interpretative questions, the proposed rules say little more than – if I give you the turn, you must take it,

        – if I show willingness to relinquish my turn, you speak,

        – if you don't, I'll carry on.

This seems rather unfair, reeking of parody rather than paraphrase, but does bring out the circularity involved in establishing rules which rely on the use of terms such as 'transition-relevance place' without describing or defining these. To be more concrete in our criticism here, let us take a sequence cited by SS&J (their data (16), *p* 716):

[4.4] S1: hey you took my ch̄air by the wȧy $_\wedge$ and I don't think that
            was very nȉce
       S2: İ didn't take your chair $_\wedge$ it's mȳ chair[9]

Has rule i[*c*] from SS&J operated (at least once) in S1's turn, or not? And in S2's turn? Compare [4.4] with a (constructed) sequence of the kind:

[4.5] S1: hey you took my chȧir by the [wȧy
       S2: İ di]dn't take your chair
       S1: you dȉ[d you know
       S2: it's $_\wedge$]mȳ chair
                                                             (fabricated)

Presumably S2 gains his first turn by the operation of either rule i[*b*], or, given that Complaint-Denial is cited by SS&J as a 'tied pair', i[*a*].[10] Further when S1 regains the turn, it may be via the operation of rule i[*b*] again, or i[*a*] (we might wish to interpret Assertion – Counter-assertion as a tied pair), or we may wish to say that S1's turn-grabbing is illegal here, as S2's second turn seems more a continuation of his first turn than a response to S1's second turn.

What is shown here is that the rules proposed by SS&J are difficult to in fact *use* with empirical data. SS&J *assume* that terms such as 'transition-relevance place', 'current speaker selects next technique' are transparent once the data is given (see here *pp* 50–1 below).

One issue that has been raised in the above discussion is whether or not a particular utterance or move by virtue of its form or function may be said itself to constitute a 'selection' technique such that the production of such an utterance or move may be said to oblige the hearer to assume the speaking turn. For SS&J the 'obvious case' is 'the fact that an addressed question selects its addressee to speak next' (*p* 716). However utterances such as questions 'do not by themselves allocate next turn to some candidate next speaker', and moreover 'addressing a party will not necessarily in itself select him as next speaker' (*p* 717). Further, 'while an addressed question requires an

answer from the addressed party, it is the turntaking system, rather
than syntactic or semantic features of the "question", that requires
the answer to come next' (p 725). It is not easy to see exactly what in
fact is being said here, but the general claim is clearly that particular
utterances or moves do *not* in themselves allocate or select next-turn
options.

The central point here is that we need a specification of what a
possible transition-point is, and what a speaker-selects-next technique
is. We further need clear criteria on which we can decide whether the
occurrent sequence of turns in a given conversation is a result of the
application of claimed turn-taking rules, or whether these rules have
in fact been broken. For what is clear is that turn-taking conventions
can be and are flouted, and deliberately so (we may of course be
obliged to say if this occurs all the time in a given case that in
consequence no or little interaction takes place). SS&J are themselves
well aware of such interpretative problems of course, as is shown by
the hedges appearing as footnotes in their paper.[11]

What emerges from the discussion however is that turn-taking
procedures are subject to the control of the speaker and/or hearer,
such that turn-selection or assignment is distinct from turn-taking.
This means that one cannot predict at any one point in time that a
change of speaker role *will* occur, though one may well be able to
distinguish on the basis of what is said, how it is said, and concomitant
behaviours such as eye-movement and body-shift, between for
example different types of silence (see footnote 26, SS&J 1974, p 715).

Such 'signals and rules' whereby potential turn-change is managed
are investigated in several studies by Duncan (eg Duncan 1972, 1973;
Duncan & Niederehe 1974).[12] In Duncan 1973, turn signals are
characterised as 'the display of at least one of a set of six clues' (p 37).
These include clues revealed in what is said (syntax, the use of various
'sociocentric sequences'), clues contained in how something is said
(specifically intonation, loudness, the phenomenon of 'drawling'),
and clues revealed in gesture and body movement. We note again that
the occurrence of a speaker turn signal (no matter how many clues are
simultaneously displayed) does not allow one to predict that a change
of speaker will actually occur. That this is so is in fact a reflection of
the distinction between communicative rule, and the use thereof in
social behaviour: that a turn is 'available', given various clues, may be
said to be 'known' to a hearer: whether or not he *takes* the available
turn however is a matter of subjective choice.

What emerges from the general discussion above is that the

complex signalling whereby turn-taking is more or less smoothly achieved in the majority of conversations is to some extent at least *independent* of what is said or done in a turn at talk. It is in fact at the moment difficult to see how a deeper understanding of the signalling devices by means of which turn-change is facilitated could *essentially* contribute towards an understanding of the structure and coherence of a discourse. I shall therefore pay little attention to these issues in developing a model for the analysis of discourse structure in Chapter 6.

What may be tentatively claimed from the discussion above is that if we can establish or assume that the structure of a conversation is essentially an interactional structure, but if, as we have concluded above, turn-changing is in part independent of what is said and done, being under the control of the interacting parties, then in the case that one speaker retains a turn at talk over a considerable period, it should be the case that the internal structure of what the individual speaker says and does is also essentially 'interactional', although there may be no overt 'interaction', in that the lecturer, bore, teacher, or whoever retains the turn at talk. Either this follows, or we have to argue and show that in an extensive turn at talk a speaker does essentially different things than when he engages in dialogic interaction in which turns at talk alternate with some frequency. In other words, the non-predictability of turn-changing in an ongoing conversation may indirectly support the contention that the structure of a 'text' is essentially an interactional structure (*cf* discussion in Chapter 2).

Complications in the identification of turn-taking signals and conventions, and the fact that turn-taking is under the control of the interacting parties lead us to assume that the identification of discourse structure is not to be found in turn-taking procedures observed in conversational behaviour.

4.3 On sequential relevance

The notion of sequential relevance is interactional −*ie* the constraints on what I can say or do given what you have said and done are social constraints.[13] To put this another way, in 'answering' a 'question', one is responding to a person, and not an utterance. Austin once more provides a useful starting-point for discussion. To the extent that Austin saw the perlocutionary act as intrinsically involved in a speech act, his theory has an interactional component.

A first important insight of Austin is that the successful

performance[14] of a speech act involves the securing of uptake (Austin 1976. *p* 117).[15] Securing uptake is distinguished from 'inviting a response' (*p* 118), such that it is not clear whether uptake is to be understood as a mental event (the implied sense) or the signalling of that mental event in a physical event or act. From a discourse analysis perspective, the former is of course an unobservable, except in that some other physical act – specifically a communicative act – may be said to *imply* uptake. For example, if I 'answer' your question, it seems reasonable for you to suppose that I have recognised that it was such. Whether we see uptake as a mental or a physical event, it signifies 'acceptance' or 'understanding' of the preceding speech activity of one's interlocutor. 'Acceptance' is here used non-evaluatively. If I assert that P, you may 'accept' that I have asserted that P, without accepting that P is the case: if I ask you to do P, you may 'accept' that I have asked you to do P without agreeing so to do.[16] (I shall later use the term UPTAKER in a technical sense to describe an interactional act of a particular kind – see *pp* 84–5.)

The requirement of uptake is then one way in which illocutionary acts are bound up with their effects. The central effect of an illocutionary act for Austin concerns however the 'perlocutionary act', which we should note is part of the speech act in the way that the co-present locutionary and illocutionary acts are. However Austin further distinguishes between the 'achievement of a perlocutionary object', and the 'production of a perlocutionary sequel', claiming that either may constitute the perlocutionary act performed (Austin 1976, *p* 118). The thought here is not totally clear: can one speak of *attempting* or *failing* to perform a perlocutionary act, or is the response the illocutionary act evokes the determining factor in deciding which perlocutionary act is performed thereby? It seems that intention and effect are confused in the notion of the perlocutionary act, and that speaker perspective and hearer perspective have to be clearly distinguished.

We may take the discussion a stage further by noting a semantic feature of perlocutionary verbs in English, *ie* verbs which denote the effect on a hearer of a verbal communication. It is relevant to the analysis of conversation to observe that perlocutionary verbs can be appropriately used to refer to a speaker's activity regardless as to whether or not the speaker intended to produce that perlocutionary effect. If you are amused by my screaming, crying, cursing, complaining, or whatever, I have amused you in behaving in these various ways. Consider here the following:

[4.6] (i)   He flattered her by talking of her husband's success
       (ii)   He insulted her by talking of her husband's success
       (iii) The lecturer made half the audience leave within fifteen
              minutes
       (iv)   The police made half the audience leave within fifteen
              minutes
       (v)   By arguing how dangerous it would be, you've convinced
              me I ought to go after all
       (vi)   I somehow persuaded him to go, although I was trying to
              do the opposite

                                                    (*Data fabricated*)

For (i) and (ii) there are two interpretations, according as we understand INSULT or FLATTER to refer only to the effect of his talking, or to both the effect and the intention. If we passivize, and delete *by him*, the non-intentional reading is the more likely, but not the only possible one. Knowledge of the world predisposes us to prefer a non-intentional reading for (iii), and an intentional reading for (iv), but the alternative reading is available for each, given appropriate contextualisation. (v) and (vi) are perfectly grammatical and acceptable: the air of paradox attaching to both derives from the fact that in the unmarked case such mismatches between intention and effect do not arise.

That perlocutionary verbs denote the effect of an utterance on the hearer, irrespective of whether this effect was intentional on the part of the speaker or not, means that it is literally the case that the effect of what one says may determine what one has done in saying it, or at the least what that which one has said *counts as* in the conversation. This lexico-grammatical fact is a reflection of the interactional nature of language use.[17]

What is suggested here then is that the response a speech act produces may in part at least determine what it is, or at least what it may be held to count as in an ongoing conversation. For the purposes of identifying utterances as particular moves in an interactional sequence, it is therefore relevant to consider the notion of sequential relevance, rather than to place the stress on unobservable intentional states. Consider here Campbell and Wales (1970), who remark in the context of interpreting children's verbal behaviour:

'. . . it may well be therefore that we should examine all three components of the communication act: the child's question or demand, the parental response to this and the child's response to the parent's action.' (*p* 255)[18]

The notion of sequential relevance has so far been considered as relevant to the possibility that the effects or behavioural consequences a piece of linguistic behaviour brings about may be said to (in part) determine what type of behaviour was occurring. The reverse notion is equally relevant, *ie* the notion that an initial piece of linguistic behaviour may be said to determine what type or types of behaviour may follow. This notion is central to the concept of discourse structure, and will be considered in some detail.

Firth noted in 1937 that 'whatever is said is a determining condition for what in any reasonable expectation may follow'. As a conversation develops, the number of options available to each speaker is conditioned by a process of 'contextual elimination' (Firth 1964, *p* 94).

Pike's (1967) reference to the 'distribution mode' of any unit of behaviour is based on the claim that many such units fill a particular slot in some larger behavioural unit, and that the structure of the whole determines the function of its parts. The conventions surrounding such 'slot-filler' expectations are strong. Goffman remarks for example that '. . . the expectation that an access ritual will be performed by a certain person at a certain time establishes a time-person slot such that anything issuing from him at that moment can be very closely and imaginatively read for a functional equivalent of an access ritual' (Goffman 1971, *p* 108). Or again, concerning questions and answers, 'Social nature abhors an empty slot. Anything can be dumped into it and read as the anticipated reply' (*p* 109). Goffman draws attention to two types of conditional relevance here. Firstly the case in which a given type of *situation* creates a 'slot' such that the type of interaction or interactional sequence which may occur there is highly conventionalised, and secondly the case in which a particular utterance creates a following 'slot', such that the interpretation given to what occurs as a 'response' to that utterance is highly conventionalised. Thus it is possible to attempt to chart the behavioural possibilities for specific types of situational settings (*eg* that of the restaurant – Ehlich and Rehbein 1972), or for the case in which a particular conversational goal on the part of the initiator of a conversational encounter limits the behavioural possibilities for the addressee (*eg* the case of asking for route directions – Klein 1977; Rehbein 1977, *p* 282*ff*; Wunderlich 1978).

We shall here concern ourselves with the notion of sequential relevance specifically as developed in the work of the ethno-methodologists. Sequences of sequentially-relevant units of interactional behaviour investigated include Summons-Answer sequences (Schegloff 1972a), Insertion sequences (Schegloff 1972b), Side sequences (Jefferson 1972), Closing sequences (Schegloff & Sacks 1973), Pre-sequences (Schegloff 1972a; Sacks 1972), and Repair sequences (Schegloff, Jefferson & Sacks 1977). Note that in this list we are largely dealing with facultative conversational behaviour-ritual or 'interactional management' concerns are handled in such sequences. Thus a Greet sequence is usually a prelude to some other conversational activity; a Close clearly follows some other matter; Insertion, Side, or Pre-sequences can only occur with respect to some other ongoing conversational business; before a Repair sequence is initiated there must clearly be a repairable. This may be accounted for by the observation that it is precisely their repetitive occurrence, their discourse-internal function that allows the investigation and characterisation of such sequences.

The characterisation of the non-ritual substantive content of conversational encounters is largely restricted however to the characterisation of the phenomenon of the 'tied' or 'adjacency' pair.[19] Instances of tied-pairs include Greet-Greet, Invite-Accept/Decline, Complain-Deny/Apologise, Request-Grant/Refuse, Offer-Accept/ Refuse, and the canonical case Question-Answer (this list is a composite one taken from Sacks, Schegloff and Jefferson 1974, p 716; and Schegloff 1977, p 85). Adjacency pairs are to be understood as conversational sequences whereby the occurrence of the left-hand element (a 'first pair part') makes the occurrence of the second pair part 'conditionally relevant'. This relevance can be carried over through an insertion sequence (Schegloff 1972b). There is a certain circularity in the characterisation of adjacency-pairs: consider the definition offered in Schegloff 1977, pp 84–5:

'Adjacency pairs consist of sequences which properly have the following features:
(i)   Two utterance length
(ii)   Adjacent positioning of component utterances
(iii)   Different speaker producing each utterance
(iv)   Relative ordering of parts (ie first pair parts precede second pair parts), and
(v)   discrimination relations (ie the pair type of which a first pair part is a member is relevant to the selection among second pair parts.'

The following points immediately suggest themselves:

(i)   It seems reasonable to assume that by 'utterance' something like interactional move is intended.

(ii)   'Adjacent positioning' seems to be contradicted by Schegloff's own observation that an insertion sequence may intervene.

(iii) The case in which one speaker poses a 'question' and then proceeds to 'answer' it is inconsistent with requirement 3 above, but does not seem intuitively to affect the relations holding between these two pair parts.

(iv)   The criteria above could scarcely be used to decide for any two adjacently sequenced utterances whether or not they constitute a pair, even if we assume it is possible to identify individual utterances or moves as 'questions', 'requests', 'apologies', and so on.

A problem of interpretation is also raised by the occurrence of two possible values for some second pair parts, while only one is given for others. Intuitively we discriminate between Accepting, Apologising, and Granting responses to Invitations/Offers, Complaints, or Requests, and Turning down, Denying, or Refusing responses, in that the former do not introduce potential conflict into the conversation, while the latter may. We may refer informally to the first listed alternatives as 'acceptances' of the preceding left pair parts, the latter alternatives as 'rejections'. The same distinction surely holds however for possible sequentially relevant responses to Questions, Summonses, Greetings, and Closes. While to 'answer' a Question or Summons, or 'return' a Greeting or Close are 'acceptance' responses, one might also presumably 'refuse' to answer a Question, return a Greeting, and so on. Therefore either Invite-Accept, Complain-Apologise and so on are adjacency pairs, while Invite-Reject or Complain-Deny are not, or alternative 'rejecting' options should be given for the right pair parts following Questions, Greets, Summonses, and so on.

Alternatively of course we need a reasoned ground to justify the claim that some left pair parts have unique right pair members, while others do not. A possible justification for this distinction is that abstaining from responding co-operatively to a Greeting, Summons, or a Question is anti-social in a way that turning down an Invitation, or an Offer are not. To put this another way it may be that firstly the status of the left pair parts for which only one 'acceptance' right pair part value is suggested is less likely to be a negotiable between the interacting parties than with other left pair parts, and secondly that the relevant behaviour which uniquely pairs with such left pair parts counts as a 'free good' in the sense of Goffman (*eg* 1971, *p* 92). However, while this suggestion may not be without relevance, there is as far as I am aware nothing in the ethnomethodological literature which accounts for the discrepancy noted between unique and multiple right pair part values. One obvious qualification to the tentative idea that unique right pair part values constitute free goods in a way that other right pair part values do not is the case of the 'question': there are some 'questions' to which the answer is far from a 'free' good: the critical issue here is how we are to understand the term 'question' however. I shall deal with the general issue of identification in the work of the ethnomethodologists below.

A further dimension to the nature of the tied-pair is introduced by the notion of 'elision' or 'ellipsis' in the work of Goffman (1976), or Merritt (1976). Goffman suggests that the nature of the link between some sequences can be viewed as the result of 'elision' or 'contraction'. Hence [4.7] (i) is a reduced or contracted form of [4.7] (ii):

[4.7] (i)   S1: are you coming?
              S2: I've got to work
       (ii)   S1: are you coming?
              S2: no
              S1: why not
              S2: I've got to work

The deleted elements constitute a 'back-pair'. Merritt refers to a similar phenomenon as 'the elliptical response', as in

              S1: do you have coffee to go?
              S2: black or white?

where S2's response is not a prelude to his replying to S1 (does not initiate a 'side sequence') but contains or implies the reply 'yes'.

Merritt suggests however that the possibility of filling in such elliptical material 'seems quite hopeless' (*p* 327). Merritt's data can be accounted for by general rules of implicature, and is further open to an interpretation on which S1's opening remark is interpreted as a 'Request', and hence S2's responding question *is* a preliminary to the response to the request – which will be the serving of the coffee.[20] (*Cf* the notion of 'execution' introduced in 3.1 above).

The phenomenon of 'elision' is widespread, and clearly requires accounting for. The H-support principle together with the possibility of re-constituting the 'elliptical' material may allow of a systematic account of what is happening in such instances. It seems intuitively plausible to suggest that the hearer *anticipates* possible subsequent moves on the part of the speaker, and, in responding to an anticipated move, adequately (if 'elliptically') responds to the original move. The notion of 'ellipsis' does not in itself have any descriptive power, but the phenomenon illustrated thereby is of central importance (I shall try to show) in conversational behaviour, and the possibility of reconstructing 'back-pairs' is less hopeless than Merritt claims (see 6.2 following).

Before this discussion of the tied pair, brief reference was made to the effects or consequences of a conversational move or utterance, and it was suggested that in order to characterise what a particular utterance counts as in the conversation, it may be necessary to look at what behaviour it leads to. We appear now to be following an opposite tendency, in suggesting that what follows a left pair part is identifiable in terms of what may constitute a right pair part for that particular left pair part value –*ie* a 'slot' is created such that what is placed in that slot will be interpreted relative to this placing. Clearly, we cannot here have it both ways. The dilemma may be made concrete in an example. Let us assume for the moment that 'Question-Answer' and 'Request-Comply' constitute tied pairs. We need not be in a position to define these precisely but may informally characterise the former in terms such as:

- request for a particular kind of linguistic act
- performing a (relevant) linguistic act,

while the latter may be characterised as:

- request for a particular non-linguistic act
- performing the requested act.

Let us then consider a (fabricated) sequence such as the following:

[4.8]   s1:   can you do a handstand?
        s2:   (does handstand)

Two possible analyses immediately suggest themselves. In that U1 produces a non-linguistic response, we might wish to claim that S2 has interpreted it as a 'command' or 'Request', via conventionalised implicature rules. The resultant tied-pair is a 'Request-Comply'. However, it seems intuitively equally feasible to say that given that U1 is a 'Question' (and the utterance has the locutionary force of a query), U2 is thereby to be understood as an 'Answer' ('X do P' entails 'X can do P'). The tied-pair is now of the 'Question-Answer' variety. There is of course an obvious artifice in isolating a two-unit sequence from its context,[21] and the data is fabricated. However while it might well be the case that the context would elucidate what S1 meant by U1, unless S2 clarifies in following talk his interpretation of U1 and of his own behaviour, it would seem that both proposed analyses are possible, according as we assign priority in our interpretative procedures to the 'effect-rule' (whereby U2 determines the nature of U1), or to the 'sequence-rule' (whereby U1 determines the nature of U2).

We may need here to look at a broader context than that provided by the two individual utterances, and also to allow of the possibility that what a first speaker 'meant' by U1, and what a second speaker interprets the first speaker to have meant thereby may be different. We may also need to allow of the possibility that insofar as the difference between analysis A and analysis B is determined by a difference in intentional or other mental states on the part of the interactants, we may not be in a position to choose between analysis A and analysis B. With particular regard to the notion of sequential relevance and the identification of interactional moves, I propose a 'hearer-knows-best' principle, such that H's interpretation of S's behaviour may be said to determine what S's behaviour counts as at that point of time in the ongoing conversation: this allows of the possibility of course that S may self-correct — ie the hearer-knows-best principle may be applied sequentially. This principle will clearly only be adopted as a matter of expedience in the case that alternative analyses deriving from the possibility of taking as it were S's or H's perspective offer themselves.

From the perspective of discourse analysis, it is a valid criticism of the work of the ethnomethodologists to remark that the units and sequences they present and discuss are ill-defined, such that the recognition of an utterance as a token of a particular discourse unit is largely a matter of intuition. It is assumed that the reader will recognise the 'rightness' of the proposed analysis somehow, given the 'real' cited data, which is often presented as though it itself justifies the analysis offered. There is further often the appearance of circularity attaching to the arguments brought forward.

The reason is that the ethnomethodologists are concerned to discover the structure of different types of social interaction rituals via the analysis of conversation. The concentration on ritual or facultative aspects of conversational behaviour has been noted above, and turn-taking procedures are also an ethnomethodological concern (see 4.2 above, pp 39–41). The central interest is not on what is said, but on what is done in interactional terms. What is said is assumed to be transparent, and intuitively interpretable as a means of interaction. Thus the links between what is said and what is done thereby are not investigated in any detail inside the ethnomethodological approach. The dilemma in discourse analysis might be said to be that linguistic and social behavioural forms are co-present in an utterance or other conversational segment. Therefore either the linguistic facts are to be taken as given, and used for the interpretation of social realities (a crude paraphrase of the ethnomethodologists' position), or the 'social facts' are to be taken as given, and used for the interpretation of the linguistic reality – specifically the coherence of the discourse. Consequently it is difficult to apply ethnomethodological terms to the analysis of actual data.[22]

A further general reservation one may have about the direct applicability of the ethnomethodologists' work to the analysis of discourse concerns its selective approach to data. Isolated sequences of discourse are analysed as revealing or interesting in the light they shed on social behaviour, but such a selective approach is open to the sort of criticism levelled against those who handle constructed data, *ie* furnish their own examples of discourse, namely that the data is selected because of its analysability. This is a perfectly warranted pragmatic approach – one has to start somewhere – but if we are looking for a model of discourse, we have ourselves to interpret the theoretical framework inside which piecemeal analyses are offered.

This does not at all mitigate the fact that the work of (principally) Sacks, Schegloff, and Jefferson reflects a perspective on the conversational use of language which has been little investigated inside linguistics. The central importance of 'placing' and of turn-taking procedures for example are little reflected in the theory of speech acts or the concerns of textlinguistics. It further seems clear that the sequential organisation of talk is governed by social constraints – *ie* the notion of sequential relevance implies the notion of *interactional* structure. What we appear to need is a system for reconciling or combining the notion of an utterance or other behavioural unit as an illocutionary act and the social perspective whereby the same utterance or behavioural token is seen as an interactional act or move.

Notes

1 While the ethnographical and sociological work of for example Fishman, Gumperz, Hymes, and Labov has been important in drawing the attention of linguists to the social parameters of language use, it would of course be wrong to suggest that the social significance of language had previously been universally neglected. Firth and his followers – what Langendoen calls 'the London school' (Langendoen 1968), Pike (*eg* 1967), and Halliday (*eg* 1973) are amongst the exceptions that spring to mind. For a view of the study of language as a branch of anthropology, see Hartmann 1974. On language as a means of *sharing* experience, see for example Cherry 1968, *p* 6; Allen and Guy 1974, *p* 11.

2 See *eg* von Wright 1963, *pp* 42 *et seq.*; Watzlawick, Beavin and Jackson 1967, *p* 48; Twer 1972, *pp* 343–4.

3 The writer has observed that if he, while reading or otherwise engaged, responds verbally to a bid for attention from a three-year-old child without lifting his eyes, the summons will be repeated as many as six times: deliberately 'attending' however immediately produces confidence and talk.

4 *Cf* the distinction between signalling and communicating made by Marshall 1970 in the field of biology.

5 *Cf* Laver and Hutcheson 1972, *p* 13: '. . . those gestures which are substitutable for verbal elements could be said to have semantic correlates equivalent to the verbal elements they replace'. It is not immediately clear what 'semantic correlates' could here mean: I prefer to substitute the phrase 'an interactional significance'.

6 What 'immediately' here means is probably a variable for different types of request, and for different situations. However, it would seem that in the case that no time of execution is specified in the issuing of the request, or implied from the surrounding co-text, the speaker desires that the addressee begin acting in such a way as to initiate events which contribute towards the execution of the request within a determinable span of time, probably in the vicinity of a maximum of sixty seconds – when a side-sequence or other negotiation is opened by the addressee, this is all changed of course.

7 *Cf* Goffman 1976, *p* 290: 'What is basic to natural talk may not be a conversational unit at all, but an interactional one . . .'

8 I will however later suggest that the ability to decode while talking simultaneously is both highly-developed and normal for members.

9 The data has been transcribed here using a less idiosyncratic (and confusing) set of conventions than that of SS&J. See *pp* 9–11 above. If in doing so I have misread their transcription, this does not critically affect the point being made here.

10 SS&J fudge here (*p* 716) by remarking that tied-pairs 'share the property of *possibly* selecting next speaker' (my italics). I shall turn to this issue below. On the notion of the 'tied pair' see 4.3.

11 *eg* (*p* 706) 'The concerns of this paper seem to us not to turn on this order of detail, and we avoid prejudicing the issue . . .' *Cf* footnote 25, *p* 714.

12 *Cf* Poyatos 1976, in which Poyatos refers to 'total body communication', some features of which are linked to turn-taking.

13 *Cf* Hasan 1977, *p* 229: '. . . the nearest non-linguistic analogue of a text is not a logico-mathematical formula, but a non-verbal social event. A text is a social event whose primary mode of unfolding is linguistic. If text can be seen as a bridge between the verbal symbolic system and the culture, this is because of the relation between text and social context: text is "in language" as well as "in culture".' Hasan here uses the term 'text' to denote what we have termed 'discourse'.

14 A certain amount of fudging is noticeable in Austin in that whenever perlocution is involved he tends to refer not simply to the 'speech act', but to the 'successful performance of the speech act', or even the 'wholly successful performance' of the same.

15 *Cf* Heal 1974, *p* 108: 'I do not fully succeed in asking a question unless the person to whom I speak grasps that I am asking a question', or Wunderlich 1974, *p* 17: 'Wie auch immer der erfolgreiche Vollzug eines Sprechakts zu definieren ist, eine der Bedingungen dafür dürfte sein, daß der Hörer den Illokutionsakt versteht.'

16 *Cf* the distinction between the moves ACCEPT and EVALUATE in Sinclair & Coulthard 1975, *p* 43, or Wunderlich's distinction between 'Verstehen' and 'Akzeptieren' (Wunderlich 1972a, *p* 23).

17 The notion that the conception of what a thing is may be equated with its immediate or remote effects is central to philosophical Pragmatism, as developed by Peirce and his followers (See *eg* the papers from Peirce and James reprinted in Hayden and Alworth 1965, especially *pp* 161, 222). See also the discussion of 'Rose's gloss' in Garfinkel and Sacks 1970, *pp* 366 *et seq*.

18 Note that in Labov 1972, the rules defining sounding refer to hearer-beliefs about speaker-beliefs – *ie* mental states – but as to when ritual sounding becomes personal insult, the critical issue is hearer-response – *ie* the case in which the person sounded on attempts to disclaim or deny the content of the sound.

19 The term 'utterance pair' (originating with Sacks) is used in Schegloff 1972b. 'Adjacency pair' is proposed in Schegloff and Sacks 1973 (*p* 295), and is used in the subsequent ethnomethodological literature. I shall use the terms 'tied pair' and 'adjacency pair' in free variation.

20 *Cf* here Winograd's SHRDLU programme, which answers a 'question' of the kind 'Is at least one of them narrower than the one I told you to pick up?' by saying 'Yes, the red cube', and not simply 'Yes' – *ie* 'The system has heuristics about what information is relevant to a person who asks a question, even if he does not request that information specifically.' (Winograd 1977, *p* 428).

21 *Cf* Gunter 1974, quoted in Goffman 1976, *p* 277: 'Yet we must see that the dialogic approach inherits many of the limitations of the grammarian's, the sins of which, after all, it was meant to correct. I refer to the sin of noncontextuality, to the assumption that bits of conversation can be analysed in their own right in some independence of what was occurring at the time and place.'

22 *Cf* Coulthard 1977, *p* 91. An illustration of the problem of identification is provided by Schegloff 1977, in which the term 'question' features prominently. It is extremely difficult to understand how Schegloff understands the term 'question' however. The clearest statement suggests that the sequentially-relevant 'answer' is the central identifying factor, though the 'special constraints' on the second pair part have not as yet been 'analytically explicated'. This suggests intuition must be our mainstay here: indeed Schegloff disarmingly claims it may not be 'useful' to distinguish 'questions' in any case (Schegloff 1977, *p* 99).

Chapter 5:

Some systems for the analysis of spoken discourse

We finished Chapter 3 by suggesting that we require a *technical* notion of the 'illocutionary act' if we aspire to producing an inventory of such acts capable of insightful application to a range of conversational data. In Chapter 4 it has been suggested that the structure of a conversational event is not a strictly *linguistic* structure, but that a conversation is structured as are other forms of social interaction. Chapter 4 concluded with the suggestion that if in discourse analysis we wish to relate conversational structure to linguistic behaviour, we appear to require a perspective whereby a conversational unit is seen as both illocution and interaction. This would suggest that in contributing to an ongoing conversation a speaker is in the unmarked case *both* communicating his own wishes, feelings, beliefs, and desires, and interacting with a fellow member, eliciting and giving responses in a dynamic process of negotiation.

In this chapter I wish to review in some detail four systematic approaches to the analysis of discourse which may be interpreted as suggesting ways of combining these two aspects of spoken discourse, before presenting a new model in Chapter 6. The discussion here will attempt to establish both respects in which the models discussed are deficient, and aspects in which they are insightful, in terms of suggesting an approach to be developed in Chapter 6 following.

The specific approaches to be discussed in varying degrees of detail are those of Rehbein and Ehlich (particularly 1975, 1976), Labov and Fanshel 1977, Klammer 1973, and finally Sinclair and Coulthard 1975. As the first two approaches do not differ essentially in terms of the type of model they suggest for the analysis of conversation, we shall review them under the collective head 'Speech Act Sequences'.

5.1 Speech act sequences

5.1.1

The work of Rehbein and Ehlich (*eg* Rehbein & Ehlich 1975, 1976) is built on the model of the interactional process presented by Labov (Labov 1971, *p* 209; 1972, *pp* 122–3: also given in Rehbein 1972, *p* 289), and further is directly relevant to the notion of the tied or adjacency pair. For we may interpret Rehbein and Ehlich (R&E) as showing that in the case that a 'rejection' as opposed to an 'acceptance' follows a left pair part (using the informal terms proposed on *p* 47 above), the conversational unit initiated by a left pair part is not brought to a potential point of closure, we move rather into a *sequence* of speech acts, rather than having a closed pair of such acts. It is the structure of such sequences that R&E may be said to investigate. We again interpret R&E as saying that given an initial act (whether a speech act, or some other act belonging to the 'pre-history' of a specific speech act), arrival at a 'possible point of subsequent action' is dependent on some 'understanding' between S and H, where we may freely interpret the 'acceptance' values for the right hand elements of adjacency pairs as showing 'understanding'. Given the non-occurrence of such an 'accepting' move however, the non-understood participant will seek to convert the 'non-understanding' of his interlocutor to a state of 'understanding', at which point the hearer will either 'accept' the proffered *'Begründung'*, or not (in their English terminology, acceptance will cause the 'reasoning' offered to become 'effective'). If the proffered 'Begründung' is not accepted, the process may be recycled. Simplifying somewhat, we may present R&E's (1975, 76) model as on *p* 56.

Some details are omitted, and the labels offered are not those of R&E. Boxes indicate speech acts, mental acts, and other acts which may be viewed as causing speech behaviour, *ie* as having interactional consequences. Diamonds indicate decision-nodes. Double lines indicate encoding processess. 'U' indicates 'understanding', which it should be stressed is not a mental understanding of the content of an utterance, but rather something like the 'acceptance' of the person responsible for the utterance so 'understood': it becomes in fact a matter of definition that when 'understanding' has been reached, a point of possible closure has been reached in the interaction.

The model is essentially one of psychological reconstruction, and the decision nodes allow of different paths through the psychological network. Consider however the distinction made by R&E between a

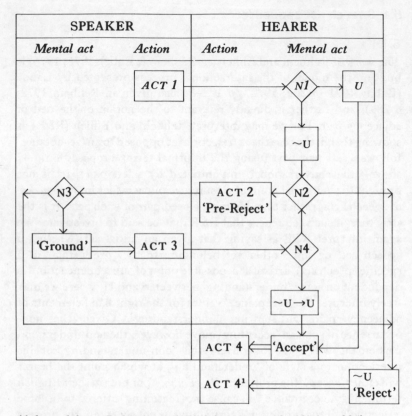

SPEAKER		HEARER	
Mental act	*Action*	*Action*	*Mental act*

(Adapted from Rehbein and Ehlich 1975, *p* 13; 1976, *p* 335).

'Begründung' as a speech act and a 'Begründungsversuch' (1975, *pp* 15 et seq.), *ie* the claim that the effects of a speech act are bound up with their nature, which leads directly to the consideration of the individual speech act as one event in a sequence of such acts. A point to ·be made here is that just as H's reaction to ACT 3 has critical significance in terms of the potential closure of this 'Handlungssequenz', so may S's reaction to ACT 4^1. Given that S1 initiates the process modelled with ACT 1, in this model it is S2 whose behaviour determines when a point of possible completion is reached. However intuition and empirical evidence suggest that this is not always so. For example, if a sequence such as the following:

- Oh sorry, I've got your pen (returning it)
- That's okay (accepting pen)

fits into the model above, what will one do with the following:

- Hey, is that my pen you've got there?
- Oh sorry, so it is (returning it)
- That's okay (accepting pen)

(fabricated)

The data is fabricated, and I do not wish to claim that any 'Reasoning' is going on here (which raises the issue of the generalisability of the model of the psychological process modelled to other conversational sequences), but surely the same structural sequence may indeed occur with a 'Begründung' sequence. Consider the case of a 'recycled' ACT 2^1, *ie* the case in which ACT 3 leads to another instance of ACT 2 on the part of the right-hand player. May not this ACT 2^1 also be a 'Begründung' of ACT 2? This would suggest that the model would be flipped over so to speak, such that the agent of ACT 1 has the option of 'accepting' ACT 2^1, and thus bringing the sequence to a possible point of closure, and is doing so withdrawing his initial ACT 1.

The brief discussion above raises the following issues concerning the application of the model in empirical analysis:

(i)   the question as to whether the number of such sequences as the one discussed above is finite – *ie* whether it is the case that for any encountered piece of data some further complex psychological network might not be set up, and thus what constraints operate in such sequencing (Consider the *Register* given in Rehbein 1977, *pp* 378–83),

(ii)   the question as to how far the reconstruction of alleged psychological networks is an empirical procedure – *ie* how such models can be tested as to their validity, and

(iii)   the question as to what degree of delicacy in such analyses is optimal for which descriptive or theoretical purposes.

The work of Rehbein and Ehlich represents a careful exploration of some psychological processes involved in the interactional process however, and has explanatory power for some speech act sequences. Of further, theoretical, importance is the attempt to suggest sequencing possibilities for more than two speech acts: the 'value' of a right pair part for example is seen as relevant to the arrival of the interaction at a point of possible closure.

5.1.2

The work of Labov and Fanshel (1977) offers certain parallels to that of Rehbein and Ehlich, and makes explicit reference to both the philosophical approach to speech acts discussed in Chapter 3 above, and the ethnomethodological approach discussed in Chapter 4.

Labov and Fanshel (L&F) analyse therapeutic discourse, and are concerned to 'explore the goals and techniques of therapy' (*p* ix). At the same time they are concerned to 'extend the scope of linguistic analysis to conversation as a whole' (*p* 349). It seems fair to say that the *local* analytic concern receives more insightful attention than the more global aim. In fact, it is not altogether easy to summarize their analytic procedures in terms of a model. We may distinguish, however, between the 'cross-sectional analyses', in which what is said is related to what is done, and the 'sequencing rules' whereby 'a number of such cross-sections are linked in a tight matrix of action and response, centering around a single topic or concern' (*p* 69). In the terms we have been developing, we shall seek to understand the cross-sectional analyses as procedures for deriving illocutionary force (what is done) from locutionary form (what is said), and the sequencing rules as indicating the interactional significance of conversational units, as revealed in their placing relative to other conversational elements. In fact, however, this distinction is neither clearly made nor consistently maintained in L&F's analyses.

In shifting from what is said to what is done via the 'rules of interpretation and production' given in Chapter 3, L&F produce some highly insightful analyses. The rules proposed bear some affinity to those for performing indirect speech acts in Searle 1975, and Gordon and Lakoff 1975. (Compare also Sinclair and Coulthard 1975, *pp* 29–32, discussed briefly on *p* 67 below.) I shall return to these rules of interpretation and production shortly.

The most explicit statement of general *sequencing* rules we find in L&F is given in the form of a table, and includes the following block of 'speech events'[1] given under the heading 'Representations':

D- EVENTS (Disputable)

A	B	A
assert	deny	contradict
give evaluation	agree	support
give interpretation	support	
give orientation	give reinterpretation	

(L&F, *p* 61)

Note that while the left-to-right columns appear to reflect turn-taking sequences (A speaks, B speaks, A speaks), and the top-to-bottom entries alternative options, this is not always so. For example, A may Contradict[2] or Support his own statement before or after B speaks (p 63). Again, the options listed in column one above for example are clearly not mutually exclusive:

> 'After presenting a series of events representing something that actually happened, the speaker will then *give an evaluation* of the significance of these events in emotional or socially evaluated terms.' (p 63)

In other words, an Evaluation may follow an Assert.

The following critical observations suggest themselves, given the direction of argumentation pursued in this book so far:

(i)   The terms used are common-sense ones, and the labels used in fact presuppose the sequencing possibilities given. On the first point, if A may give an Evaluation, Interpretation, or Orientation, why not an 'explanation', 'summary', or whatever? If either A or B may Support, why is it that only A may Contradict, while only B may Deny? What is the difference? On the second point, 'deny' or 'agree' clearly presuppose a speech action to be denied or agreed with: giving a Reinterpretation differs from giving an Interpretation only in that the former presupposes the prior occurrence in the relevant segment of discourse of the latter.

(ii)   There is further overlap, as 'meta-linguistic' speech actions co-occur in any cross-sectional analysis. Thus any of the speech actions above is at the same time to be classified as (roughly) Initiating, Continuing, or Ending (p 61). However, these 'metalinguistic' functions would seem to a large extent to be presupposed by the labelling attached to other speech actions to which they are to be ascribed. For example, it would seem to be true as a matter of definition that a Deny or Agree may not be an Initiate, that an Assert may not Continue or End.

(iii)   Sequencing possibilities are not made explicit in such a schematic presentation, in part because turn-taking is not necessarily built into the sequencing blocks given. For example, in the block given above, if A, following B's turn at talk, contradicts himself (or herself)[3], this may presumably count as either a Contradict or Support with reference to B's intervening speech action, according as this was an Agree or Deny. In the latter case, A's Support will presumably constitute a Retreat – a category appearing in column three under the heading

Requests, but not appearing under Representations. The *former* case, that in which A contradicts himself after B has agreed with or supported A's assert, seems in fact intuitively highly unlikely. It is difficult to find any *system* at work here.

In short, the terms and categories used here seem ad hoc, sequencing rules are not specified explicitly, turn-assignment problems are not clarified in connection with sequencing possibilities, and illocutionary and interactional aspects of talk are not distinguished in the labels offered for different types of 'speech actions'.

In a sense however, this very confusion gives rise to the most insightful aspect of L&F's approach. For some of the rules of interpretation and production given are, we may say, 'discourse-sensitive' – *ie* in order to determine what is done, L&F also take account of *where* a particular type of utterance occurs, in terms of its location in a sequence of speech actions. Consider for example the following two rules:

Rule for Embedded Requests
'If A makes a request for action B, and B responds with a request for information, B is heard as asserting that he needs this information in order to respond to A's request' (*p* 91).

Rule for Reinstating Requests
'If B has responded to a request for action from A by making a request for information, and A gives that information, then A is heard as making the original request for action again' (*p* 93).

These rules capture interpretive/productive procedures inside one possible sequential sequence. The structural phenomenon interpreted is the 'insertion' or 'side' sequence[4] of the ethnomethodologists, and the Rule for Reinstating Requests captures the claim of Schegloff that the 'conditional relevance' of a left-pair part is carried over through an inserted sequence (see *p* 46 above). *Recursion* is structurally accounted for here, as in the 'recycling' possible in the Rehbein/Ehlich model discussed above, in that following the Rule for Reinstating Requests, the Rule for Embedded Requests may again apply. Further, multiple embedding is captured as a structural potential, as a request for information is a sub-type of the request for action. (See L&F, footnote *p* 92, and compare Schegloff 1972b, *p* 79).

In the light of rules such as those for Embedding or Reinstating

Requests, L&F claim that 'the rules for interpretation and production have absorbed much of the complexity that has appeared elsewhere in discussions of sequencing' (p. 111). Having then made a distinction between rules of interpretation/production and rules of sequencing, L&F now appear to be claiming that the former make the latter redundant. What rules such as the two given above do however is to give an interpretative account of a *specific* sequencing possibility: they do not in themselves specify a set of sequencing possibilities. In order to do this (and thereby make separate sequencing rules redundant), L&F would need to give similar interpretative rules for each and every possible conversational sequence. This would clearly be inefficient, fail to capture generalisations concerning interactional structure, and lack psychological plausibility in terms of the learning of such rules. We do not therefore find in Labov and Fanshel a model which makes the illocution/interaction distinction redundant: on the contrary, the weaknesses in the model discussed support the necessity of making that distinction.

5.2 A tagmemic model

In Klammer 1973, a tagmemic model is developed to establish the 'Foundations for a theory of dialogue structure'. That language is to be viewed as social behaviour is stressed: the perspective is similar to that of Pike or Halliday. For our own analytic purposes we feel a small, but possibly important, reservation needs to be made when we read that 'the original motivation for the study grew out of a concern with written texts, in which phonological structure is necessarily obscured' (*p* 38), and when we further observe that the data cited has every appearance of being fabricated for illustrative purposes.[5] In fact, the interest of Klammer's work lies more in the model it suggests than the dialogue structures it develops and describes. As Klammer presents the foundations of a *theory*, this is perfectly reasonable, but we shall wish to assess his theory with reference to the analyses it allows, of course.

Dialogue paragraphs (DP's) are conversational units which combine in certain ways in conversations. Klammer is largely concerned to demonstrate the internal structure of different types of DP's however, and we shall therefore restrict ourselves to this structural scope. The central claim is that an utterance as an element in a DP has both a 'grammatical' function, as an 'initiating', 'countering', or 'resolving' unit for example, and a 'lexemic' function such as 'question', 'remark', or 'proposal'. The relationship between the two is one of 'manifestation', such that for example an Initiating Speech (Sp-I) may be made manifest in a Question, and the following Resolving Speech (Sp-R) in an Answer. Such a pair forms a non-compound, simple DP. The lexemic pairs given are simply

Question – Answer
Remark   – Evaluation
Proposal – Response

It is intuitively clear that Questions, Remarks, and Proposals seem to match grammatical choices of mood – interrogative, declarative, imperative respectively – and that we appear to have 'adjacency pairs' here. The nature of the link between these lexemic tagmemes and grammatical categories of mood, and between the left and right pair parts – in the terminology of the ethnomethodologists – is however not explored in Klammer's paper. One problem here is that if grammatical and lexemic function are to be kept distinct, how is it possible to define the right pair parts of the lexemic pairs above such that their *grammatical* function is not contained in such definitions? For example, can an Answer to a Question be other than a Resolving Speech, in the case that the Question was an Initiating Speech?

In a Complex, as opposed to a Simple, DP, an Initiating slot is followed by one or more 'countering' slots (SP-Cs), and the occurrence or non-occurrence of a 'Resolving' unit (Sp-R) will determine whether or not the resultant DP is itself 'resolved' or 'unresolved'. If the final exchange contains an Sp-R, the whole DP is 'resolved'. Klammer here remarks:

'. . . simply to take Utterance and Response, or Elicitation and Response, as primitives in language study will be inadequate as a means of language analysis. There must be at least a third basic category, corresponding to our Sp-C, which is both a reply in terms of the speech which precedes it and an elicitation in terms of the speech that follows it' (*p* 34).

In addition, Klammer's system allows of DP 'margins', or 'peripheries', which may precede or follow the nuclear exchange in a DP and 'act as an important means of linking and transition within longer stretches of dialogue' (*p* 42). One type of postnuclear margin is the Terminating Speech (Sp-T), commonly manifest in the lexemic tagmeme 'Compliance' or 'Dissatisfaction'.

There is much to criticize here, though we have presented only the basic notions in Klammer's system. None of the lexemic or grammatical tagmemes are defined, which makes for interpretative difficulties. We note though that just as some right pair parts have multiple values in the ethnomethodologists' work (p 47 above), so here the 'positive' or 'negative' value of a lexemic tagmeme does not affect its potential grammatical function. Thus for example (p 36):

A: Chuckleberry had a misspent youth
B: You're very wrong about that

constitutes a Resolved DP – the Sp-R being presumably an 'Evaluation' in lexemic function. However when a lexemic function such as Question or Remark manifests a Countering slot in the grammatical structure of a DP, it seems intuitively obvious that the 'positive' or 'negative' value of the lexemic Answer or Evaluation critically affects the question as to whether or not the DP is resolved. For example Klammer gives (p 40):

A: Chuckleberry had a misspent youth
B: Do you think yours was any better
A: No, I guess not

as a Complex Resolved DP, the grammatical structure being Sp-I, Sp-C, Sp-R, and the lexemic structure Remark–Question-Answer. However, a possible token for the Answer would be 'Well yes I do actually' or something such. It is intuitively obvious that this 'answer' does not 'resolve' the DP in the way that 'No I guess not' did. The utterance 'Well yes I do actually' would then perhaps not be deemed to be an Sp-R in grammatical structure, but perhaps an Sp-C: to be consistent we shall then apparently re-analyse the utterance lexemically as a Remark, not an Answer. But this seems adhocery.

Consider then the case in which the alternative 'Answer' I have just suggested is followed by a non-agreeing 'Evaluation' by B of A's original utterance, such that the constructed sequence appears for example as:

[5.1] A: Chuckleberry had a misspent youth
      B: Do you think yours was any better?
      A: Well yes I do actually
      B: Well I think Chuckleberry's youth was perfectly okay

The data seems a simple case of embedding, but as far as I can see cannot be adequately handled in Klammer's analytic schema. It can be analysed, of course. The problem is, it can be handled several ways, and there appears to be no ground on which we may say we should choose one of these possibilities rather than another. We could for example call B's second utterance an Sp-T margin, manifest as a Dissatisfaction in lexemic function. The whole sequence could then be analysed as either

Sp-I, Sp-C, Sp-C, Sp-T or Sp-I, Sp-C, Sp-R, Sp-T,

with the latter possibility to be preferred if Terminating moves may only follow Resolving moves. Again, on the evidence of *p* 35, where the following analysis is cited:

Sp-I A: Chuckleberry had a misspent youth
Sp-C B: Do you think yours was any better?
Sp-C A: Even if it wasn't it's none of your business
Sp-C B: Please don't raise your voice
Sp-C A: Chuckleberry *did* have a misspent youth

we might view the second B utterance in [5.1] as an Sp-C. As Sp-Cs may not follow Sp-Rs in Klammer's system (and indeed a Resolving Speech is badly named if it is immediately followed by a Counter), the whole sequence would now have to be Sp-I, Sp-C, Sp-C, Sp-C. A third possibility is suggested by a citation on *p* 33; which we reproduce as given:

'(Previous dialogue between A and B)

Sp-I A: Chuckleberry did *too* have a misspent youth (exits)'

It appears we may now view B's second utterance as initiating a new DP, bound in some way to the preceding one, which we may still analyse as Resolved or not. Our analysis is now:

$$DP1: Sp\text{-}I, Sp\text{-}C, \left\{ \begin{array}{c} Sp\text{-}R \\ Sp\text{-}C \end{array} \right\} ; DP2: Sp\text{-}I.$$

There seems little to choose (other than what our intuitions might propose) between these various accounts. We should temper this remark by observing that Klammer's article is based on his unpublished doctoral thesis, in which the issues we have raised are doubtless dealt with in greater detail. The point though surely is that unless the different lexemic and grammatical functions invoked are precisely defined and distinguished, the structural apparatus allowed by Klammer's system is far too powerful. Unresolved simple DPs may have only one element of structure. After an Sp-I, n Sp-Cs may occur, and a following Sp-R may or may not occur. Further we have possible 'margins' which may precede or follow Sp-Is and Sp-Rs. Our central and critical interpretative problem concerns the identification of lexemic functions which may manifest the Sp-R in grammatical structure. Klammer's model is therefore difficult to apply to data, the lack of criteria for identifying the lexemic and grammatical tagmemes being the major difficulty.

However, of real interest and importance is the distinction between 'grammatical' and 'lexemic' function – *ie* the notion that units of dialogue are to be identified on two interrelated levels. The nature of this interrelation is however not very thoroughly investigated in Klammer's article. He notes (*p* 42) that grammatical structure is 'usually' sequential and linear, while lexemic structure is not necessarily determined by contiguity, as lexemic functions (Questions and Answers, and so on) are related to each other 'logically and semantically'. The only instance in which there is a non-direct match between a left pair part in lexemic function (Question, Remark, or Proposal) and an Initiating or Countering element in grammatical structure, and a further match between an Answering, Evaluating, or Responding lexemic tagmeme and a Resolving element in grammatical structure concerns the case in which one speaker inside one turn produces two utterances, each of which has a lexemic value, but which *together* count as an Sp-I in Grammatical structure. The corresponding lexemic tagmemes (right pair parts) then *together* manifest the Sp-R by the following speaker. This seems a relatively uninteresting case in which a one-to-one mapping is not discernible. Klammer himself suggests that the relations between lexemic structure and grammatical structure require further investigation (*p* 42).

Summarising the above, we may claim that the distinction between 'grammatical' and 'lexemic' categories is far from clear – lexemic categories such as 'Answer' or 'Response' would appear to have a *grammatical* function built into them for example. Further the problems of identification and application with this model are considerable. However, a tagmemic model such as Klammer's offers a means of combining the notions of interactional structure and illocutionary force, and a notion such as that of the 'discourse paragraph' would seem to have more general and complex structural potential than that of the tied or adjacency pair.

5.3 'Situational' and 'Discourse' categories
in a rank-scale model

The work of Sinclair and Coulthard (1975) bears some affinities to
that of Klammer above (*cf* also Hasan 1977). The qualifications and
emendations proposed in Coulthard and Brazil 1979 do not essentially
alter the strengths and weaknesses of the 1975 model in my opinion,[6]
and I shall therefore concentrate on the 1975 model in this discussion.
The descriptive model used is Hallidayan, such that units of the
lowest rank – *Acts* – are defined functionally, and higher-rank units
are defined in terms of possible combinatorial structures of
lower-rank units. Inside such structures, some elements are optional.[7]
Ranks of discourse events are schematically related to grammatical
units and external non-linguistic events as follows (*p* 24):

Non-linguistic organisation	Discourse	Grammar
course		
period		
topic	lesson	
	transaction	
	exchange	
	move	sentence
	act	clause
		group
		word
		morpheme

Of central importance is S&C's notion of discourse function. The
lack of a one-to-one correspondence between grammatical form and
discourse function – between clause and Act – is to be accounted for in
'situation' and 'tactics' (*p* 28). The former term while imprecise
concerns features of the type we are familiar with from our discussion
of indirect speech acts, and includes 'all relevant factors in the
environment, social conventions, and the shared experience of the
participants' (*p* 28). The latter term concerns the factor of 'placing'
which is stressed in the ethnomethodologists' work on conversation.
S&C claim that 'It is place in the structure of the discourse which
finally determines which act a particular grammatical item is
realizing, though classification can only be made of items already
tagged with features from grammar and situation' (*p* 29).
      The distinctive feature of S&C's notion of discourse function

concerns their tentative exploration of the relations between these two factors, utterance value in 'situation', and utterance value in 'tactics'. Klammer's distinction between lexemic and grammatical function seems not dissimilar. We shall in fact wish to see whether this distinction can be interpreted as that between illocutionary act and interactional act or move.

Consider first the relation between a declarative sentence and a 'statement', or an interrogative and a 'question'. There is no one-to-one mapping here, as both the logical sense of the sentence and the situational context in which it is used determine which situational category the utterance belongs to. S&C present what we may call grammatico-situationally determined interpretative rules whereby for example an interrogative clause is to be interpreted as a 'command to do' if it contains certain grammatical features (presence of one of a set of modal verbs, second-person subject) and if the predicate describes a proscribed action which is physically possible at the time of utterance (p 32). Such interpretative rules 'predict when a declarative or interrogative will be realizing something other than a statement or a question'. There is a direct parallel here to procedures in Searle for deriving illocutionary force from locutionary force (to use our terms rather than Searle's). Searle's conventions for indirect requesting are re-formulated as interpretative rules with situation–specific constraints.

We feel justified then in claiming that S&C's situational categories are illocutionary acts whose force is determined by the logical sense of the utterance and situational points of reference bearing on its use. However the value of an utterance in 'situation' (its illocutionary value) and its characterisation in 'tactics' are non-identical. S&C present the following table (p 29):

Discourse Categories	Situational Categories	Grammatical Categories
informative	statement	declarative
elicitation	question	interrogative
directive	command	imperative

and discuss the relationship between the situational categories and the discourse categories as follows:
'The definitions of the discourse acts, informative, elicitation, and directive, make them sound remarkably similar to statement, question, and command but there are major differences. While

elicitations are always realized by questions, directives by commands, and informatives by statements, the relationship is not reciprocal . . . Statements, questions, and commands are only informatives, elicitations, and directives when they are initiating, an elicitation is an initiating question of which the function is to gain a verbal response from another speaker. . . a question which is not intended to get a reply is realizing a different act from one which is; the speaker is using the question for a different purpose and we must realize this in our description.' (*p* 34)

What this suggests is that a Question may somehow be defined over and above grammatical features such that it is not necessarily an Elicitation, a Command such that it is distinct from a Directive, and a Statement such that it does not overlap with the definition of an Informative. As none of the situational categories are defined in S&C, a host of interpretative problems arise. Compare the following two analysed extracts from Text H (*pp* 92, 94):

[5.2] (i)		ACT	MOVE
	– What do we do with a saw	*Elicitation*	*Opening*
	– Cut wood	*Reply*	*Answering*
	– Yes	*Evaluate*	
	You're shouting out though	*Comment*	*Follow-up*
(ii)	– Scissors	*Starter*	*Opening*
	What do I cut with scissors	*Elicitation*	
	– Paper paper	*Reply*	*Answering*
	– Yes paper	*Evaluate*	*Follow-up*
	Somebody's shouting out at the back	*Directive*	*Opening*
	– (non-Verbal)	*React*	*Answering*[8]

On what ground may we interpret the utterance 'You're shouting out though' as a Comment in [5.2] (i), while the utterance 'Somebody's shouting out at the back' in [5.2] (ii) is to be identified as a Directive? The answer must be that their placing is different. However this does not help us, as in both instances the placing is 'post Follow-up'. Despite this it is intuitively clear that intonation and pausing might reveal that the relevant utterance in (ii) above does not belong to the preceding Exchange in the way that the Comment in (i) might be felt to do.

What then of the situational value of these two acts? The Directive in (ii) above is a Command, as Directives are always realized by Commands. What of the Comment in (i)? According to S&C a Comment 'is realized by statement and tag-question' (p 42), though this is hedged by an 'almost always' on p 36. However one is reluctant to interpret the utterance 'You're shouting out though' as a Statement in situation, as our knowledge of the world gives us to assume that shouting out is a proscribed activity in this setting, and it should therefore be read as a 'command to stop' (p 32).[9] Note also that if the Comment were of the form 'But don't shout out please', its interpretation as a Statement as opposed to a Command would evidence the only combination of grammatical and situational categories which S&C did not come across in their data (p 29). It appears then that the Comment in [5.2] (i) above is a Command in situation, just as is the Directive in (ii). If this is so, the question is how we can interpret the notion of a Command such that it does not 'request a non-linguistic response' – ie such that it does not have a Directive discourse function (p 41).

I would suggest that a Command *does* have a Directive function in that it must count as a Request to do, regardless of its placing in discourse structure, but in S&C's system Commands which are non-directive in discourse structure are distinguished from those that are by their subordinate discourse function – ie in the structure of the discourse, Commands which appear as other than head of an Opening Move are subordinate in function to some other Act. This leads to circularity in the notion of discourse structure. The point is clearly of importance: I shall try to reinforce it by examining the Acts Clue and Starter.

A Clue is 'Realized by statement, question, command, or moodless item[10]. It is subordinate to the head of the initiation and functions by providing additional information which helps the pupil to answer the elicitation or comply with the directive' (p 42). A *Starter* is remarkably similar: it functions to 'provide information about, or direct attention or thought towards, an area in order to make a correct response to the initiation more likely' (p 34), and is also realised by statement, question, or command (p 40). The difference between the two is their structural potential: a Starter may appear only as pre-head in an Opening Move, while a Clue is an optional post-head element (p 26).

The argumentation is clearly circular: Acts are to be 'functionally' defined and then occur as elements of structure in Moves, Exchanges, and Transactions. We may not then validly distinguish one act from another by virtue of their respective structural potential.

How though are Starters and Clues to be distinguished from Informatives, Elicitations, and Directives? A Statement, Question, or Command is classifiable as Starter in the case that the teacher does not allow an answering Move, but retains the speaking turn. In a sequence of Statements and other illocutions, it is ('usually') the final one which is initiating, and by not relinquishing his turn the teacher 'pushes down' preceding Statements, Questions, or Commands to act as Starters (*p* 35). The problem then arises, however, how a Statement, Question, or Command may appear in *post*-head position in an opening Move –*ie* the existence of the Clue appears to contradict the argumentation for the identification of the Starter.

The distinction between a Clue and a Directive is illustrated by reference to a teacher-utterance 'look at the car': 'It does not have the status of a directive because its function is not to cause a pupil reaction. If the whole class simply looked at the car the teacher would be very annoyed; the children are to look at the car in the light of the elicitation "Can you think what it means?" (*p* 38). Note that the children *are* though to look at the car – *ie* the Command has a Directive function in that it requests a non-linguistic response. Similarly a Starter was defined as 'providing information about, or directing attention or thought'. . . *ie* as being Informative or Directive. The *subordinate* role of the Clue or Starter is built into its definition, and is what distinguishes these Acts from Informatives, Elicitations, and Directives.

The structure of Moves therefore is handled inside the definitions of the Acts of which the Move is composed, and the informative, Elicitatory, or Directive function of Statements, Questions, or Commands is part of their illocutionary force, whether they appear as 'Informatives', 'Elicitations', 'Directives', or not in discourse function. The critical factor is that they appear as head of an Opening Move, and not as subordinate elements.

Having discussed the relation between the situational and discourage categories in some detail, I wish to turn to the notion of Exchange structure, and ask how far the analyses given insightfully characterise the given data. Clearly, if the above argumentation is accepted, difficulties of analysis will follow.

Consider the case in which what is a Question in situation functions as a Reply in tactics.[11] We might expect an insertion or side sequence as in the work of the ethnomethodologists, or a Counter in Klammer's terms, but none of these analyses matches S&C's data, in which the Reply is the complementary and appropriate linguistic response to an Elicitation, whose function it is to request such an act, while, however, the same utterance is a Question in situation. Consider the following:

PUPIL: Does it mean there's been an accident further along the road?
TEACHER: No
PUPIL: Does it mean a double bend ahead?
TEACHER: No (Taken from text D, cited on p 35)

We do not have 'Elicitation-Reply' sequences here in discourse structure, but sequences of the latter two elements of Opening-Answering-Follow-up sequences, such that the 'questions' are Replies and the 'answers' are Evaluations.

On the interpretation I have argued above, what is indisputable here is that the pupil Replies are also eliciting in that they 'request a linguistic response – specifically some sort of evaluation from the teacher. This elicitatory function belongs to their questionhood.

The characterisation of what is actually going on in Opening-Answering-Follow-up sequences occurring in pedagogic settings is highly complex.[12] What we need somehow to take into account here is that the teacher Elicitation is a pedagogic *strategy*, designed to achieve pedagogic goals: 'Questioning' is a well-established teaching *technique*. For example we may say that in a 3-part sequence the teacher may be seeking to indirectly 'inform' the class as a whole: thus in ratifying a student-Reply – *ie* Evaluating it positively – the teacher achieves the goal he could have achieved by directly 'informing' the class. Indeed, if no ratifiable student-Reply is forthcoming, he may be obliged to directly inform himself (see for example S&C, p 72). It is common knowledge that teacher 'questions' are often different in kind from non-pedagogic 'questions' (as noted by S&C, pp 36–7): I am suggesting that this may be seen to have consequences not merely as regards the characterisation of the 'questioning' illocution in situation, but as regards the peculiar structure of the Exchange initiated by such a 'question'. An informal parallel might be found in children's verbal games in which a 'question' is asked, merely in order that its 'answer' provide an opportunity for a ritual insult.[13] Again in this type of sequence, we would say that the initiating 'question' is clearly used strategically – the Follow-up contains the punch-line.

I do not propose to attempt to provide an analysis of the structure of teacher Elicit Exchanges, but simply suggest that strategy plays an important role here, and the analysis in S&C, specifically in the case that a Question appears as Reply, is less than satisfactory.

The claim made here is consistent with the observation that S&C's analyses tend to get into difficulties as soon as pupils initiate Exchanges. Consider the following two Exchanges, taken from Texts D and H respectively (*pp* 86, 107):

[5.3]

		MOVE	ACT
(i)	– Miss they showed you		
	a film about . . .	*Opening*	*Inform*
	– ah yes	*Accept*	*Follow-up*
(ii)	– Please can I go		
	to the toilet	*Elicit*	*Opening*
	– Climb over that way	*Reply*	*Answering*

[5.3] (i) is a Pupil-Inform Exchange, (ii) a Pupil-Elicit Exchange. In (i) – and this is the standard analysis for Pupil-Inform Exchanges – the Opening is followed by a Follow-up; to be consistent here S&C not only require specific turn-taking rules for such pupil-Inform Exchanges, but also a distinct Act, the Pupil-Inform, as an Informative Act is defined such that 'the only response is an acknowledgement of attention and understanding' (*p* 41).

A further and final important issue to discuss in Exchange structure is the relation between Statement and Informative, indeed the status of Informatives as Acts which may realise Opening Moves is worthy of discussion. For if the function of an opening Move is to 'cause others to participate in an exchange' (*p* 45), how can an Informative Act be said to be a possible realisation of such a Move? Directives and Elicitations are defined as functioning to *request* appropriate responses, but Informatives are not. There is a certain amount of careful hedging here: 'an informative is an act whose function it is to pass on ideas, facts, opinions, information and to which the appropriate response is simply an acknowledgement that one is listening' (*p* 28). The passing on of ideas etc is arguably the function of a Statement in *situation* – just as the function of finding out whether or not a pupil knows the answer is a *situational* function – this is why the teacher asks *Questions*, not why he produces *Elicitations* (*pp* 36–7).

I shall propose no alternative analysis here but one may register a doubt at the least as to the parity of Informatives on the one hand and

Elicitations and Directives on the other as concerns their co-membership of the class of potential exponents of Opening Moves. We note incidentally that there appear to be no cases of teacher-Inform Exchanges in which the Follow-up slot is actually filled. If it *cannot* be filled – an empirical issue, but one suspects it may well be so – then this suggests that something other than an Opening Move is being performed when a non-subordinate teacher-Informative occurs.

I have tried to interpret the distinction between value in 'situation' and value in 'discourse' in Sinclair and Coulthard 1975 as reflecting the distinction between illocutionary value and interactional value, as this latter distinction has been raised in Chapters 3 and 4. However, Sinclair and Coulthard's distinction, while suggestive, is neither clearly worked out in theory, nor in its application does it lead to insightful analyses in every instance. A central problem seems to be that while a three-part Exchange structure is clearly discernible in classroom discourse, we have no apparatus for knowing whether this Exchange structure might not be the result of a teaching strategy, and thus not appropriate both to some exchanges occurring in the classroom setting and to Exchanges found in other, non-pedagogic settings. Problems concerning turn-taking, and concerning the status of the discourse function of Statements or Informative Acts have also been touched upon.

In the several approaches discussed in this chapter we have found three distinct ways of reconciling the notion of a conversational unit as an illocutionary act with its functioning as an interactional act or move. We have discovered however neither a model inside which this distinction is clearly made, nor an analytic system directly or indirectly based on this distinction which has explanatory power for other than a limited range of data.

A further problem we have not found other than hinted at is that of discourse structure above the level of the 'speech act sequence', 'discourse paragraph', or the 'exchange'. I shall attempt to resolve at least some of the difficulties raised in this chapter and preceding ones in the model and analyses presented in what follows.

Notes

1 Also called 'interactional terms', 'verbal interactions', and 'speech acts' – all on *p* 60.

2 For the length of this discussion, terms used by L&F will be given with initial capitalisation.

3 See L&F, p 63: 'The speaker may also provide a set of normative guidelines, which serve to orient the listener to a particular line of behaviour; here she can be said to. . .' It seems likely here that 'she' – ie 'the speaker' – is to be understood as Rhoda, and not in a generic sense: this clearly raises the question of the generalisability of the categories offered.

4 One may in fact justifiably query whether the Rule for Reinstating Requests actually operates in the form given. The complying response to an embedded request of the type 'What did you say?' clearly 'makes the original request for action again' in a way that the complying response to an embedded request of the type 'How long do you want to borrow it for?' does not. In terms of 'making' a certain speech act again, one would like to distinguish these two cases, which L&F do not do.

5 eg   'BARNEY: Now that Chuckleberry is here, we can
                              discuss what you said about him, Arnold
             ARNOLD: I really have to be going
       CHUCKLEBERRY: Don't try to avoid the subject, Arnold' (p 37).

6 Apart from the important work on intonation, the major innovation is an attempt to re-classify Moves so as to be able to extend the three-part Exchange structure in S&C 1975 to non-pedagogic discourse (p 28). In order to do this Coulthard and Brazil are obliged to set up a Response which is at the same time an 'Initiation' in terms of its structural relation to the following third structural element, the Follow-Up (p 42). (cf Klammer's claim quoted on p 62 above.)

7 Terms and categories for S&C's system will be given with initial capitalisation in this discussion, to avoid a proliferation of inverted commas. Thus in what follows Act and Move are not to be identified with the notions of interactional act and interactional move, as we have attempted to introduce these latter terms. Some parallelism is nevertheless clearly discernible.

8 In this transcription I have adopted a top-to-bottom display rather than the left-to-right display found in S&C.

9 There is a possible counter-argument here concerning the pastness of the shouting out in (i), and its non-pastness in (ii). There is a valid distinction here, but it is not a distinction between a Command and a Statement, but between two types of Command – we might for example distinguish between a Command to stop and a Command not to do again.

10 Note the inconsistency here. *Statement*, *Question*, and *Command* are situational categories, not grammatical ones. Presumably 'moodless items' are themselves to be interpreted in situation as statements, questions, commands, or as exponents of some further categories.

11 Coulthard and Brazil (1979) devote some attention to this problem (see note 6 above).

12 See eg Edmondson 1978b, 1979b; Rehbein 1979.

13 'What's fifteen and fifteen? – Thirty – Your face is dirty' is an innocuous example.

Chapter 6:

Illocution plus interaction:
an integrative model

The model for the analysis of discourse to be presented here is based on the considerations brought forward in the foregoing chapters, which therefore underpin and in part justify what follows in this chapter. Further and more importantly, the model is based on and applied to conversational data. Before entering into a detailed account, I shall here give a short account of the data base used in developing the model, and then give a brief overview of the analytic system.

The data consists of simulated two-party face-to-face conversations, covering a controlled range of situations. Six 'interactional bases' were set up as likely to lead to a spectrum of conversational behaviour. The interactional bases used were as follows:

(i)   X wants, Y do P
(ii)   P needs to be done, where P is a variable, but that something be done is in the interests of both X and Y
(iii) Y did P, P bad for X
(iv)   Y did P, P good for X
(v)   X did P, P bad for Y
(vi)   X believes that P, Y believes that -P

The data were originally collected as part of a research project concerned with the teaching and learning of communicative skills.[1] In this project further data were collected in which German learners of English played out a variety of situations based on the six configurations above, in every case assuming role X, when role Y was played by a native-speaker of English. This accounts for the fact that interactional bases 3 and 5 differ only in the X-Y role constellation: we wished to have data in which the learner was both 'complainer' and 'complainee'. However for my purposes in this study, category 5 may be seen as a duplication of category 3.

The motivation for setting up these six (or more strictly speaking five) interactional bases was the belief that they could be expected to lead to a variety of different types of BUSINESS TRANSACTION. The term is proposed for any conversation which produces a significant outcome in terms of the behaviour of either X or Y, or in terms of the relations between them. Thus the achievement of mutual understanding, if not agreement (6 above), the reciprocation of a social good (4), the restoration of a state of social harmony between X and Y (3, 5) are considered matters of 'business' just as much as the arriving at collective decisions concerning individual or collective action involving X and/or Y (1 and 2 above). Searle's 1976 classification of illocutionary acts was a starting point for the establishment of these six interactional bases, and likely sequencing possibilities were also considered, such that no distinctive interactional base was proposed as likely to produce promissory acts, on the intuitive assumption that bases 1 and 2 could well lead to behaviour of this type. There was clearly no intention that overlapping should *not* occur: it is intuitively clear for example that 'representatives', while to some extent most appropriate to base 6, would likely occur in all encounters built on these interactional bases.

For each of these six bases four social role constellations were used, arrived at by systematic variation along the two dimensions of social role relationship (X = Y, X<Y) and social attitude ({±} familiar). We thus arrive at 24 *situational bases*. For each of these a situation was constructed, and situational pre-histories for the participants X and Y were written.[2] A random distribution of male/female identities for X and Y was built into the personal histories which formed part of the situational pre-histories such that 6 male-male, 6 female-female, and 12 male-female pairings occur in the 24 situations.

The 24 resultant situational bases may be briefly characterised: A-D represent systematic variation of social role relationship as follows:

A: [X < Y] / [+ familiar]
B: [X< Y] / [− familiar]
C: [X = Y] / [+ familiar]
D: [X = Y] / [− familiar]

1A: Sixth-former requires reference from French-master
B: Baby-sitter wants to back down on a previous arrangement

C: Sheila wishes to borrow records off a flatmate

D: Boy meets girl: he wishes to take her off from a party

2A: Lodger's gas-fire explodes: his landlady investigates

2B: Hitch-hiker and driver witness traffic-accident, and stop to help

2C: Two friends discuss how to turn down a third-party who wishes to accompany them to London for the weekend

2D: Two travellers discover by accident that they seek the same destination

3A: Student working on a farm discovers that the farmer has not marked up his tally correctly

3B: Patient returns to doctor's surgery as prescribed antibiotic has given her a painful rash

3C: Richard has forgotten to hand in a university paper for Leslie: she discovers this

3D: Returning to her books in the library, a student finds her place occupied

4A: Having finished her studies, student takes leave of her kind landlady

4B: Woman discovers art folder in a park, and returns it to its owner

4C: Joe has borrowed some money off his parents, in order to help out his friend

4D: Shopkeeper witnesses accident involving parked car. Later assists returning car-owner

5A: Landlady hears student lodger returning late; next morning bathroom is in a mess. She confronts lodger over breakfast

5B: Librarian notices student returning book has copiously annotated the text

5C: Joan has borrowed (and stained) her friend's suede jacket: her friend discovers this

5D: Student seeking to work is disturbed by riotous party above. She investigates

6A: Jim talks politics to his girl-friend's father: their views and backgrounds differ

6B: Lady is disturbed by behaviour of West Indian youths in tea-shop: she voices her feelings to a student customer who does not share them

6C: Two friends, supporting rival football teams, meet after a match featuring the two teams in question

6D: Travelling by train, young man seeks to engage woman in conversation by reading out to her an 'amusing' article concerning 'Women's Rights': she is not amused.

The positional role of X was kept consistent with that of a student for all 20 situations. Students of the University of Essex were invited to enact or play out these situations, and from the multiple recordings made two were selected for each of the twenty-four situations constructed as the data for this study. The necessity of *selecting* from among the 2+ recordings of a particular situation was occasioned by clear cases of 'breaking down' or 'over-acting': selection was also based on the performers' own assessment of their performance, which they listened to and commented on in terms of its 'naturalness'. A clear problem here is that students were asked to play not only role X, but also role Y. In situations in which X and Y are rough social equals (C and D), the situational role of Y is not inconsistent with the social role of the students assuming this situational role, but this is clearly not the case in a situation of type A or B, in which X < Y.

I do not propose to go into details concerning the elicitation of data in empirical conversational research[3], nor to detail the procedures used in collecting the data on which this study is based. It is however necessary to refer to two obvious objections that might be raised concerning the status of the data used here.

Firstly, the conversations were audio-recorded, while it may be generally accepted that video-recordings provide a richer and more reliable data-base. This must be conceded. To mitigate the force of this objection however the following points are relevant:

(i)   Feasibility, in terms of equipment, personnel, and finance, is unfortunately a factor which cannot be ignored in research design.

(ii)   Non-verbal acts which seemed of potential significance in terms of the progress of the conversation were noted by the observing researcher both during the recordings, and during the immediately following play-back in the presence of the subjects. Given that simulation was involved, it was at times necessary to ask subjects, for example, 'When you said that, would you already have handed him his drink, or would you be about to do so?' Such reconstructions were seldom necessary, but always possible.

(iii)   The analyses proposed are not delicate enough to be concerned with factors such as proxemics, eye-contact, hand-movements, and so on. We are essentially concerned to discover conversational structure. That non-verbal clues are of great significance in accompanying and modifying the effect of verbal communications is clear: noted in our transcriptions are only such however as have a *structural* function.

A second and more critical limitation that must be made in connection with the status of the data used concerns the fact that it is elicited or simulated. As noted above, a central issue here is when an individual is called upon to play a role which carries with it a social authority which that individual himself does not possess. A tendency to play some stock or cliché figure might operate here.

Note however that it is not the case that subjects were asked to *tell* or *describe* what they would do if placed in such and such a situation[4], they were asked to *do*, as though they were in such and such a situation. Nonetheless it may be claimed with some justification that what one does when *asked* to behave in a certain situation may be different from what one would in fact do if actually in a certain situation. Even if it is however conceded that behavioural differences may be observed in simulations, this does not invalidate the data collected via simulation for our investigatory purposes. Our central concern is the elucidation of discourse structure, such that what is critical is not whether person A would behave differently in a non-simulated but parallel situation, but whether the set of possible modes of behaviour is non-identical in the simulated and the non-simulated instances. In other words, that differences in terms of the choice of options made in a simulation as opposed to a non-simulation may be observable is not critical: it is only if the options available differ in the one case that data obtained via simulation becomes totally unreliable. The distinction between social and communicative competence is again illuminating here. The fact that our data were obtained via simulation does not therefore invalidate those data for our research purposes, though a more delicate description, concerning for example differences in social behaviour brought about by differing role constellations, would have an insecure foundation if based on simulated data of the kind used in this study. The data is deemed reliable and valid for my purposes therefore, though in drawing any conclusions concerning differences in social behaviour observed in the data used, one must be highly tentative, given the provenance of the data.

When data is produced as evidence in what follows, it will not always be taken from our corpus. Fabricated data, as hitherto, will be explicitly stated to be such. The non-fabricated data whose provenance has been sketched above will be presented using the non-refined and hopefully transparent conventions given at the beginning of this study (*pp* 9–11 above).

Having discussed the source of the data used in developing the model to be presented, I wish to give a brief summary of the system.

A COMMUNICATIVE ACT is characterised as both an INTERACTIONAL and an ILLOCUTIONARY ACT (as in a tagmemic model, *cf* Klammer above). Interactional acts are 'realised' or 'manifest' in one or more illocutionary acts. The underlying structure of a conversational episode is an interactional structure – *ie* it is the sequential relevance of interactional acts which gives coherence to a conversation, and this is reflected in the textual cohesion of the substance of the conversation – *ie* what is said. Interactional structure is critically determined at a level of analysis above that of the interactional act, namely that of the INTERACTIONAL MOVE, as it is at the level of the interactional move that turn-taking operates. Thus interactional acts combine to form interactional moves, and interactional moves are sequenced in various ways to produce EXCHANGES. Exchanges of different kinds exhibit different types of linkage, thus combining to form PHASES of a conversation. An ordered sequence of Phases may be said to describe the structure of an ENCOUNTER. In investigating interactional structure, we shall concentrate on exchange structure and exchange linkage. As elements of interactional structure are both interactional acts and illocutionary acts (in the unmarked case), we shall refer to *discourse* or *conversational* structure when considering interactional structures manifest in verbal (and other) behaviour. The distinction is in a sense a theoretical one, though it is hypothesised that non-verbal interactions are structured as are conversational encounters. A purely non-verbal encounter however we would not wish to call a conversation. Thus the distinction between interactional and illocutionary act is valid for descriptive purposes. Further, structural elements in a conversation may be realised by non-verbal means – *ie* interactional acts may be realised other than by illocutions inside a conversation.

An exchange is so defined that it produces OUTCOME: the nature of the outcome is determined by the illocutionary (and other) acts which realise the elements of which the exchange is composed. At higher levels of analysis (Phase, Encounter), exchange outcomes may also be systematically related, as determined by the structure of the Phase or Encounter itself.

In describing interactional structures, we distinguish between possible structural configurations which can be said to define the framework inside which substantive interaction can take place (a conversation is one type of substantive interaction in that things get done when things get said), and the actual occurrent sequences of interactional acts which occur in substantive interactions. The distinction may be glossed as that between 'deep' and 'surface' structure, and reflects that between communicative and social competence on the part of speakers (pp 7–8 above). In ongoing conversations speakers use their familiarity with 'base' or deep' interactional structure in order to achieve conversational goals (a conversational goal is a conversational outcome desired by one of the interactants). The implementation of conversational STRATEGY is characterised as systematically accounting for the non-direct matching between underlying interactional structure and the actual occurrent sequence of communicative acts in an observed conversational encounter.

The possibility of strategic play essentially derives from the claim that the mechanisms for turn-taking are under the control of the interacting parties, predominantly the party who at any one point in time holds the speaking turn. Thus I may 'assume' you 'agree' with me that P, and retain the turn at speaking, having 'asserted' that P, in order to go on to other communicative acts. A move to be informally glossed as your 'agreeing' that P may therefore be said to belong to the underlying discourse structure, though there may be no behavioural token with which this alleged 'agreement' may be matched.

Similarly, in the realisation of communicative acts – ie the process of saying something, the production of the substance of a conversational episode – various 'lubricative' verbalisations are strategically employed to further the conversational goals of the speaker. Some of these we characterise as a class of conversational FUMBLES: they do not constitute communicative acts, but do constitute elements of verbal communicative activity. In grossly simplified terms, therefore, we wish to develop an analytic apparatus in which interactional structures are manifest in sequences of illocutionary acts. In conversational behaviour, speakers employ strategies, based in large part on their interpretative ability to anticipate hearer response, and further make selected use of fumbles and other 'gambits' to lubricate the ongoing conversation, and directly or indirectly support their conversational purposes.

The above overview is clearly deficient in terms of adequately defining the terms introduced – a fuller exposition is to be found in what follows.

6.1 Interactional structures characterised

A communicative act has a function with respect to both the structure of the interaction of which it forms a part and with respect to the attitudes, feelings, and beliefs of the speaker making it. It is both an interactional and an illocutionary act. Here we concern ourselves with the *interactional* structure of an encounter, the acts, moves, exchanges, and phases of which an encounter is composed. In an attempt to clarify the relation between interactional and illocutionary behaviour, we may cite Goffman 1971, *p* 134: 'Because face-to-face conduct pertains to quickly changing displays, the main method for collecting evidence of conformance is to watch (and listen to) the actor himself as he engages in these displays in one's presence. Therefore we can easily think that what is being studied is communication. It is not. Language may not be involved, and when language is involved, as when an individual pronounces a word incorrectly, conduct is still at issue, the conduct of speaking.'

The formulation here is perhaps not totally lucid, but it seems clear that while face-to-face conduct is not always communication, and while communication may not necessarily involve the use of language, communication is most often a form of face-to-face conduct, and any use of language is an instance of communication, or at least attempted communication. Therefore if one wishes to claim that the structure of social action and the structure of conversation are two different things, and at the same time hold that communication is social activity, it follows that conversations, as a type of communicative event, are structured as social activity, and at the same time may be described as 'language' – a series of verbal acts made coherent by the social structure in which they are realised. This is the viewpoint adopted here. To emphasise the point, consider Goffman's distinction between 'ritual' and 'substantive' work undertaken by a member who has offended a fellow-member. Goffman claims that the issue is one of 'indicating a relationship, not compensating a loss' (Goffman 1971, *pp* 147–8). The simple point to be made here is surely that in an ongoing conversation a speaker may 'indicate a relationship' *in* 'compensating a loss', or offering to do so. The opposition may be insightful for expository or polemical purposes, but it is not a question of *alternatives*, but rather of characterising what is happening (the same event) from two different perspectives.[5]

As a preliminary to the notion of interactional structure as it will be developed here, and because of the centrality of the notion of an Exchange in interactional structure, it is of interest to investigate the notion of exchange informally.

In everyday terms, an exchange consists of the passing of a good from A to B, and a reciprocal passing of a good from B to A. Thus, if two people exchange greetings or presents, two goods are transferred. However, the passing of a good from A to B may be said itself to consist of two acts, which we may informally term 'offer' and 'acceptance'. Thus if two people in a room are said to be 'exchanging glances', we understand this to mean that repetitions of eye-contact occur, and not that A glances at B, without B's acknowledging this look, and then subsequently B glances at A, without A's noticing or taking cognizance of this. Again shaking hands with somebody normally implies more than simply shaking somebody's hand as one might shake a bottle of ketchup. Thus we may say that a one-way passing of goods involves a two-way 'exchange' of acts. A source of confusion in the analysis of discourse is that in the unmarked case the 'goods' that are 'exchanged' are in fact communicative 'acts'. For example we may informally refer to 'offering' and 'accepting' both 'suggestions' and 'criticisms', but if we talk of the offering and acceptance of a *present* for example, we are not referring to an *exchange* of presents, but to a *giving* of presents. Further to refer to an 'exchange' of criticisms is only meaningful if two members criticise *each other*.

In short, we need to distinguish three distinct elements of conversational behaviour which are all related to the non-technical notion of an exchange, namely *uptaking*, *replying*, and *reciprocating*.

All three notions permeate and give structure and meaning to conversational behaviour. The notion of reciprocation is of course implicit in the H-supportive maxim proposed earlier, and links with a very basic notion of social obligation, and it is against the background of this social law that we refer to 'owing a favour', 'fulfilling a social obligation', 'paying somebody back', and so on.[6]

The case of ritual exchanges in which the appropriate 'reply' is in fact a reciprocation' is thus finely organised such that while an 'exchange' in a technical sense – a tied pair of sequentially relevant and complementary illocutions – is taking place, the fact that the 'goods' exchanged are often identical ('Hi' – 'Hi': 'Goodbye' – 'Goodbye') means that neither party is placed under social obligations – the ritual allows an Exchange to take place (a minimal unit of social contact) without either party exhibiting superior social skill. (In this connection the status of formulae such as 'how are you' is of interest. Here we see that while 'how are you' – 'fine thanks' constitutes an Exchange of illocutions, this exchange is felt by some responding members to place them under a social obligation to reciprocate by enquiring after the health of the co-member.)

We have briefly suggested that the notion of the 'exchange' here informally investigated may be seen to link with three central features of conversational behaviour – uptake, the sequentially relevant reply, and the notion of reciprocation. This will be demonstrated in the system of interactional structure developed in the following sections (6.1.1-6.1.3).

6.1.1 Interactional acts in move structure

The smallest units of interactional structure are interactional ACTS, which combine to form an interactional MOVE. The simplistic structure of the move may be described in Sinclair and Coulthard's terms as a Pre-Head, Head, Post-Head structure, in which the first and third elements are optional. We propose the terms

   (Uptake)   Head   (Appealer)

such that the UPTAKER validates the preceding *move* performed by the previous speaker as a contribution to the ongoing discourse, the interactional function of the head derived from the type of move of which it is the head exponent, and the APPEALER solicits Uptake from the hearer: Appealers link closely with signals for managing turn-change, and are grammaticalised for example in the form of tags of various kinds in English. An Uptaker therefore looks back, as it were, creating a link with the preceding move, while an Appealer looks forward. Central interactional acts (the heads of interactional moves) are therefore cemented into the discourse structure via the *facultative* interactional acts of Uptake and Appealer:

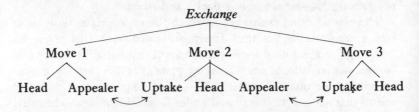

The optional nature of Uptakers and Appealers in the structure of the interactional move can readily be explained in that with many moves, the item which realises the head of the move itself implies or presupposes uptake – thus if I 'agree' to your request that I do P via an utterance of the form 'okay', it is clear that I have heard and interpreted your request. Similarly, as suggested above, the interactional work that may be done via an Appealing act may be done via many other means. It is indeed implicit in the nature of many illocutions which may appear as heads of interactional moves that some form of relevant response is required of the hearer by the performer of such an illocutionary act. Indeed, very few instances of Appealers occur in the corpus on which this study is based.

A rationale for the phenomenon of Uptake may be provided by considering what a speaker is enabled to do in utilizing this interactional slot. Firstly there is the issue of face. Given the general social desirability of H-supportive behaviour, and given that a head interactional act may constitute a 'contradiction', 'disagreement', and so on, the possibility of Uptake allows a speaker to pay ritual lip-service to H's social standing vis à vis himself, in that he may ratify H's preceding head illocution as a contribution to the discourse before producing the head of his own move. Secondly, the phenomenon of Uptake may be said to help reassure the previous speaker that the communication channel is open, and that the Uptake-producer both can hear and is listening. Thirdly, it seems likely that Uptake may be used to signal a willingness or readiness to assume the speaking role, without actually constituting an interruption. Fourthly, Uptake gives a replying speaker time in which to formulate and encode his communicative intentions in the light of what he has just heard. This last function is also filled by other devices (see 6.4.1 below), but it seems highly plausible to suggest that Uptaking also serves a gap-plugging function.

Note that we have chosen to make Uptake an optional pre-head element in the structure of the move. Alternatively, one might make it an obligatory act in the performance of any interactional move, and then claim that a certain sub-set of possible head acts themselves contain or imply Uptake. This alternative presents a neater generalisation, but a more clumsy descriptive procedure. Further, the four interactional functions of Uptaking suggested above cannot be said to be carried by an act which is simply 'implied' or 'contained' in some other act. We therefore choose to make Uptake an optional pre-head structural element for descriptive purpose.

The phenomenon of Uptake is so prevalent that it will be illustrated very briefly here. Our later citations will provide ample further illustration. Appealers in the form of tags occur not infrequently, but in other forms relatively seldom. Consider the following extract:

[6.1]　(Situation: Y has just discovered that X has borrowed her jacket
and spilt wine of it)

Y:　yeah well it's gonna be pretty hard to remove really isn't it

X:　well ₘ most I can do is offer to get it dry-cleaned

Y:　yeah but I mean it's not gonna come out with dry-cleaning
wine spots don't I mean . . .

(5C11.5)[7]

In this extract Y uptakes at the beginning of her two turns at
speech, and produces an Appealer at the end of the first. One reason
for not considering the form *well* as constituting an instance of Uptake
is that it may often *follow* or indeed precede ('well yes, but. . .') an
instance of uptaking. The major reason however is of course that an
utterance of the form *well* cannot be said to constitute a
communicative act. However we are not yet in a position to consider
the verbal tokens by means of which interactional acts are realised
until we have characterised the illocutions which may occur in
different slots in interactional structure.

6.1.2 Interactional moves in exchange structure

While the interactional act is the smallest unit of interactional
structure, and while a move exhibits structure in terms of the acts of
which it may be composed, interaction cannot be held to have taken
place until an exchange can be said to have occurred. This means of
course that an utterance cannot be held to constitute a communicative
act unless it constitutes an element of structure inside an exchange.
The reason is clear: as the name suggests an exchange consists of at
least two interactional moves, and it is at this level of analysis that
turn-taking operates – *ie* in the case of the minimal exchange
consisting of two elements, the second move is made by the addressee
of the first. As we are handling exclusively two-party interactions, we
may say that moves in exchange structure are performed by
alternating speakers.

An encounter then consists of at least one exchange, which may
therefore be considered the minimal unit of social interaction. The
simplest form of the exchange consists of two elements, the first of
which is a stimulus for the second, which is a response to that
stimulus. Thus we have the two-part exchange, the 'pair' or 'round' in
ethnomethodological terms. An exchange is here to be understood
however as a potentially 'closed' unit: when an exchange is completed,

both participants are in a position to close the matter in hand, to proceed or revert to other business, possibly to terminate the encounter – an exchange produces *outcome*. Interactional friction has been avoided, loss of face has been avoided, the interaction has reached a point of possible further development or indeed termination. The second element *satisfies* the first. these two elements of structure we wish to term PROFFER and SATISFY.[8]

It follows as a matter of definition that in Satisfying A's Proffer, B is acting in a manner consistent with A's purposes in making that Proffer: in Austin's terms, a Satisfy communicates to A that his perlocutionary intent has been successful. Note that if this is to be the case, the Proffer must be such that A in making that Proffer can be said to at least implicitly communicate what will constitute a Satisfying response to it, and further B in producing that Satisfy will do so in the knowledge that what he does may be held to count as Satisfying that Proffer. This is by no means always the case, for example with a Proffered illocution we shall characterise as a Complain. It follows that an exchange may have more than two elements of structure, a 'satisfying' outcome has to be worked towards, negotiated by the interacting parties.

A Proffer by definition initiates an Exchange, and a Satisfy by definition produces an outcome. No exchange may be terminated other than by a Satisfy move. However it is not always the case that the occurrence inside the structure of an exchange of a Satisfy brings that exchange to a point of closure, as Satisfys always work with respect to the immediately preceding valid interactional move: the nature of the move which is Satisfied therefore determines whether the total exchange is brought to a point of closure, or whether the outcome produced by the Satisfy is merely 'local'. Proffer-Satisfy sequences we may diagrammatically represent thus:

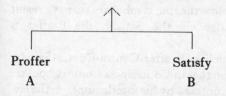

Proffer   Satisfy

A   B

The non-directional bracketing above the line represents a closed sequence, and the arrow placed thereon signals outcome.

Given a Proffer, it is intuitively clear that to Satisfy that Proffer is not the only option open to the recipient. One alternative we wish to term the CONTRA. A contra implies acting in a way inconsistent with the perlocutionary intentions of the interlocutor, insofar as these are deducible from his immediately preceding conversational move – *ie* what he has just said and done. A Contra counts interactionally as an attempt on the part of the producer of the Contra to cause his conversational partner to withdraw the preceding Proffer. If a Contra is then itself Satisfied, such that a Proffer-Contra-Satisfy sequence results, the exchange is closed, but the outcome may be 'negative', as interactionally the outcome is the withdrawal of the initiating Proffer: the situation which caused the original Proffer to be made may well not be 'satisfied' or resolved by the cancellation of that Proffer. However, a 'negative' interactional outcome may imply a non-negative situational outcome for the participants. For example, if a 'suggestion' that a married couple go out for the evening is 'turned down' by one party, and this Contra is 'accepted' by the other, who Proffered the 'suggestion', it may no longer be necessary to talk on the issue of the evening's activities, as 'staying in' is the implicit alternative to 'going out', and in withdrawing a suggestion to do the latter, one of the partners may be held to have accepted the alternative presented by the former. We shall therefore represent a Proffer-Contra-Satisfy sequence as producing outcome, although that outcome might be held to be 'negative':

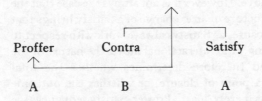

The left-directional arrow below the line symbolises that as a result of the closure of the exchange via the Satisfy, the Proffer is 'withdrawn' or 'cancelled'.

Consider now a sequence such as Proffer-Contra-Contra-Satisfy. We make it a matter of definition that in Contraing a Contra a speaker re-enacts the move which was Contraed by his interlocutor – *ie* the law of excluded middle applies ($\sim \sim P \rightarrow P$). The four-move sequence above is closed, as in Satisfying the immediately preceding Contra, the last speaker both Satisfies the original Proffer, and withdraws his own preceding Contra:

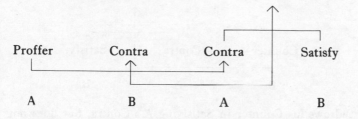

Longer sequences in which 2+n Contras occur between the initiating Proffer and the terminating Satisfy are possible.

Proffers may then be followed by either a Satisfy or a Contra: Contras may likewise be followed by a Satisfy or a Contra. A Contra has itself to be Satisfied however before the Exchange can be said to be terminated. A third possibility following a Proffer we wish to term the COUNTER. A Counter counts as an attempt by a speaker to cause the content of a preceding move (which we shall assume for illustrative purpose to be a Proffer) to be amended, qualified, or withdrawn in the light of the content of the Counter. We distinguish a Counter from a Contra as a matter of definition only, on the basis of the effects of the move. If a Counter is Satisfied, the preceding Proffer is not necessarily withdrawn, but the outcome of the Counter-Satisfy sequence amends or modifies the content of that original Proffer. In the case that the Satisfaction of the move following a Proffer *does* bring the total exchange to a point of termination we shall wish to claim that the move was not a Counter, but a Contra. In the case that a Counter is Satisfied, and the Satisfier retains the turn at talk he may *re-present* the substance of his original Proffer in a RE-PROFFER. This possible structural configuration is illustrated in the following sequence:

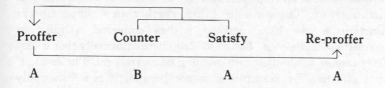

In 'accepting' the content of a Counter A does not withdraw his preceding Proffer: its substance is affected however by the outcome of the Counter-Satisfy sequence, whose outcome is therefore 'local' – *ie* exchange-internal. Note further that with a Counter the law of excluded middle does not apply – *ie* a speaker can withdraw a Counter without thereby Satisfying the move immediately preceding that withdrawn Counter. Thus in the following sequence:

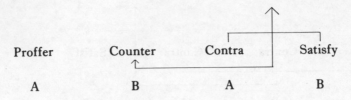

Proffer	Counter	Contra	Satisfy
A	B	A	B

B withdraws his Counter in Satisfying A's Contra, but does not thereby Satisfy A's original Proffer: he may proceed to produce a further Counter or Contra, or indeed a Satisfy; A may also Re-Proffer. The exchange is still open to negotiation. We may put this another way by saying that in Contraing B's Counter A does not re-present the substance of his original Proffer, as happens with a Proffer-Contra-Contra-Satisfy sequence, which is a closed exchange sequence.

An obvious objection one might make to the distinction between the Counter and the Contra needs to be 'countered' or if possible 'contraed' here. The objection is that the different structural potential of these two moves is in fact their only difference in definition. If an outcome resulting from a move other than a Proffer being Satisfied is 'local', such that the exchange is not terminated, the Satisfied move is to be termed a Counter: if, however, this outcome resolves the exchange, the Satisfied move is to be understood as a Contra. This is true.

The empirical status of these interactional structures is put to the test however when we are confronted with conversational data, in which an interactional move is composed in the unmarked case of *communicative* acts, not simply interactional acts — *ie* the illocutions by means of which interactional moves are made in conversational behaviour provide an empirical basis for the elements of interactional structure set up. The question is then whether the Counter-Contra distinction as we have defined it has empirical validity in conversational behaviour. I wish to claim here informally that it has. Effects cannot be predicted in ongoing conversations. The 'excuse' that is effective for example is so not because it is substantially different from non-effective excuses, but simply by virtue of the fact that it is 'accepted'. Similarly, in argumentative discourse, logic does not win arguments, speakers do: in other words, 'bad' arguments may and do persuade, where 'good' arguments may fail. In pedagogic exchanges of the kind analysed by Sinclair and Coulthard, to give a third informal instance, what counts as a 'correct' pupil-response is determined by the teacher: if 'wrong' answers are 'accepted' by the teacher, they thereby become by definition 'right' answers.

The Proffer, Satisfy, Counter, and Contra, together with the Re-Proffer constitute a basic move inventory which is sufficient for the analysis of the major part of the corpus used. One important additional move set up on the basis of the corpus used has yet to be discussed – this is the PRIME. It seems highly likely however that the structural potential of the exchange is not exhausted by the characterisations provided for the moves found in our corpus. Before the PRIME is discussed therefore, two further moves, the REJECT and the RE-RUN will be tentatively introduced, though we have no empirical basis in the corpus used for requiring these two moves. It will be seen that The Prime, the Reject, and the Re-Run have a common feature, namely that they appear to be discourse-specific interactional moves – their status and function is bound up with the peculiar nature of verbal interaction whereby the interaction itself may be a topic of talk.

In a REJECT a speaker 'rejects' the preceding move as a communicative act: a Reject does not imply or presuppose Uptake – on the contrary, the Reject implies that the preceding communicative move was not conversationally licensed. If a Reject is Satisfied, the preceding move (let us assume it was a Proffer) is annulled or cancelled as is the case with a Contra. However, a Re -Proffer would be a further consequent possibility. If a Reject is withdrawn (it may be Contraed, and the Contra then Satisfied, for example), its withdrawal does not imply Satisfaction of the move preceding the Reject, but simply validates that move as such in the discourse. The original move which was Rejected is now 'accepted' in that it may be countered, Contraed, or Satisfied. This means of course that to Contra a Reject is not to re-present the substance of that which was Rejected. Graphically, the following are illustrative:

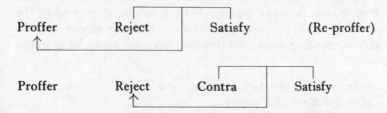

Consider as an informal example the distinction between 'turning down' a 'request', and objecting to the request's being made or to the manner in which it is made. If such an objection is withdrawn, clearly the speaker who withdraws his objection does not thereby acquiesce to the 'request' – he has not responded to the content of the 'request' at all, we would say informally. However, if the objection is 'accepted', then the accepter clearly withdraws that 'request': he may go on to re-present that 'request' in a different form, but in doing so he is conceding that his first attempt did not get off the ground. Anticipating somewhat, I would suggest that in the case that the substance of a 'complaint' is disputed – *eg* a hearer denies authorship of the complainable – the interactional move involved is a Reject. An alternative analysis whereby a 'complain' is labelled an 'accuse', such that Satisfaction of a Proffered 'accuse' implies promotion of the 'accuse' to the illocutionary status of a 'complain' would also seem feasible, but appears to violate our theoretical standpoint that it is interactional structure which accounts for the dynamics of conversational processes, rather than illocutionary sequencing. It seems likely therefore that a more thorough analysis of the structure of the exchange would lead to the inclusion of a further distinctive move – the Reject.

Just as the non-occurrence of uptake can lead to a Reject, so can inappropriate uptake lead to a RE-RUN. In fact, this does not occur in the data analysed. Consider however the case in which a speaker A makes a Proffer, and on the evidence provided by B's subsequent move believes that his Proffer has been misconstrued, and seeks then to change this state of affairs. His first task is to make B aware of the fact that in his opinion the communication process is not working optimally. Secondly he has to re-present his misconstrued Proffer in such a way that the misinterpretation is not repeated. Thirdly in doing so, he tacitly cancels or invalidates both B's move and his own misconstrued Proffer. He proffers therefore a *Re-Run*. In the illustration above we have referred to more than *interactional* proceedings – the above is simply one case in which it appears a Re-Run might be appropriate. A Re-Run therefore rejects the intervening move of one's interlocutor, and substitutes for the speaker's preceding move. A fabricated instance would be as in the following:

– John, pass me the dictionary will you
– Here (proffers dictionary)
– No, the Oxford

If we simplify somewhat (the relation between a 'request' and the performance of the requested act is a complex one – see *pp* 36–8 above), the structure here might be shown as

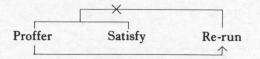

Proffer	Satisfy	Re-run

The graphic presentation suggests that the Re-Run substitutes for the preceding Proffer, and annuls or cancels the outcome of the preceding pair of moves. (The 'cross' results from the arrow-head leaving the 'closed' exchange meeting the left-directional arrowhead emanating from the Re-Run). It can readily be seen that such a structure cannot be described in the terms we have so far developed. Re-Runs do not however occur in the data used for this study: it seems likely that much conversational work is concerned to ensure that Re-Runs are not necessary in fact. They are clearly non H-supportive. (Schegloff, Jefferson and Sacks, 1977 argue persuasively that talk is so structured as to favour self- as opposed to other-correction: a Re-Run in these terms constitutes an other-correction).

Finally we may introduce the PRIME. Primes may occur as initial elements in exchange structure, but are to be viewed as 'pre-Proffers'. The move which Satisfies a Prime is itself a Proffer, such that a Prime-Satisfy sequence does not produce outcome except in the sense that the Satisfying move is itself the 'outcome' functioning as a Proffer.[9] Diagrammatically a Prime-Satisfy sequence may be represented as follows:

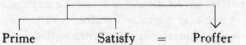

Prime	Satisfy	=	Proffer

Consider the following case:

[6.2]   (Situation 2B: X and Y have just witnessed a traffic accident)

X: what shall we <u>do</u> what shall we <u>do</u> oh <u>dear</u>
Y: erm now now now oka<u>y</u> now ∧ let's ∧ the first thing to do is keel <u>calm</u> ∧ let's keep <u>calm</u>
X: <u>right</u>

(2B21)

The structure evidenced here is

Prime   Satisfy   =   Prime   Satisfy

As the Prime has potentially enormous power as a descriptive element, it is necessary to attempt to restrict this and to account for the necessity of introducing such an interactional move. That an Exchange may be Primed follows from the peculiar status of language as both a system of reference and a mode of action, such that what is referred to in a communicative act may in fact be some preceding communicative act. It follows that among other things communicative acts may be 'requested', 'offered', 'criticised' and so on. This is well-known. We need then to distinguish the case in which the goods which are for example 'requested' in a communicative act are such that they can only be delivered in or through some subsequent verbal act, from the case in which the requested goods may be delivered by other means. Further we shall wish to distinguish the case in which such a 'request for a communicative act' may be a non-Priming Proffer ('Please say you'll come') from the case in which such a 'request' may be a Prime ('What do you think we ought to do?'). If the content of the requested communicative act is specific, then we may say that to 'request' this communicative act is in terms of interactional structure no different in kind from a 'request' for a packet of cigarettes.[10] However if the 'request' for a communicative act does not express a specific content, then when the requested communicative act is produced, its status in the conversation is so to speak a matter of negotiation between the conversing parties. In other words, the 'request' in the latter case may be functioning as a Prime in discourse structure.

It is of interest in considering the distinction between Priming and Proffering moves to consider the procedures observable in formal debates or discussions, in which one person is assigned the role of chairperson, regulating turn-taking, topic, and other structural aspects of the discourse. Such a chairperson may call for contributions to the ongoing discussion, assign X a turn, and thank X for his contribution after his turn. X's contribution itself may however be in the form of a 'question', a 'reply' to a previous point, a 'suggestion' for future action, and many other things. The chair may then call upon Y to speak, and Y may 'agree' with X, 'disagree', and so on. Y in turn will be thanked by the chair for his contribution. From the chairperson's perspective, the contributions of X and Y constitute Satisfys of the Proffered 'request for contributions' with which the Chair opened the debate. The thanks we interpret as initiating a Post-exchange (see 6.1.3 below), showing that Proffer-Satisfy exchange units are occurring. However from the perspective of the participants in the discussion, the chairperson's opening 'request for contributions' constituted a Prime, and the moves made by X and Y count as structural elements in a (possibly) coherent discourse. We understand in the context of a formal debate or meeting that the chairperson has a 'neutral' perspective on the debate, merely enforcing conventionalised rules for its conduct. The Prime in informal discourse however can be seen to be a means of eliciting a Proffer, in interactional terms, similar to the 'request for contributions' in the hypothetical debate described above.

Primes occur infrequently in the corpus used. It seems a reasonable hypothesis to suggest that this may be related to the fact that we consider only two-party interactions. Whether or not Priming increases as the number of participants in a conversation increases is however an empirical issue. It is also possible that the simulated nature of the data investigated in part accounts for the infrequency with which Priming is to be observed in it: in many of the situations set up in order to elicit this corpus, at least one participant had a relatively well-defined conversational goal. Whether or not Priming occurs more frequently when this is not the case is again however an empirical issue.

I have now covered the categories of moves in exchange structure. In attempting to illustrate some exchange structures, we face the considerable difficulty that the surface texture of what is said (and done) – *ie* the means by which interactional structures are realised in conversational behaviour – is complicated by other factors we wish to explore later in this exposition. In discussing briefly several data extracts, we shall therefore concentrate solely on the 'basic' interactional structure of the ongoing talk. Consider the following extract:

[6.3] (Situation 3A: X is picking fruit on Y's farm: a dispute develops as to how many baskets X has picked)

    X: I've done se͝ven seven Mónday and Tuésday and Wédnesday you kńow it's not unusual I'm going to do seven on Thùrsday I do it every dày you know it's seven pound a

    Y: it did rain though eárlier ∧ are you súre you∧

X: no I've been picking all the t̲i̲me I've got me w̄aterproofs_M
Y: who ∧ who was ch̲ecking the tally this m̲orning

                                                                (3A13)

If we accept for purposes of exposition here that X's first turn at
speech may be deemed to be one move, namely a Proffer, it is clear
that Y's following move does not constitute a Satisfy. It cannot be a
Contra as Y later appears to 'accept' X's claim that he has been picking
all the time – *ie* X's Contra. If then Y's first move in this extract were
to be understood as a Contra, in apparently Satisfying X's Contra
to it, Y would be cancelling or withdrawing his own Contra, and in
fact Satisfying X's original Proffer. This is however not the case: Y
continues by opening further negotiations as to how many baskets
have been picked. Y's first move is therefore a Counter: its withdrawal
brings only a local negative outcome, X's original Proffer is not
Satisfied by the withdrawal of the Counter. The structure evidenced
here is therefore

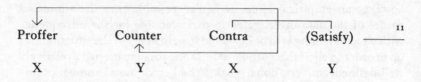

Proffer   Counter   Contra   (Satisfy) ───── [11]

   X   Y   X   Y

Note that we have allowed here a Contra to be Satisfied implicitly:
in raising a new issue ('Who was checking the tally this morning') Y is
addressing X's original Proffer, and not the immediately preceding
Contra. We have more to say on this issue in 6.2. The notion of
interactional structure evidenced here is a dynamic one. In
(implicitly) Satisfying X's Contra, Y both annuls his own preceding
Counter, and ratifies the substance of X's Contra as a local discourse
outcome. This outcome (a shared belief that Y continued picking
despite the rain) now belongs to the shared discourse world operant at
this point in the conversation.

An identical structural sequence occurs later in the same encounter.
Here however it is X who Counters, and who then withdraws this
Counter in Satisfying Y's Contra of that Counter:

[6.4] (Situation 3A: as for [6.3] above)

X: I'm s̲ure I did s̲even h̲onestly ∧ you ∧ for i̲nstance this this
    girl ab̲ove er Elisabeth G̲osforth ∧ she's done two four ∧ she's

> done si- síx ∧ it's a bit unúsual isn't ít for a Thúrsday ∧ cos
> she did she's done fóur and fóur and twó before [are you
> suré you didn't
>
> Y: well I díd] nów I had a wórd with Elisabeth yésterday
>   actually cos I (follows long account)
>
> X: yéah wèll now well if] you sáy that then obviously ∧ er but
>   I'm absolùtely súre I did séven . . .
>
> (3A14)

If we again simplify drastically, we may say that X's opening
'suggestion' concerning Elisabeth Gosforth is a Counter to Y's
earlier-stated non-acceptance of X's claim that he has picked seven
baskets. Y Contras this Counter, and X Satisfies this Contra – this
time explicitly. Note that X then immediately restates his position
('I'm absolutely sure. . .'), thus making it clear that his Satisfy of Y's
Contra to his Counter does not imply an abandonment of the position
implied by that Counter (namely that he picked seven baskets). The
given section of X's latter turn at speech above therefore contains two
moves, a Satisfy followed by a Re-Proffer.

[6.5] (Situation 3D: X returns to her library seat to find that it has
       been occupied in her absence by Y)

> X: excúse me but I think you've got my pláce
>
> Y: oh I'm térribly sórry but I'm in this terrible rúsh I've just
>   gót to get this páper finished ∧ I've just ∧ got hálf an hour
>   reading this bóok ∧ I'm sorry do you mínd [it just means
>
> X: well lóok ∧ I've got to] well lóok I wouldn't wouldn't
>   ótherwise but erm ∧ you knów I I've got this próject I've got
>   to finish by the end of térm and I haven't dóne much today
>
> Y: yéah I've got the same próblem I've just got ţo read this
>   periódical about about twenty mínutes that's áll
>
> X: well couldn't you júst read it   couldn't you take one of those
>   cháirs . . .
>   (Intervening dialogue omitted)
>
> Y: okáy (bustles to rise)
>
> (3D21)

X's initial Proffer here is Contraed by Y in her 'request' to retain
X's place. X Contras this Contra. X's Contra is then Contraed by Y,

who in doing so re-presents her Contra to X's initiating Proffer. X again Contras such that the content of her 'suggestion' that Y take another chair represents her current position.

In Satisfying this Contra therefore Y brings the exchange to a point of potential closure. The structure evidenced here is therefore

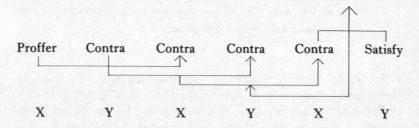

Proffer	Contra	Contra	Contra	Contra	Satisfy
X	Y	X	Y	X	Y

The following is a final illustration:

[6.6] (Situation 5C: Y has just discovered that X has borrowed her jacket and spilt wine on it. She has drawn X's attention to her discovery.)

X: well ₘ most I can do is offer to get it dry-cleaned

Y: yeah but it's not gonna come out with dry-cleaning wine spots don't I mean I presume it's wine cos it's red

X: hmm ₘ well have you got any ∧ sort of evidence that it won't come out with dry-cleaning

Y: only that wine-spots don't usually come out it's suede suede's a very ∧ difficult material to get cleaned anyway ∧ and any kind of ∧ alcohol or grease-spots or anyth[ing just

X: ahum]

Y: don't come out of suede

X: well can you not get it re-textured or anything like that . . .

                                                            (5C11/2)

Again we have to consider the given extract independently of the preceding and following structure. We assume a preceding exchange-initiating Proffer on the part of Y, the general tenor of which we might informally gloss as complaining in tone. The structural sequence we propose for the given extract is as follows:

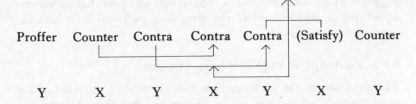

Proffer   Counter   Contra   Contra   Contra   (Satisfy)   Counter

Y   X   Y   X   Y   X   Y

Again we assume that in proposing re-texturing in her last turn at
speech in the given extract X is implicitly abandoning her offer to have
the jacket dry-cleaned – *ie* a Satisfy is found in the interactional
structure given above for which there is no clearly matching verbal or
other behavioural token. There is here an argument that the
verbalisation represented as *ahum* in the transcription can be
interpreted as a Satisfy, but as we have already allowed non-expressed
Satisfys following Contras, we do not need to argue this interpretation
(see however 6.4.2 below). It can be seen that the Counter with which the
extract ends is a Counter to the original Proffer with which the
extract opens, or more precisely the Proffer we understand to have
opened the exchange from which an extract is given above.

We conceded prior to citing the data above that our analyses are
here extremely incomplete. Two issues that have arisen inside what
has been said are firstly that some moves can apparently be made
implicitly – specifically a Satisfy following a Contra, and secondly that
while turn-taking is claimed to operate at the level of the move, this
appears not to be so above the level of the exchange – indeed following
a Satisfy of a Counter or of a Contra to a Counter, it appears that either
speaker may make the next move. This is so: following a Satisfy either
speaker may produce the next move, though it is clear that the options
open to the one or the other are not likely to be the same.

We have assumed in presenting different interactional moves that
with the exception of the Satisfy what may *follow* any individual move
is not restricted – *ie* any move other than a Satisfy, an 'accepting'
move, is itself 'Proffered', in the sense that it may be followed by any
of the possible moves which may follow a Proffer itself (save that a
Prime may not be followed by a further Prime, of course). There are
clearly however limitations operating here in conversational practice –
for example there is no instance in our data of a Counter being
Countered. We need here however to distinguish between the
structural potential of the exchange and the actual structural
sequences which may be observed in conversational behaviour. We do
not feel justified in attempting on the basis of a limited corpus to

suggest what the limitations operating on potential discourse structures might be, beyond the structural potential built into the move definitions given.

6.1.3 Exchange linkage in phase structure

The structure of the exchange has been described in terms of the moves which may occur in an exchange, and the implicational interrelations holding between them. Similarly, the structure of a conversational Phase will be described simply in terms of different types of exchange linkage. Linkage may be subordinate or co-ordinate. A HEAD Exchange may be preceded by a PRE-EXCHANGE. As Pre-Exchanges are not a basic type of subordinate exchange, but a type of subordinate exchange resulting from a conversational strategy used by the speaker initiating such an exchange, the Pre-Exchange will be explored and illustrated in 6.2 below. Here we shall simply define it in structural terms. A Head exchange may also be followed by a POST-EXCHANGE. Embedded inside a Head exchange we may find PRE-RESPONDING EXCHANGES. These three types of Exchange are linked via subordination to the Head exchange they precede, follow, or occur within. It is structurally possible for subordinate exchanges to contain subordinate exchanges – *ie* recursion can and does occur. Two types of co-ordination are suggested: CHAINING and RECIPROCATION. Head exchanges may be chained or reciprocated, but while *multiple* chaining is possible, only *two* exchanges may be reciprocal, as a matter of definition. Subordinate exchanges may be chained, and multiple chaining is again possible, but reciprocally-linked Pre-, Post- and Pre-Responding Exchanges do not occur in our data, and in this instance we are prepared to claim *may* not occur. Two subordinate exchanges may not be reciprocally linked. We thus have three types of subordinate linkage, and two types of co-ordination. Each will be developed and illustrated below.

A note on pre-exchanges

Pre-Exchanges are directly parallel to 'Pre-Sequences' in the ethnomethodological literature. They are defined such that the *outcome* of such an exchange directly leads to the initiation of a following Head (or other) exchange. This means that a Pre-Exchange is in part identified and defined by its consequences, and also that turn-taking is consistently determined by move sequence *after* a Pre-Exchange – *ie* the Speaker who initiates a Pre-Exchange will initiate the following exchange. That this is so is taken as an indication that *strategy* is operant here. The generalisation we proposed earlier (*p* 99 above) was that after a Satisfy *either* party may perform the next move. Diagrammatically, Pre-Exchanges will be linked to the exchange which follows them as follows:

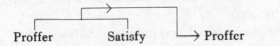

Proffer   Satisfy   ⟶ Proffer   . . . .

A note on post-exchanges

Given the negotiable nature of communicative acts, and given for example that the distinction between a Counter and a Contra is based on the effects of the communicative act deemed to have the status of the one or the other as an interactional move, it is perhaps to be expected that for the active participants in ongoing transactions, the arrival at a point of possible closure may require confirmatory or other action. Post-Exchanges allow of this possibility. Post-Exchanges serve to firm the outcome of a preceding exchange, and most commonly consist of two elements only, *ie* have a Proffer-Satisfy structure. Insofar as the initiation of a Post-Exchange gives the other conversationalist an opportunity for come-back however, and insofar as it is matter of common experience (and empirical observation) that people can and do have further thoughts on previously-negotiated outcomes, the initiation of a Post-Exchange may lead to the re-opening of business which appeared to at least one of the interactants to be potentially closed. In such a case, the structure of the Post-Exchange will clearly be more complex. Thus details concerning a previous outcome may be raised in a Post-Exchange. Post-exchanges may be substantive or ritual.

Post-exchanges optionally follow Head and indeed subordinate exchanges, and commonly bridge the business and closing phases of an encounter. In such cases they function similarly to the 'Pre-Closing' sequences investigated in the work of the ethno-methodologists. Post-Exchanges may be graphically related to the preceding exchange whose outcome they firm or make more precise as follows:

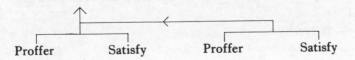

Proffer   Satisfy   Proffer   Satisfy

In illustrating Post-Exchanges from our conversational data, we shall point to some additional complications concerning the structure of conversational episodes, thus anticipating later sections of the descriptive apparatus being developed.

[6.7] (Situation 1A: Y(X's school-teacher) has just been filling out
       part of a form for him)
       Y: yès erm right ∧ (completes form) (mutter) wèll (hands over
           form) that's <u>that</u>
       X: (accepts form) òh ∧ thank you very <u>much</u> Mr Sinden
       Y: oh well
       X: I'll be seeing you agàin [before . . .

                                                                    (IA22)

We wish to claim that Thanks-Minimization sequences typically realise Post-Exchanges, though it is not of course the case that Post-Exchanges are typically realised by Thanks-Minimization sequences. This involves the claim of course that a 'thanks' (which is characterised, together with a 'minimization' in 6.3 below) is occasioned by a preceding conversational *outcome* in the case that it initiates a Post-Exchange. This is consistent with the position we take

[6.8] (Situation 1B: X and Y have just negotiated a solution to the
       problem arising from X's inability to keep a baby-sitting
       appointment made with Y)
       X: . . .but perhaps we can <u>do</u> that I'll <u>bring</u> my friend
           roùnd tonight
       Y: yeàh [okay
       X: what time] would you li̇ke
       Y: oh <u>any</u> time about eight thirty'll be [<u>fine</u>
       oh∧] <u>yės</u> allright <u>fine</u> ∧ well I'll bring her round toni̇ght
       Y: yèah

                                                                  (1B14/5)

with regard to illocutionary acts in 6.3 below, and also with the observation that when a 'thanks' is occasioned by a communicative act (an 'invitation', or a 'compliment' for example) a minimization may not follow. (As minimizations are not always realised in British English, clearer evidence is provided by a language such as German).

In [6.8] (p 102), a first 'firming' Post-Exchange is followed by a second concerning a detail of the outcome which has just been firmed, before a third Post-Exchange leads directly to the close of the encounter.

More than one Post-Exchange may occur therefore. This is further illustrated in the following extract, in which the repeated initiation of firming exchanges by Y may be accounted for (apart from temperamental factors as regards the individual playing Y's role) by the situation, in which X has been physically hurt. The reiterated initiation of Post-Exchanges evidences Y's concern for X's well-being therefore, as she thereby gives him a further opportunity to express his needs:

[6.9] (Situation 2A: X is Y's lodger: his gas-fire has just blown up as he has tried to light it. The conversation which follows the advent of Y on the scene concludes as follows:)

    Y: allright ∧ I'll just go and get your [tea then

    X: okay]

    Y: and I'll come back and we'll have a nice [little chat

    X: okay∧] okay

    Y: allright

    X: right

    Y: and don't you worry about anything

    X: thank you Mrs Walker

    Y: allright (opens door)

    X: thank you (exit of Y)

Note here incidentally that the 'thanking' moves do not initiate Post-Exchanges: informally we would say here that X is thanking Y for her 'expressions of sympathy' *ie* a communicative act is the thankable, not a conversational outcome.

The neat sequence of pairs illustrated in extract [6.9] above is not always or even usually to be found in examining Post-Exchanges. We shall wish to claim in fact (6.4 below) that a Satisfy of any Proffer in a *ritual* exchange may be realised non-verbally, or – and this is a hypothesis which a more detailed analysis of non-verbal communicative behaviour might confirm or refute – that in the absence of any alternative to a Satisfy, the initiator as source of the Proffer is justified in acting as though a Satisfy had been forthcoming. Note that this is different from the *strategic* assumption of a Satisfy – as when we saw that a Satisfy to a Contra following a Counter may be absent from the surface texture of the conversation in that the speaker responsible for the Contra retains the turn at talk, simply *assuming* that his Contra is valid as determining outcome. Not all Post-Exchanges are however ritual, of course: only in the case that the outcome of a Post-Exchange is identical to a previous exchange outcome is the Post-Exchange a ritual one. Thanks-Minimization exchanges functioning as Post-Exchanges in discourse structure are however a case in which ritual is indulged, and, as we have said, minimizations do not always occur:

[6.10] (Situation 4B: Y has returned X's folder to him at home – he had left it on a park bench)

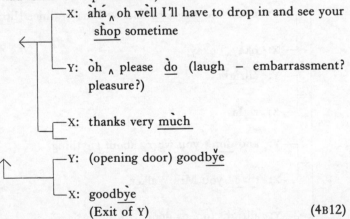

X: aha ∧ oh well I'll have to drop in and see your shop sometime

Y: oh ∧ please do (laugh – embarrassment? pleasure?)

X: thanks very much

Y: (opening door) goodbye

X: goodbye
    (Exit of Y)   (4B12)

The 'thanking' move here firms the outcome of the preceding exchange, as the 'invitation' from Y is elicited – it is not a Proffer, but a Satisfy. Our broad transcription was incapable of discovering any behavioural token for any following minimization here. To justify this analysis is not possible until we have explored the notion of illocutionary act and exchange outcome more thoroughly (see 6.3 and 7.1 below). It is clear that the claim that a particular element of interactional structure may have a zero-realisation (or indeed a non-verbal realisation, when no attempt is made to make empirical observations as to what form this might take) is a serious weakness in an analytical system unless the conditions under which this is possible are rigorously delimited. On what grounds are we to distinguish a three-element exchange from a sequence of two two-element exchanges, the latter element of the second of which is not realised? We wish to claim that the notion of illocutionary outcome as developed below (*pp* 137–9, 193–4) resolves this difficulty.

Pre-responding exchanges

As the name suggests, a Pre-Responding Exchange differs from a Pre-Exchange and a Post-Exchange in its placing. It may occur after any move other than a Satisfy with the qualification that as Pre-Responding Exchanges may be chained, a second or subsequent Pre-Responding Exchange may immediately follow an initial or preceding Pre-Responding Exchange, and in such a case will follow in sequenced time a Satisfy concluding a preceding subordinate Exchange of the same type. Note however that in such a case the structural linkage will be between the move preceding the *initial* Pre-Responding Exchange and the outcome of the chained Pre-Responding Exchange, and not between the outcome of the initial exchange in the chain and that of the chained exchange following it. If we assume a Pre-Responding Exchange is initiated following a Proffer, therefore, and that a second *chained* subordinate exchange follows, the linkage may be represented graphically as follows:

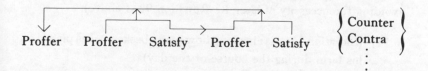

It is perfectly feasible, though no instance occurs in our data, that multiple embedding should occur, as for example in the following configuration:

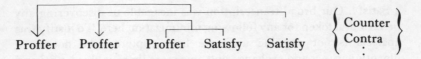

Proffer   Proffer   Proffer   Satisfy   Satisfy   { Counter }
                                                       { Contra }

(It will be clear that Pre-Responding Exchanges bear some affinity to 'side' or 'insertion' sequences in the work of Sacks, Schegloff, and Jefferson).

A Post-Exchange served to 'firm' the *outcome* of a previous *exchange*, while a Pre-Responding Exchange serves to 'firm' the content or significance of a preceding move. Further, just as a Post-Exchange may either be ritual or have content – *ie* negotiate a detail concerning the outcome of the preceding exchange, so, in the case of a Pre-Responding Exchange, the outcome may be identical to the content of the move preceding the Exchange, or may add specification or detail to the content of the preceding move. The distinction reflects in part a distinction between checking on the content of the preceding communicative act as a locution, illocution, or interactional move, and checking on the *significance* of the preceding communicative act, in terms of its implications. (*cf* Candlin et al's (1976) distinction between 'task-oriented' and 'meta-communicative' 'functions'). This distinction however concerns the illocutions used to realise the Proffer initiating a Pre-Responding Exchange: it is not reflected in interactional structure.[12]

Finally, note that turn-taking at the level of the move in interactional structure is not disturbed by the insertion in interactional structure of Pre-Responding sequences – *ie* a Proffer initiating such a subordinate exchange cannot be made by the performer of the move preceding that Proffer.

A first illustration is of a case in which the outcome of the Pre-Responding Exchange does not substantially affect the nature of the move preceding. Such 'firming' work, we may suggest, not only serves a time-gaining function for the responder, but is also a means of avoiding the necessity of later Re-Runs (*pp* 92–3 above):

[6.11]   (Situation 3A: Y is checking how many baskets X has picked on
         his farm during the course of the day)
    →   Y: yes ∧that's six baskets for you today then Peter
         X: six
         Y: yup
         X: you mean seven   (3A11)

The following illustrates more substantive Pre-Responding behaviour:

[6.12] (Situation 1C: X has been talking about her difficulties in finding records to take to a party later on in the evening, and knows that Y is very careful concerning his own large record collection)

   → X: well (exhalation) (tongue click) well I ∧ I wondered I mean really ∧ I don't know how to put this but ∧ (inhales) could we take some of yours along (exhales)

    Y: (deep breath)

    X: (quickly) we'll be very careful

    Y: (exhales, shifts in chair) ∧ which ones

    X: well I mean ∧ that's partly up to you ∧ I mean you know the sort of stuff I like ∧ but ... (extended justification of request in the form of explanation of situation, undertaking in the case of accidents etc)

    Y: mm (inhales) yeah okay erm (all said on exhalation)

                                                 (1C13)

X's second turn at speech here (edited in the above) clearly has itself structure: however we are not yet in a position to offer an analysis of it. [13] The extract is therefore considerably shortened. In another version of the same situation, several Pre-Responding Exchanges occur before the requestee(Y) eventually 'agrees' to lend X some of his records: the following extract records the beginning of this process of negotiation:

[6.13] (Situation 1c: as in [6.12] above)

X: . . .the thing i̠s̠ (self-conscious giggle) re̠a̠lly erm we
needed some re̠cords and er (laugh) ∧ I mean I k̠now̠
you've got a very good collection er ∧ and I was gonna
ask if I could b̠o̠rrow some but er

Y: a̠h

X: you'd probably want to b̠e̠ there ∧ while they're being
pl̠a̠ying cos I know you're very ca̠reful[14] about your
re̠cords

Y: (inhales) ye̠ah well er ᴍ there ∧ there's not gonna be a
di̠s̠co or anything at the pa̠rty [I mean

X: n̠o̠] it's just that S̠i̠mon's been asked to bring along
some re̠cords and erm well I mean you know what
hi̠s̠ taste is li̠ke

Y: well ∧ it depends on other pe̠o̠ple bringing re̠cords
that the party exi̠s̠ts or the music for the party exi̠s̠ts

X: ye̠ah I thi̠nk so . . .

                                                        (1c22/3)

Chained exchanges

In the above extract, the two cited sequential Pre-Responding
Exchanges are *chained*: they are co-ordinate in having the same
function with respect to the same preceding communicative act.
Chained exchanges will be diagrammatically shown to be such in that
their outcomes will be graphically linked as follows:

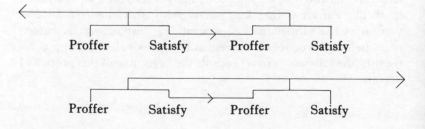

Proffer   Satisfy   Proffer   Satisfy

Proffer   Satisfy   Proffer   Satisfy

The directionality of the linked outcomes will depend on whether Pre-Responding/Post Exchanges are chained, or Pre-Exchanges are linked in this fashion.

Consider informally a purchasing transaction in a shop. The purchaser may request in one turn at speech goods a to n, and the seller will then, we may assume, seek to produce each of these requested goods. Alternatively, the purchaser may request a good a, and when this is produced by the seller, continue by requesting a good b, and so on, until the outcome, we may assume, is identical to the outcome in the first instance, the case of the 'block' order. It seems intuitively obvious that in the case of the piecemeal ordering a series of subtransactions together constitute a transaction essentially similar to that instigated by the block order. These sub-transactions are chained.

The notion of chaining clearly requires further specification –ie the descriptive power of such a form of linkage needs to be restricted. The following four characterising features are suggested:

(i)   Chained Exchanges may be re-ordered or collapsed into a single exchange (cf the case of the bulk order above), such that the content of the Proffers which initiate chained exchanges may be contained in one Proffer: the same holds for the Satisfys or other responses to the individual Proffers.[15]

(ii)   Exchanges which are chained must be of the same type – note that while two exchanges which are reciprocally linked are as a matter of definition not chained, *pairs* of reciprocal exchanges may in fact themselves be chained. This constitutes a necessary but not a sufficient condition for chaining. Chained exchanges must belong to the same phase of an Encounter.

(iii)   The illocutions which realise the Proffer slots in chained exchanges are essentially of the same kind – they are compatible.[16]

(iv)   There is a common theme to be found among the illocutions which fill the Proffer slots in chained exchanges.

That these four characteristics can scarcely be said to provide strict identificational criteria for the recognition of chained exchanges is undeniable, and that this is so is not surprising. It may be stressed again that in the model being set up, the notion of interactional structure is taken as given, such that it is against his background knowledge of what a speaker might be doing interactionally that a hearer interprets the significance of what he has heard.

Several instances of chaining have been cited already: we provide here one further illustration. The extract is edited to reveal the structural pattern of chaining: the chained exchanges are Pre-'Execution' Exchanges (see p 184 below).

[6.14] (Situation 3B: doctor (Y) and patient (X) in doctor's consulting-room)

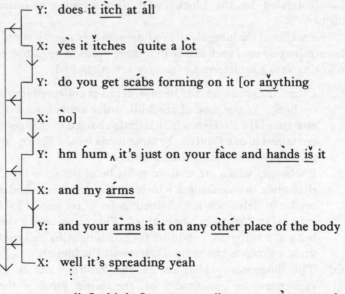

X: well can you ∧ can you prescribe anything for the allergy I mean will it go away I mean it's quite nasty to look at

Y: does it itch at all

X: yes it itches   quite a lot

Y: do you get scabs forming on it [or anything

X: no]

Y: hm hum ∧ it's just on your face and hands is it

X: and my arms

Y: and your arms is it on any other place of the body

X: well it's spreading yeah

Y: well I think I can prescribe some ointment for you...

(3B12)

The 'question-answer' sequences are all relevant to the rash which is to be treated: the information elicited by the doctor piece-meal could in theory have been elicited in a 'block' by means of an utterance such as 'tell me about it', 'describe this rash for me' and so on. The illocutions are essentially similar, and the embedded exchanges which are chained are of the same type.

Reciprocal Exchanges

In examining the term 'exchanges' in everyday use we distinguished between uptaking, responding, and reciprocating as leading to a type of 'exchange' following an initial act of some kind. The notion of 'responding' may be said to underpin the technical sense in which the term Exchange has been adopted in our schema, and we have included Uptake as a particular kind of interactional act in the structure of an interactional move. Here we wish to argue that the notion of reciprocation is relevant to *exchange* linkage, Reciprocal exchanges being co-ordinated in a particular way. It was suggested in discussing the notion of reciprocation that there is a powerful law of social sharing which supports reciprocal activity between members. It can be seen in fact that the social desirability of H-supportive behaviour, coupled with the fact that interaction necessarily involves two participants itself implies some notion such as reciprocation.

By a reciprocal exchange is meant an exchange whose outcome may be said to 'reciprocate' the outcome of a preceding exchange, which it therefore reciprocates, The notion of reciprocation here essential involves a reversal of speaker-hearer benefits and costs in the negotiated outcomes of the two exchanges deemed reciprocal.

As we noted earlier there is often in ritual interaction a nice blend of reciprocal and firming work, in that for example, in what we may informally term a 'request-comply-thanks-minimization' sequence, the thanks-minimization sequence both firms the outcome of the preceding head exchange (and is therefore a Post-Exchange), and is a ritualised reciprocal exchange, in that thanks is itself a socially beneficial good, proffered by a speaker here in reciprocation of the requested good his interlocutor has delivered, or undertaken to deliver. Reciprocity is most evident in the structure of phatic talk, where mutual stroking — *ie* 'I'll scratch your back, you scratch mine' — is the order of the day.

Note that a reciprocal exchange may be initiated by either party, thus retaining the generalisation that turn-taking above the level of the exchange is a matter of negotiation between speakers, and is not determined by interactional structure. Thus following the case in which X 'agrees' to do a social good for Y, either X may 'request' a reciprocating 'favour', or this may be 'offered' by Y. Note further that compensatory offers following complaints do not necessarily initiate reciprocal exchanges, though clearly some notion of social justice may be said to underpin such behaviour. Nor does a remark of the kind 'I'll let you have it back tomorrow', following the borrowing of a sum of money or of some other good necessarily initiate a reciprocal exchange. When two exchanges are reciprocally linked, their outcomes will be shown as converging, as follows:

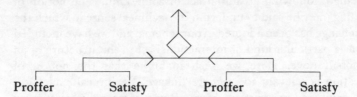

Proffer   Satisfy   Proffer   Satisfy

In the first illustration below, we wish to claim that the 'exchange' of names which takes place consists of two exchanges, although only the Satisfy of the second appears in the observed conversational behaviour of the two participants – *ie* X *assumes* Y might like to know his name, and 'tells' her accordingly: here we trespass on territory to be covered in 6.2 below once more:

[6.15]   (Situation 1D: Two students have just met at a social function)

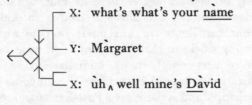

X: what's what's your n\`ame

Y: M\`argaret

X: \`uh ∧ well mine's D\`avid

Y: aha y\`ou're doing the same co\`urse are you

(1D12)

'Small talk' may in fact in part be characterised by simple exchange structures, and chained reciprocal exchanges. Consider the extract from another version of the same situation given in [6.16].

Simplistically we may say here that X asks Y to tell about herself, and when she has done so, tells her about himself, and having volunteered more information about himself than he had previously obtained from Y, feels justified in asking her to reciprocate by telling more about herself. This is of course a totally informal analysis. The interactional structure which reflects and justifies it evidences a Post-Exchange ('no'-'no'), and as we shall argue below (see 6.2 following) the utterance 'I've been in London most of the time' is to be seen as belonging to the first bracketed exchange in the graphic

[6.16] (Situation 1D, X and Y meet at a semi-formal party)

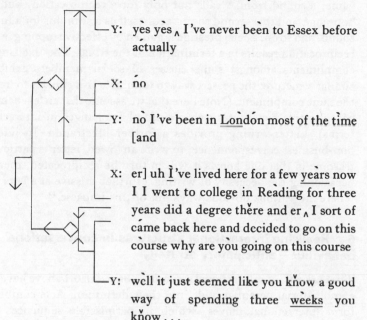

X: . . .you arrived today

Y: yes yes ∧ I've never been to Essex before actually

X: no

Y: no I've been in London most of the time [and

X: er] uh I've lived here for a few years now I I went to college in Reading for three years did a degree there and er ∧ I sort of came back here and decided to go on this course why are you going on this course

Y: well it just seemed like you know a good way of spending three weeks you know . . .

(1D21)

representation of interactional structure shown. X's following turn at talk is analysed as evidencing a Satisfy to an *assumed* Proffer, and a Proffer ('Why are you going on this course') which is Satisfied by Y in her final turn at talk in this extract. Note that X's Satisfy is seen as reciprocating *both* the preceding and the following exchanges: this is because the structure of his own biographical narrative (we are obliged to use these informal descriptive terms until we have given an account of our analysis of illocutionary acts) is complex — crudely, we may say he 'volunteers' more information than is necessary to reciprocate that which he receives, and is therefore justified in requesting more from his interlocutor. Two 'levels' of reciprocity may be detected here therefore, as shown graphically alongside the given extract [6.16] above.

Informally we may see this operation as a type of 'reciprocal chaining', and it may be appropriate to offer some observational support for the claim that reciprocity in social dealings can and does operate in the 'chaining' fashion illustrated. If we think of Labov's account of sounding in Harlem for example (Labov 1972) it seems intuitively clear that according to the rules of this particular social game, a sound from A calls not only for a reciprocation, but for a 'topping', and this second sound acts itself as a stimulus for a further sound, and so on. Social prestige is gained by effective topping: a weak reciprocation results in a termination of the ritual. The 'exchange' of compliments amongst some classes of social members exhibits a similar structure: the neatest way to terminate this ritual is to 'return' the same compliment. (Note here that we assume that an 'exchange' of compliments constitutes two reciprocal Exchanges in interactional terms). Letter-writing provides a further illustration. In informal non-business correspondence, to write an 'owed' letter is particularly irksome in that one knows it will in turn be reciprocated, therefore occasioning the necessity of writing a further missive at a later data. There are various obvious ways out of this impasse.[17]

6.2 Realising interactional structures in conversational behaviour – anticipatory strategy

The elements of interactional structure posited in 6.1 above have their combinatorial potential built into their definition. Acts combine to form interactional moves, which in permissible sequences form exchanges. Exchanges may then be linked in various ways, thus forming Phases. It is posited that an Encounter consists of an ordered sequence of phases, though the only structural possibility we feel justified in positing at this level of analysis is that of (Ave)-Business-(Vale).[18]

However interactional structures do not exist in vacuo. Interactional structures are evidenced in conversational behaviour, and in other social activity. In the terms of the model we propose, slots in interactional structure are filled by units of behaviour: in the case of a conversational encounter, these units of behaviour will commonly be locutions having in their context of occurrence an illocutionary value.

When we seek to match elements of interactional structure with observed behavioural acts performed by interacting parties, we find that a simplistic one-to-one substitution of illocutionary or other behavioural acts for each interactional act in interactional structure does not account for more than a restricted range of conversational behaviour. There are several reasons why this is so. The critical notion of communicative strategy will be explored in this section, while in 6.4

below some other aspects of the actual performance of communicative acts will be discussed, which again affect the surface texture of what is said.

The central point to be systematically explored and illustrated in this section is that speakers *use* their knowledge of interactional structure in their conversational behaviour. In the terms we have suggested, interacting members have a *social* as well as a *communicative* competence. They employ conversational strategies, which are largely devices used in the interests of achieving conversational goals. The main and obvious feature of conversation which allows of strategic play is that turn-taking is under the control of the interacting parties. If the speaker wishes to retain the turn at talk at all costs, there is in fact little that the hearer can do about it. This is of course not quite true: he can resort to violence of one kind or another, or he can disengage from the interaction by not listening or by simply removing his person from the scene. But in neither case could it be said that such an act constitutes a structural element inside the ongoing conversation (such acts are considered in 6.4 below). Similarly, if a speaker wishes his interlocutor to assume the turn at talk, but the hearer does not wish to assume it, the speaker must either carry on talking, or let the conversation peter out.

By a conversational strategy we wish to denote the manipulation of interactional structure in conversational behaviour, in the interests of achieving conversational goals. Note that while 'strategy' may be deemed to imply a disguised or cloaked act whose purpose is not transparent,[19] this is *not* implied by the notion of conversational strategy: hearers use interpretative strategies as much as speakers behave strategically, and thus conventionalisation occurs, such that what we shall term a strategy may be generally recognised as such inside a particular language community. I shall wish to claim however that it is in the implementation of conversational strategy that the creative aspects of language use are most obviously to be found.

For this reason a full account detailing every possible conversational strategy is not possible. We shall detail several of the most commonly met strategies by investigating more fully Pre-sequences, and then labelling as distinctive *supportive* moves three types of turn-internal communicative acts which have a strategic function with respect to the head act of the move they support. These will be labelled GROUNDING, EXPANDING, and DISARMING moves. This is a device adopted for descriptive purposes: we shall seek to show that such supportive moves are to be derived from the elements of interactional structure developed in 6.1 above. Further we shall consider the case in which more than one illocutionary or other act may fill one slot in interactional structure, but no supportive function is discoverable. Such conversational behaviour will be termed ADDITIVE strategy, leading to a MULTIPLE-HEAD act in move structure. Finally we shall consider other strategic ploys, including the case in which a Satisfy is 'assumed' by a speaker in his continuing turn at talk.

6.2.1 Pre-exchanges

A Pre-Exchange is initiated by a speaker to check on whether a condition for the achievement of a particular conversational goal holds – *ie* that a Satisfy for his intended Proffer is a feasible interactional move for his interlocutor. A Pre-Exchange Proffer checks on an anticipated Counter or Contra. There is thus a systematic relation between the content of a Proffer initiating a Pre-Exchange and the content of a possible Counter or Contra to the Proffer initiating the head exchange which may follow the Pre-Exchange.

Consider the following (fabricated) sequences of communicative acts, and let us assume the initial items are to be viewed as Proffers in interactional structure:

[6.17] (i)   – Can you open the window please John
             – I'm a bit cold myself actually

     (ii)   – Shall we watch the Western on tele later?
             – I've got to work tonight

We are not in position to decide whether the 'replies' given here are Contras or Counters but it seems intuitively clear that these are the most likely possibilities.[20]
Consider then the following (fabricated) sequences:

[6.18] (i)   – Don't you find it a bit stuffy in here?
             – Yes, it is rather
             – Yeah, do you think you could open the window?

     (ii)   – Have you got to work tonight
             – Not particularly, no
             – Oh, shall we watch the Western on tele later?

Pre-Exchanges are evidenced here. There are two sides to the strategic use of this type of subordinate exchange. Insofar as H 'agrees' that the room is a bit stuffy, or claims that he is not particularly busy, he is scarcely in a position to Counter or Contra the

following 'request' or 'suggestion' via an illocution whose
propositional content is incompatible with that of the Satisfy move in
the Pre-Exchange – *ie* having agreed that the room is stuffy, or he is
not engaged, the second speaker in [6.18] (i) or (ii) is not in a position
to produce the Contra/Counters given in [6.17]. On the other hand,
the second speaker in [6.18] (i) and (ii) might have responded to the
initiating 'questions' by saying

'No, I'm a bit cold myself actually' or

'Yes, I'm going to be busy all evening',

in which case S may in fact withhold the intended 'request' or
'suggestion'. By checking beforehand in a Pre-Exchange he has
avoided putting H into a position where he will Contra or Counter his
intended 'request' or 'suggestion'. The strategy is consistent therefore
with the general maxim supporting H-supportive behaviour in
conversational activity.

Pre-Exchange Proffers are often recognisable as such by hearers –
thus in the case of a 'Pre-Invite', to use ethnomethodological
terminology, a hearer may may well be aware that the content of his
'reply' to the Proffer initiating a Pre-Exchange may have
consequences he is not prepared to accept: a common procedure here
is to initiate a Pre-Responding Exchange ('Why do you ask?' etc)
before unwittingly entering into a commitment. The possibilities for
strategic play are here considerable.[21] We stress once more however
that it is not the existence of alleged intentional states which
determines the occurrent interactional structure, though we may refer
to commonly observed and intuitively psychological states in order to
explicate and provide a rationale for particular configurations in
discourse structure.

Conventionalisation can and does occur, in that what might have
counted as a Proffer initiating a Pre-Exchange may be known by a
speaker to be recognisable as such by his hearer, such that that Proffer
may be said to communicate his illocutionary goals. It can be seen in
fact that this is a plausible analysis of the conventionalised forms of
making requests given in Searle 1975 and Gordon and Lakoff 1975,
for example. Thus a Proffer of the form 'Could you open the window'
is not likely to be responded to by an utterance of the form 'Yes I could
why' – or at least in the case that such a 'response' were forthcoming, it
would be interpreted as deliberately non-co-operative. Consider then
a possible sequence such as

– 'Don't you find it a bit stuffy in here?'

– 'Allright I'll open the window'.

Through interpretative anticipation the hearer has 'taken the hint' —*ie* anticipated the speaker's conversational strategy. (*cf* Goffman and Merritt, and the notion of 'elision', *p* 48 above). At this point in the discourse, we shall be able to claim that the utterance which was Proffered counts as a 'request' in that it is Satisfied as such. That the first speaker may go on to claim that his original Proffer was not intended as a 'request' is true. If this occurs then the status of the 'response' as a Satisfy is in jeopardy, as the outcome of the exchange will be subject to further negotiation between the conversationalists. Again there are various strategic ploys possible here. Through intonation, pausing, facial display, a speaker may Proffer a Pre-Exchange Proffer, or a *supportive* move (see 6.2.2 below), and make it clear that a 'response' is called for, hoping that the hearer will interpret his illocutionary point without his having to be more explicit. This strategy is followed perhaps most commonly in the communication of 'bad news' ('I'm afraid there's been an accident'/'It's about your son Johnny'/'I'm afraid I have some bad news for you'). In other cases the strategy is adopted in order to force the hearer to articulate the speaker's illocutionary point, in which case he is at a disadvantage in terms of the social acceptability of a non-Satisfying response. The hearer may then deliberately *withhold* the relevant interpretation, simply Uptaking, and thereby force the speaker to be more explicit. An example follows:

[6.19] (Situation 1C: X wishes to borrow some records off Y, but knows he is very particular about his collection. She has introduced the topic of the party she wishes to attend)

X: yeah ∧ problem is they haven't got many records ∧

Y: yeah

X: well ∧ Simon promised ∧ to take some along ∧

Y: yeah

X: well you know Simon's collection and I mean it's virtually non-existent and most of it's absolute rubbish and it's just not the sort of thing they like there

Y: so

X: well (exhalation) well I I wondered I mean er really ∧ I don't know how to put this but ∧ (inhales) could we take some of yours along

(1C12/3)

Again, it has to be said that the question as to whether or not Y is aware of X's perlocutionary intent in this extract before the actual 'request' is made is indeterminate. The discourse structure cannot meaningfully be said to be different in the case that X does realise what Y wants from the case that X does not. The essential claim we wish to make here is that Pre-Exchanges may be systematically related to possible 'replies', and are therefore to be seen as the result of strategic exploitation of interactional structures of the type expounded in 6.1 above.

Pre-Exchanges are also commonly used to establish a topic – *ie* to introduce various presuppositions into the operant discourse world – and thus 'prepare the ground' for a following Proffer initiating a Head Exchange:

[6.20]   (Situation 1B: Y, X's baby-sitter, calls round to try to get out of an appointment)

X: oh hellŏ Mrs Norton

Y: oh hellŏ Susan

X: yes erm well I'm afraid I've got ∧ afraid I've got a bit of a problem

Y: you mean about tomorrow night

X: yes ∧ erm you [know I

Y: oh dear]

X: know that that you said

Y: yeah

X: er you wanted me tomorrow night

Y: uhŭh yeah

X: well I just thought erm (clears throat) I've got

something else on which I just didn't think
about when I arranged it with you you know
and er

Y: (sighs) yes

X: I'm just wondering if I could possibly back
down on tomorrow

(1B11)

Such Pre-Exchanges can be seen as anticipating Pre-Responding
Proffers, and seem another means of avoiding the necessity for
Re-Runs in ongoing talk.

Pre-Exchanges may also be strategically employed to gain advance
commitments ('Can you do something for me?'), as we have
suggested. However if a hearer refuses to commit himself in advance,
but seeks further specification, the resultant interactional structure is
quite different from that of a Pre-Exchange followed by a Proffer:

[6.21] (Situation 2A: X and his landlady Y have been handling a
situation in which X's gasfire has exploded)

Y: allright ∧ would you do me one favour

X: what is [that Mrs Walker

Y: would you woul]d ∧ go down to the Colonel and
∧the Major and tell them what has happened in
your room so that they won't do the [same
thing

X: okay∧]

(2A13)

In his first utterance in this extract X neither Satisfies nor Contras
Y's preceding Proffer: he initiates a Pre-Responding Exchange, such
that while we may feel intuitively that in her first utterance Y was
strategically introducing a Pre-Exchange, this is not reflected in the
discourse structure which results following the nature of X's
response. Interactional structures are viewed independently of the

illocutionary (and other) acts which realise their structural elements, though there are clearly strong ties between the two 'levels' of analysis. What we wish to stress once more however is that in discourse interaction, alleged intentional states cannot themselves be taken to be determinants of discourse structure.

A final instance of a Pre-Exchange which evidences strategic planning on the part of its initiator is as follows:

[6.22] (Situation 3A: Y (a farmer) and X (a farm-worker) are disputing how many baskets of fruit X has picked in the course of the day)

        X: I'm I'm] sure I've done seven today honestly this is my last basket ₘ you know I was gonna knock off what is it four-thirty erm is it four-thirty yeah I was gonna ₐ knock off I always do seven this is my last one I've [been counting

        Y: what ₐ what] time did you start today Peter

        X: er I started er at eight-thirty yeah

        Y: eight-thirty and what time do you normally start

        X: oh I start ₐ at that ₐ every time yeah I've done seven you can see it's on your list

                                    (3A12)

The Pre-Exchange is intended by Y here to lead to a Counter – this is an intuitively based judgement, but for expository purposes seems acceptable. The following 'question' ('What time do you normally start') might also have resulted in a Pre-Exchange, but Y sees as it were the drift of the argument, and Contras the (implicit) Counter before the farmer is in a position to verbalise it. Compare Y's strategy in the above with his behaviour in the following:

[6.23] (Situation 3A: as above)

        Y: it did rain though earlier ₐ are you sure you ₐ

        X: no I've been picking all the time

                                    (3A13)

Here no Pre-Exchange is initiated: Y is in a position to 'assert' that it rained earlier in the day, and therefore produces this 'information' as a supportive move preceding his Counter.[22] However in [6.22] above Y is not in a position to 'assert' when X commenced working: he elicits this 'information' via a Pre-Exchange. There are close links therefore between the strategic use of Pre-Exchanges, and that of supportive moves, to which we now turn.

6.2.2 Supportive moves – grounders, expanders, disarmers

The relationship between Pre-Exchange initiations and potential Counters, Contras (and maybe Rejects), is a systematic one. We introduce the notion of SUPPORTIVE move in order to claim that the anticipation of types of potential hearer-responses in such supportive moves is again a systematic one. Supportive moves occur therefore only in conversational behaviour (at the 'surface' level), not in underlying interactional structure, whence however they are systematically derivable via the notion of anticipatory strategy. Crudely we may say that a GROUNDING supportive move is a Satisfy of an anticipated Proffer initiating a Pre-Responding Exchange ('Before you ask me *why* I want you to close the window, I'll tell you why'), an EXPANDING supportive move may likewise anticipate a Pre-Responding Proffer, and may also Contra an anticipated Counter ('Before you ask me *how* you can do P, as I request, or before you object that you *can't* do P as I suggest, I'll tell you how you can'), a DISARMING supportive move may also anticipate a Pre-Responding Proffer, but also be seen as a Counter to an anticipated Reject ('Before you *object* to my asking you to do P, I'll apologise in advance for asking you').

The above characterisations are highly informal. We shall investigate more closely Grounding, Expanding, and Disarming supportive moves in turn, and illustrate each in operation in conversational behaviour.

Grounding

Let us imagine the case once more in which A wishes to ask B to open the window. The notion of a Grounding supportive move derives, we wish to claim, from A's knowledge that as a response to such a Proffered 'request' B might for example say 'Why don't you open it yourself?', 'What for?', 'Why ask me?', and so on – the potential interactional status of such 'replies' is a matter of empirical investigation, but they might for example initiate Pre-Responding

Exchanges, or might constitute Rejects or Counters.

In 'answering' such 'questions' – *ie* in Contraing such Rejects or Counters, or in Satisfying such Pre-Responding Proffers, A might say for example 'I've got my hands full here at the moment', 'It's a bit stuffy in here', 'You're not busy at the moment', and so on. These utterances may then be used by A as supportive moves in requesting B to open the window:

'John, I've got my hands full here at the moment.
Could you open the window for me. It's a bit stuffy in here.'

(*fabricated*)

In other words, in that H is conversationally licensed to 'request' reasons, grounds, or justifications for a communicative act addressed to him by S, S may provide such supportive communicative acts in producing a Head communicative act.[23]

As the above fabricated example illustrates, more than one Grounding supportive move may be used in the performance of a Head interactional act. Further, multiple embedding is possible –*ie* a Grounder may itself be Grounded. Note that what is Grounded is a communicative act – specifically an illocutionary act: I may refer to a state of affairs in a communicative act, and go on to 'expand' that reference by saying why or how it came into being – in giving reasons for its being the case that P, I am not Grounding my 'observation' that P –*ie* the supportive move in such a case is likely to be an Expander, not a Ground, though we shall be obliged to concede that there are fuzzy edges as regards this distinction.

Grounding is sufficiently common for the absence of such supportive behaviour to appear marked:[24]

[6.24] (Situation 2D: X and Y are discussing how best to get to an appointment)

Y: ...I wonder if we shouldn't erm ⌃ perhaps we could share a taxi or something ⌃ it see – it doesn't seem too far ⌃ really [if there are aren't any one

X: no it shouldn't cost too much between the] two of us

Y: no if there aren't any one way street systems or something strange ...

(2D21/2)

Both X and Y produce supportive moves Grounding the 'suggestion' that they take a taxi.

The notion of 'Grounding' is a conversational as opposed to a logical form of linkage. It is necessary to say this as again we stress that any chain of logical reasoning that one might choose to reconstruct in order to precisely characterise the logical connection between head and supportive moves inside one turn at speech has little or no empirical validity, save by reference to what is actually said (and done) in the observed conversational episode, including of course the consequences and effects of that action. For example, one might well imagine a situation in which the observation that the distance to be travelled was a short one might be seen as a reason for *not* taking a taxi: in this extract however X's response to the observation from Y shows that it has been interpreted as supporting the idea of taking a taxi, in that it Contras a potential Counter to that 'suggestion' concerning the high costs involved.

Communicative behaviour does not 'work' because it is 'logical', but may be seen to be 'logical' in that it 'works' – *ie* is effective in leading to outcomes acceptable to the participants.

Expanding
The relation between an Expanding supportive move, and the outcome of a following exchange is nicely illustrated in the following two extracts from different versions of the same situation:

[6.25] (Situation 1C: Y returns from a day at the university to find X at home)

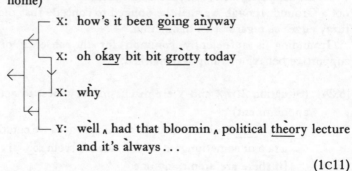

X: how's it been going anyway

X: oh okay bit bit grotty today

X: why

Y: well ∧ had that bloomin ∧ political theory lecture and it's always . . .

(1c11)

These two exchanges are chained: note that the utterance *why* does not serve to elicit a Grounding of the preceding communicative move, but might be informally glossed as implying 'Tell me more!'. In the following version of the same situation, Y 'tells more' without an explicit stimulus from X:

[6.26] (Situation 1C: as in [6.25] above)
 Y: hello
 X: oh hello did you have a good day at the university
 Y: er ∧ fairly tiring lectures were long and tedious but er
 ∧apart from that it was okay...

(1C21)

This phenomenon is so common that just as one may hazard a social law whereby the Grounding of 'requests' for example is normative (the social law one might posit would claim that a requester be prepared to produce Grounds for his 'request' upon demand, and that a requestee has a social right to 'demand' such grounds), so in encounters or phases of talk we may term 'phatic' (following Malinowski, 1923), largely characterised by 'contact', 'social', or 'small' talk, there appears to be a norm of social competence concerning the giving of biographical information as to one's person which has roughly the form:
 'When a free verbal good is requested,
 give more than is asked for!'
A person who does not follow this social norm we characterise as 'difficult to talk to' This norm may of course be deliberately flouted in order to discourage the conversational advances of a partner:[25]

[6.27] – Hello nice party isn't it
 – yes
 – do you know John and Mary well
 – yes I do
 – oh erm you've been here before then have you
 – no
(fabricated)

An Expanding or Grounding supportive move may appear immediately before or immediately after the move it Grounds or Expands. Thus
 'John, can you lend me ten pounds. I've gone and forgotten my wallet, and just remembered it's Cleopatra's birthday'
reveals an alternative realisation of the same anticipatory strategy evidenced in
 'John, look, I've gone and left my wallet at home, and I've just remembered it's Cleopatra's birthday today, I was wondering can you lend me ten pounds'

(fabricated)

In the case that the supportive moves precede the head communicative act, direct comparison with Pre-Exchanges is possible: indeed, a hearer may react to a pre-posed Grounding move for example before its supportive function in the discourse is evident. Again a speaker may often request some acknowledgement of the content of a Grounding or other supportive move prior to proceeding to the head move. In either case, the supportive moves may assume the interactional status of Pre-Exchange Proffers. In the case that the supportive move follows in time the head move it supports, a time-gap may be taken as communicating to S H's non- co-operation, and in a sense therefore as stimulating the supportive move – here a detailed analysis of proxemics, eye-contact, gesture, and other paralinguistic procedures might well be insightful.

That multiple embedding or recursion may occur with respect to Grounding or Expanding moves follows from the same possibility with respect to Pre-Responding Exchanges, and the sequential possibilities inside the structure of the exchange.

It should be noted here that it was claimed (*p* 106 above) that Pre-Responding Exchanges may have a 'firming' function in that they serve to check on the locutionary or illocutionary content and function of the preceding Proffer or other move. It follows that Grounding and Expanding moves, and Pre-Exchange Proffers, may Satisfy by anticipation the Proffer of such a Pre-Responding Exchange.[26] In other words the Head move may be 'expanded' or a Pre-Exchange initiated in order to specify the locutionary or illocutionary point or purpose of that contiguous or following head move. Thus strategic moves such as

'Could I ask you something'
'I just wanted to tell you John'
'That's my opinion anyway'

and so on (examples fabricated) are to be seen as strategic moves which clarify the scope and illocutionary purpose of the Head thus supported, precluding potential misinterpretations, and thus avoiding the necessity for re-runs or repairs. In the data analysed in this study, such supportive moves are in fact not to be found, but they certainly do occur, and could be characterised by the use of a term such as 'Clarifiers'.

Disarming
In a Disarming supportive move Rejects or particular Pre-Responding Proffers are again anticipated. Consider the following table in which

possible 'responses' might be anticipated as shown alongside:

Possible H-moves	anticipated in	S supportive moves
Who do you think you are barging in like this?		I'm sorry to bother you but. . .
You're always bossing me around – get off my back		I hate to sound as though I'm bossing you around but. . .
Why do you hate me so		I don't want to be aggressive but. . .
Don't interrupt		I don't wish to interrupt but. . .

Such supportive moves we shall term DISARMERS[27]: they are both H-disarming and defensive, self-protective devices. The strategy is again based on the speaker's knowledge that to deny a potential office before it is committed forces the hearer into non- co-operative, face-losing behaviour if he nonetheless attempts to claim that the offence is a real one.[28] Barker (1975) pertinently notes that 'verbal defensiveness can be viewed as the use of components of the speech act to *control* the verbal behaviour of an addressee by restraining the latter's set of possible responses' (p 37), and suggests a 'megamaxim of self-defence', which might be formulated as

'Criticize yourself before somebody else can!'
or more succinctly
'Call your own violations!'
Barker interestingly suggests that such defensive mechanisms – the use of such Disarming supportive moves in our terms – may give insight into what Barker calls 'the rules of pragmatic competence' (p 42). Thus Barker relates Gricean rules of quantity, quality, relevance, and manner (Grice 1975) to such Disarmers as

'This is a minor point, but. . .'
'I'm not sure of this, but. . .'
'I don't wish to change the subject, but. . .'
'This may be a bit unclear, but. . .'

(fabricated)

However it seems necessary here to distinguish between communicative and social competence once more. Gricean

co-operative principles underpin the former, as the derivation of
illocutionary force from logical sense (= locutionary force + content)
relies at least in part on such principles. Their strategic exploitation
however is a matter of social competence, as is the use of Disarming
supportive moves. Barker's 'megamaxim' is a strategy therefore
whose appropriate use reflects social competence.

Some instances of Disarmers may be briefly cited:[29]

[6.28]   (Situation 1B: X is seeking to arrange another baby-sitter for Y
         for the following evening)
         X: yes I'm quite sure she'll be able to come round you know
              later this evening you know if it's convenient for you then
         Y: yeah erm ˄
         X: I know it's sort of troubling you again but erm ˄ you know I
              I wou – you know I'd like to sort of resolve the problem for
              you if we can ˄

                                                              (1B13)

There is clearly some heavy face-work being indulged by X here:
the Disarming 'I know it's sort of troubling you again' plays its part.
Several turns later in the same version of the same situation, Y has
occasion to use a Disarmer:

[6.29]   (Situation 1B: as in Extract [6.28] above)
         Y: yeah okay if you can bring her round okay erm ˄ I don't
              want to have to ˄ erm say anything er ˄ angry to you but
              ˄erm as I've said ˄ it's happened to me before I ˄ I've had
              other babysitters they don't turn up
         X: uhm
         Y: and I'm just about you know getting to the point where ˄ I
              think I'm gonna have to er employ ˄ someone slightly older
                                                              (1B14)

In this instance we are inclined to feel that Y does in fact have it in
mind to say something angry. Perhaps, having said that she does not,
she feels thereby licensed to do so. In the following illustration, the
Disarmer is recognised by the hearer as such: she in fact anticipates
the Head which the Disarmer is intended to support:

[6.30] (Situation 1C: X has asked Y if she may borrow some of his
        records; negotiation has been considerable)
        X: yeah yeah well erm you know I'll make a special effort ∧ for
            once (laughs)
        Y: yeah ∧ but I mean I don't wish to be fastidious about it
            lending these records out but
        X: yeah ∧ I know you know just takes one scratch and er ruin
            er record's ruined

                                                                    (1c25)

Here we see that in fact just as a Pre-Exchange initiation may
function as an illocution as would the Proffer or other move it is
designed to lead to, so can a supportive move itself serve to
communicate the illocutionary point it may be intended to support.
Thus a (fabricated) sequence such as
  – It really is getting a bit late darling
  – Well I want another drink
is perfectly interpretable, though the point at issue – the imminent
departure of the conversationalists – is not referred to in the locutions
used.[30]
  Grounders, Expanders, and Disarmers are simply instances in
which a supportive move is made in anticipation of a possible response
to that which is thereby supported. The sub-categorisation of
supportive moves into these three categories is neither a delicate nor
we hazard, an exhaustive one. Supportive moves do not enter into
discourse structure in terms of the graphic conventions we have been
proposing, as the head communicative act of an interactional move is
'supported'. In the analyses we give later (6.5), supportive moves will
be labelled as to type, and explicitly related to the heads they support.

6.2.3 Multiple heads in move structure

Supportive moves account for a range and variety of cases in which in
conversational behaviour more than one move may occur in a
speaker's turn at talk. We have argued and attempted to demonstrate
that such supportive moves can be seen to derive from subordinate
exchange elements – *ie* they may be seen as Satisfys to anticipated
Pre-Responding Exchange Proffers. We have also claimed that
supportive moves can be seen as Contras to anticipated Counters or
Rejects. The nature of the tie between the Head of the interactional
move and the supportive move or moves accompanying it can be seen

as one of Grounding, Expanding, or Disarming. Consider now
however the case in which a *Contra* is anticipated, and a *Contra* to that
anticipated Contra is offered by a speaker. As the Contra to a Contra
to a Proffer re-presents the value of the original Proffer, and as we saw
with supportive moves that the supportive move may precede or
follow the head of the move it supports, it follows that given two
communicative acts in one turn at talk – the one in theory to be
interpreted as a Contra to a Contra to the other – it may well not be
possible to distinguish *which* of these two moves is to be deemed the
Head, and which the Contra to an anticipated Contra. The *content* of
the two communicative acts may give no indication as to 'supportive'
or 'subordinate' linkage, and the *placing* of the two acts relative to one
another is not necessarily any indication as to their relative status, by
analogy with the possibility of pre-posing or post-posing a supportive
Ground, Expand, or Disarm. In such a case we shall refer to the two
communicative acts as *together* realising the Head of the interactional
move. We thus allow of more than one illocutionary act filling one slot
in interactional structure in such a case, and may refer to the
MULTIPLE head of the discourse move.

En passant we may note that the above case is different from the
case in which let us say several Proffers are 'collected' together and
uttered in one turn at speech, as a strategic alternative to the issuing of
one Proffer in one turn at speech, a second following its Satisfaction,
and so on. In this latter case a chained sequence of head exchanges
would have resulted, and the phenomenon of 'collection' can be seen
as a re-ordering of elements of interactional structure, crudely of the
form:

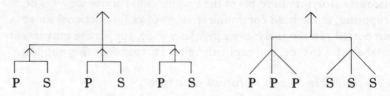

$$\text{P} \quad \text{S} \qquad \text{P} \quad \text{S} \qquad \text{P} \quad \text{S} \qquad \qquad \text{P} \quad \text{P} \quad \text{P} \qquad \text{S} \quad \text{S} \quad \text{S}$$

Such a 're-ordering' we have posited in the fabricated example of
the bulk order in a purchasing transaction.[31] The difference between
such a re-ordering conversational procedure, and the collective head
strategy being here investigated is intuitively clear, though in analytic
practice we may well come across indeterminate cases. However, if we
consider informally the case of a Proffered barrage of 'complaining'
communicative acts, for example, it is strongly counter-intuitive to

suggest that here we have a re-ordered sequence of chained exchanges, such that an alternative for the 'complainer' would be to utter a first 'complaint', and when this has been negotiated to a happy outcome, to utter a second, and so on.

To posit plausible psychological motives for the ADDITIVE strategy resulting in multiple-head moves is not easy. Nor is it our purpose to do other than offer intuitive psychological accounts of strategic behaviour in order to provide a rational motive for the existence of the claimed strategic moves. As a generalisation based on the corpus examined we suggest that speakers appear to resort to additive strategy when in a situation in which face is a matter of considerable importance – *ie* when fighting as it were for their own social standing. We observe a much higher density of multiple Head realisations in situations based on the ⌐X did P, P bad for Y⌐ interactional constellation, on the part of both the X and Y role players.

The following is an extract from a situation in which additive behaviour occurs:

[6.31] (Situation 1B; X has got out of a baby-sitting appointment with Y, but while alternative arrangements for the evening in question have been negotiated, it is clear that Y is not yet happy with the conversational outcome up to this point)

Y: ...erm could I just ask you do you think this is gonna happen ∧ frequen[tly

X: oh no] no no no I this is ∧ purely an oversight on my part ∧it was [just the

Y: yeah]

X: wrong thing I put in my diary and I really ∧ I just can't understand how it happened to be quite honest cos I'm usually so methodical about these things...

⋮

Y: ...and I'm just about you know getting to the point where ∧I think I'm gonna have to er employ ∧ someone slightly older

X: oh well well I don't think that will arise I'm quite sure it won't happen [again

Y: yeah]

X: you know and I'll do my very best once I say a thing ∧ I'll
     usually ∧ carry it [through
Y: yeah]
X: without an – it's just ∧ I I just feel terrible about it I really
     do you know to think I'm letting you dosn right on this
     first ∧ instance . . .

                                                    (1B13/4)

In the two discontinuous segments of this extract Y produces
illocutions which we need not at this stage attempt to characterise
precisely, but which we may deem 'accusatory', 'criticising', or
'threatening' in tone. In each case X 'responds' with a Collective move
consisting of more than one utterance, and more critically more than
one illocution. The strategy is perhaps based on the assumption that
the more she says the more likely is it that her conversational goal of
restoring her own face will be successful (in this instance we may say
that the more Counters she produces the more likelihood there is that
the multiple-headed move will function as a Contra in the discourse).
Note incidentally that the presence or absence of sentence connectives
here would appear to make little difference to the discourse structure
to be discerned. Compare the following:

[6.32] A: this is purely an oversight on my part it was just the wrong
            thing I put in my diary and I really I just can't understand
            how it happened to be quite honest cos I'm usually so
            methodical about these things
       B: this is purely an oversight on my part cos I put the wrong
            thing in my diary but I really I just can't understand how it
            happened to be quite honest I'm usually so methodical
            about these things
       C: this is purely an oversight on my part and it was just the
            wrong thing I put in my diary I really I just can't
            understand how it happened to be quite honest I'm usually
            so methodical about these things

                                                    (fabricated)

Version A is simply transcribed from [6.31] above, omitting the
interspersed Uptaker from Y: versions B and C are fabricated
variations on this recorded behaviour, in which different sentence
connectives are employed, including insertion or deletion changes. It
would be wrong to say that the use of sentence connectives in

conversational behaviour is arbitrary, and that they are in free variation in many contexts, but what I think can be said is that the presence or absence of particular sentence connectives cannot in itself be taken as *determining* discourse structure (*cf pp* 17–18 above).

It can be seen from the above example that the distinction between an Expanding supportive move, or a Grounding supportive move, and Additive conversational behaviour may well turn out to be fuzzy-edged when one seeks to apply it to real data. This is of course regrettable, but seems to reflect the conversational facts. We use the notion of Multiple heads as a last resort in our analyses, but have sought to argue here that such multiple head moves do occur in conversational practice, and can be systematically related to interactional structures.

6.2.4 Other anticipatory strategies illustrated

The use of Grounding, Expanding, and Disarming supportive moves can be said to be conventionalised, in that we have posited maxims concerning their use, the following of which maxims is a matter of social competence. Such maxims we may formulate as follows:

- When exacting work from your conversational partner, be prepared to justify and ground your act!
- When a free verbal good is requested, give more than is asked for!
- Call your own violations!

A social norm underpinning the use of multiple illocutionary acts is less easy to formulate, though some similarities with the motivations for such behaviour and the three maxims posited are to be seen: the contexts in which Additive behaviour occurs are most commonly contexts in which 'self-justificatory' work is being done, a Gricean principle of quantity is superficially being flouted, as in the second maxim above, and further some element of disarming strategy is also discernible in Additive strategy. Pre-Exchanges may also be based on these maxims, or, perhaps most commonly on the implementation of the general maxim favouring H-Supportive behaviour, as in theory a 'negative' response to a Pre-Exchange Proffer may Satisfy that Proffer, even though it invalidates the following Head Proffer that the Profferer might have intended to make. Thus a hearer may 'indirectly' Contra or Counter a Head Proffer in Satisfying a Pre-Sequence Proffer. In brief, the strategy underpinning Pre-Exchanges is consistent with the H-supportive maxim.

These systematic instances of conversational strategy by no means exhaust conversationalists' anticipatory powers. A speaker may for

example in the course of negotiations following a communicative act
initiating a Business (let us assume a Proffer made by himself)
anticipate possible Counters or Contras, and produce a Counter or
Contra of his own which would be a possible subsequent move in
Exchange structure if the anticipated Counter or Contra from H had
occurred. Indeed, in order to be able to do so, a speaker may himself
articulate H's possible Counter or Contra in order to be able to dispose
of it. This is a direct analogy to the strategy commonly observed by the
opening speaker in a formal debate. Consider here the following
extract:

[6.33]   (Situation 3A: Y and X disagree as to whether X has picked six
         baskets of fruit, or seven)

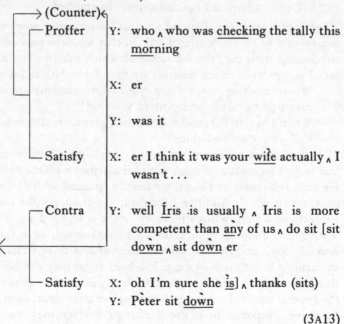

	Proffer	Y:	who ∧ who was checking the tally this morning
		X:	er
		Y:	was it
	Satisfy	X:	er I think it was your wife actually ∧ I wasn't . . .
	Contra	Y:	well Iris is usually ∧ Iris is more competent than any of us ∧ do sit [sit down ∧ sit down er
	Satisfy	X:	oh I'm sure she is] ∧ thanks (sits)
		Y:	Peter sit down

                                                                    (3A13)

The possibility that Y himself made a mistake in 'checking the tally'
has already been mooted by X, and later withdrawn. However here it
is Y, not X, who raises the issue as to who was checking the tally
earlier, and in remarking on Iris's competence Y would seem to be
Contraing a 'suggestion' that she, Iris, is responsible for an error in
scoring. Such a 'suggestion' is not actually made however – there is no
verbal or non-verbal token one may point to as representing such a

Counter (it would be a Counter and not a Contra as the verbalised
Contra to it is Satisfied by X – 'Oh I'm sure she is', but in doing so he
does not withdraw his claim to have picked seven as opposed to six
baskets). We cannot say here that in saying 'I think it was your wife
actually' X can be held to have Countered Y's position that X has not
picked seven baskets, because the information contained in this
utterance is produced as a Satisfy to a Proffer by Y. Y's defence of his
wife's competence is therefore a Contra to an anticipated or assumed
Counter by X. In presenting the structure of conversational episodes
in which other-speaker moves are assumed, we shall adopt the
procedure of simply inserting the anticipated move in brackets in
interactional structure. This will allow turn-taking at the level of the
exchange to continue to operate. If this is to be the case with regard to
the above example, note that the subordinate exchange with which the
extract opens cannot be a Pre-Exchange, as it is Y who produces the
Proffer: it will be a Pre-Responding Exchange *following* the 'assumed'
or anticipated Counter from X. If verbalised this Counter might then
have some form such as 'Well somebody made a mistake this
morning'. This analysis is consistent with our strong intuition that in
asking who was checking the tally in the morning Y is already
anticipating X's line of thought. The notational procedure suggested
is also convenient in a case such as the following:

[6.34]   (Situation 1B: X has just told Y she cannot baby-sit for her the
following evening as arranged, as she has something else on)

> ┌─ Proffer   Y: when did you find out
> │
> └─ Satisfy   X: it was erm yesterday
>
>   Proffer ←   Y: (Clicks tongue) it's a pity you
>   [couldn't let me know yesterday
>
> ┌─ Contra   X: and it's the first time I c]ould let you
> │   know
> │
> └─ Satisfy   Y: uhm oh dear

(1B21)

A difficult issue of interpretation here is the question as to whether
or not Y's masked utterance ('it's a pity you couldn't let me know

yesterday') counts in the discourse or not. How one is to decide such
an issue empirically is difficult to say. Given the notion of anticipatory
strategy however, and the convention suggested, the question
resolves itself into a decision as to whether or not to place brackets
around the interactional move at issue. The analysis offered above
assumes that the utterance does so count: the first exchange is a
Pre-Exchange, and it is assumed that Y's 'complaint' ('it's a pity. . .')
has the status of a Proffer: the subsequent discourse allows one to
believe that X's following 'excuse' is 'accepted' ('uhm oh dear'), *ie* that
the Contra is Satisfied. The example demonstrates quite clearly that a
cline operates between 'assumed' or anticipated interactional moves,
and their manifestation in observable communicative acts.

We have already suggested that some Satisfy moves may be
assumed by the speaker, who does not relinquish his turn at speaking
but 'takes it for granted' that his word is so to speak the last to be said
on the topic being negotiated. In the data investigated this occurs only
in the case of a Contra move, for which the Satisfy necessary to bring
the exchange to a close is assumed.[32] Additionally, we have suggested
on the basis of our corpus that a Satisfy, in this case to a Proffer, in a
ritual exchange (whether 'firming', 'greeting', or 'closing') may be
assumed even in the case that the hearer has the opportunity to assume
the turn at talk following that Proffer. These observations are offered
as generalisations based on the corpus investigated: it is not claimed
that we have specified the full range of possibilities for anticipatory
strategy here. On the contrary, we shall wish to suggest that the
potential for anticipatory strategy is possibly unlimited. The creation
of a complex text – be it a novel, a sermon, or whatever – is we shall
wish to claim to be seen as a complex manipulation via anticipatory
strategy of discourse structures of the kinds we have detailed in 6.1
above (see 7.2 below).

6.3 Illocutionary acts characterised

Interactional structures are realised in conversational behaviour. In
6.2 above we have attempted to suggest how conversational strategies
employed by speakers in ongoing conversations can be said to
systematically relate 'underlying' interactional structures to observed
sequences of communicative acts – *ie* discourse or conversational
structures. We now consider the substance of conversational
encounters, *ie* the elements which manifest interactional structure in
conversational behaviour. These elements are largely verbal acts,

though we have claimed that non-verbal acts may also realise elements of discourse structure in an ongoing conversation. Here we are concerned to characterise the verbal acts by means of which interaction occurs in discourse. A verbal act which realises an element of interactional structure is a *communicative* act. In other words a communicative act is both an interactional and an illocutionary act.[33] An illocutionary act communicates a speaker's beliefs, feelings, attitudes, or opinions with respect to a specific event or state of affairs. Illocutions are the counters used by speakers to negotiate conversational outcomes. The sense in which we use the term 'illocution' is not identical to the way this term is commonly used in Speech Act Theory, as we wish to consider illocutions as independent of their placing in discourse structure. For descriptive purposes we need to separate illocutionary and interactional function, and are led to suggest that what are termed 'illocutions' in the literature are sometimes illocutions as we propose to use the term, sometimes communicative acts, whereby the illocutionary and the interactional function of the verbal act are conflated in the notion of 'illocution', and sometimes conversational *outcomes*. This conclusion has already been anticipated at several points in 3.1 above.

It is clear that terms such as 'agree', 'accept', 'turn down', 'contradict', 'comply', and so on describe what a speaker may be said to do with respect to a preceding communicative act, be it a 'suggestion', 'criticism', 'offer', 'statement', or 'request'. Therefore such terms describe the significance of a communicative act with respect to its function and placement in the total discourse of which it forms a part. If however we wish to develop an analytic apparatus in which illocutionary value and interactional value are characterised distinctively, we shall not wish to use such terms as denoting categories of illocutionary activity. In fact we seek to analyse conversational behaviour such that what is meant by 'turning down an offer' or 'complying with a request' is made explicit. It follows that if a first speaker 'requests' that H do P, and the second speaker, H, 'turns down' this 'request', we need to characterise exactly what it is H may be said to be doing in illocutionary terms. That this illocution realises let us say a Contra slot in discourse structure will then characterise what it is to 'turn down a request'. In this case we suggest that an utterance such as 'no I won't' is itself a RESOLVE, communicating H's intention to undertake a future action ~P, as in the interests of H. There is then a mis-match between S's illocution in favour of a future act P on the part of H as in the interests of S, and H's illocution in favour of a non-compatible future action on his own part as in the interests of himself.

This seems intuitively acceptable. Consider however an illocutionary notion such as 'Promising', already briefly discussed on *p* 26 above. Here we need once more to distinguish between a concept of for example 'Promising' evoked by a particular lexical item of English – in this case the verb PROMISE – and a technical term designed to describe a particular type of empirically-observed conversational behaviour. For our purposes the following two fabricated exchanges both contain an illocutionary act we might term 'promising':

- I'll carry your bag if you like
- Thank you, please do

- Carry my bag, will you please
- Sure, if you like

Let us refer to the first speaker in the first exchange as 'he', the second as 'she', and assume the same role constellation in the second exchange. In both exchanges he communicates a willingness to perform a certain act, in both exchanges she communicates a desire or wish that he perform that certain act. Both exchanges are (potentially) closed, and the outcome is the same in both cases. We shall wish to say that the illocutions are also the same in both cases – *ie* it is 'requesting' and 'promising' that is going on here, as much in the first exchange as in the second. Following the same lines, we shall claim that 'agreeing' to a 'suggestion' for joint action most commonly involves making that same 'suggestion':

- Let's go to the pictures tonight
- Good idea, let's do that   *(fabricated)*

It seems likely that this approach is counter-intuitive. The reason is precisely that the locutionary and illocutionary terms which are available as part of the lexis of English, and which have been taken over in various approaches to speech acts, often carry strong connotations concerning the interactional status or function of the acts so described.

In the light of the claim that illocutions and interactional acts are to be distinctively characterised, and following the observation that many of the 'illocutionary' terms available in English are in fact non-neutral so to speak with regard to the discourse function of the acts they refer to, we face a difficulty of nomenclature in attempting to catalogue illocutionary acts for our analytic purposes. Wilful avoidance of everyday terms seems unusually presumptuous, but to take over commonly-used terms such as 'promise' may be totally misleading in the light of the definitions offered for the illocutionary acts to which these everyday terms are ascribed. We shall follow the procedure of using common-sense terms as labels for types of illocution where possible, though some available terms will be avoided as misleading and inappropriate ('offer' and 'promise' are cases in point).

Before categorising some types of illocution, we may make two preliminary distinctions. Firstly, as a communicative act is itself an event, a subsequent illocutionary act may seek to communicate a speaker's feeling, beliefs, and so on with respect to that communicative act. To put this another way, an illocution may concern some discourse-internal act or state of affairs, or some discourse-external act or state of affairs, though the latter may be *referred to* already in the ongoing discourse. Thus if I 'thank' you for 'offering' to put the cat out, my 'thanks' is a discourse-internal illocution; if I 'thank' you for actually putting the cat out, my illocution is a discourse-external illocution. In discussing Grounding supportive moves we have already introduced the distinction implicitly as we distinguished the case in which, following my remark that John is out, I say *why* he has gone out (Expanding this 'remark') from the case in which I say why I *tell* you that he is out (Grounding the 'remark'). Illocutions may be discourse-external, or discourse-internal therefore.

Secondly, an illocutionary act is in the unmarked case made via a locutionary act consisting of a locutionary force marker and a propositional act, which together constitute the logical sense of the utterance. However many tokens by means of which illocutionary acts are performed are highly ritualised, such that it does not make much sense to refer to the semantic meaning of the verbal token – its total meaning may be said via conventionalisation to be pragmatic. An utterance such as 'hello' is an obvious case in point: 'exclamations' such as 'oh' and the like also offer difficulties if we seek to discover the propositional content of such verbalisations. Some illocutions may be made by ritualised verbal expressions therefore, while others – the majority – are derivable from the logical sense of what is said – the locution.

The two distinctions above are of course not unrelated. It is precisely utterances whose illocutionary point may be said to concern the ongoing process of interaction itself which may be performed by ritualised expressions. Discourse-internal illocutions tend to be capable of formulaic realisation to a greater extent than do discourse-external illocutions.

The distinction between discourse-external and discourse-internal illocutions concerns the act or state of affairs referred to or addressed in the illocutionary act. An illocutionary act of 'thanking' for example may be both discourse-internal or discourse-external. In characterising illocutions we shall first list some members of the class of illocutions which may be either discourse-internal or discourse-external, before producing a further set of illocutions which are defined as having exclusively discourse-internal relevance.

The categories proposed are designed to elucidate the data corpus investigated. The list offered is therefore not claimed to be exhaustive or refined. Further sub-categorisation is clearly possible. It is assumed that whether or not this is desirable is determined by the purposes of the analyses made.[34] Reductio ad absurdum a highly delicate illocutionary inventory might include a category such as 'invite the addressee to take a seat in the immediate vicinity of the speaker'. A less delicate analytic schema, on the other hand, might well subsume 'invitations' under a category such as 'request' or 'mand'. The question as to what might constitute a theoretically optimal degree of delicacy is here left an open one: some notes on possible sub-categories will be appended to illocutionary categories as they are introduced.

6.3.1 Discourse external/internal illocutions[35]
Definitions will be offered under the following heads:

(i)   What is the speaker seeking to communicate with regard to his own person, beliefs, attitudes, or opinions? A specification of the nature of the act or state of affairs addressed by the illocution will be given when necessary.

(ii) Given the nature of the universe, and the fact that speakers are assumed to have reasons for performing illocutionary acts, what states of affairs may be said to be implied by such an illocutionary act?

(iii) What relations hold between the illocutionary act being defined, and other illocutionary acts defined earlier, or to be defined later? Alternatively or additionally, how might the illocutionary act in question be further sub-categorised?

A full exposition under each of these three heads will now be offered for each category introduced.

A: *Request*
(i)   S (speaker) wishes H (hearer) to believe that S is in favour of H's performing a future act A, as in the interests of S.
(ii)   In making a Request, S may be said to give H reasons for believing that he wishes H to do A. In making a Request, S is assuming that it is not impossible that H will do A as a result of his making that Request.
(iii) 'Request' is here used as a neutral term, covering different intensities of volition and social role relations between S and H. Further a requested act A may be of the form ~P, *ie* a 'prohibition' will be taken as a form of Request. Requests will be sub-categorised along two dimensions, one concerning the expected proximity in time of the requested act A to that Request, the other concerning the nature of the requested act A, specifically the case in which the requested act is a communicative act, which, if forthcoming as a result of the request, will itself form part of the structure of the ongoing discourse. Such Requests for communicative acts will be considered as discourse-internal illocutions in 6.3.2 below.

A1: *Now-request*
In additional to A(i) to (iii) above, the following additional specification holds:
   The act A is such that it may be performed by H, or more precisely sub-acts contributing to the performance of A may be initiated by H, within a period of time subjectively interpretable as contiguous to the time of utterance of the Request (see *pp* 36–7, 52 n 6). S is then in favour of H's performing a future act A 'now'.

A2: *Then-request*
This category complements A1 above. A(i) to (iii) hold, with the following further specification:
   The act A is such that its execution by H cannot be held to be requested by S in time immediately subsequent to the time of utterance of that Request. The notion of immediacy is here a potential matter of negotiation: in the unmarked case the absence of a non-immediate time specification in the locution by means of which a Request is made can be taken to imply that the

Request is a Now-Request. The now/then distinction detailed here for Requests is valid for all illocutions concerning a future act A on the part of S or H.

B: *Suggest*
(i)   S wishes H to believe that S is in favour of H's performing a future act A, as in the interests of H.
(ii) In making a Suggest, S is assuming that it is not impossible that H will do A as a result of his making that *Suggest*.
(iii) A sub-categorisation in terms of Now- and Then- Suggests is assumed. Suggests differ from Requests as concerns the party S wishes H to believe he believes will benefit from the act A. As A may affect both S and H, strategy clearly plays a role – *ie* S may wish H to believe he believes A is in the interests of H, when in fact S believes A to be in his own interests. It is to be expected then that in identifying an illocution as a Request or a Suggest, unclear cases may arise. This is perhaps to be seen less as a weakness in our analytic schema than as a reflection of the negotiable status of some illocutionary acts. It is also to be expected that a speaker may himself characterise as a 'suggest' a locution which clearly has a Requesting illocutionary function (and vice versa):

> 'I suggest you keep your mouth shut when you've got nothing to say'
> 'Go and see your doctor, I beg of you'
>
> *(fabricated)*

C: *Propose*
(i)   S wishes H to believe that S is in favour of an act A, to be performed jointly by S and H,[36] as in the interests of both.
(ii) There will clearly be a common ground between S and H deemed by the speaker to be sufficient to justify his Propose.
(iii) Proposes can be interpreted as conditional Resolves (see G below) – *ie* 'I will if you will'[37] or as combining in one act the force of a Request and that of a Willing (see D below) – *ie* 'You act in my interests and I'll act in yours'. Proposes may be sub-categorised as being of Now- or Then-.

D: *Willing*
(i)   S wishes H to believe that S is not against performing a future act A, as in the interests of H.
(ii) That S will be deemed to have reasons for performing a Willing

implies a situation involving H which the act A in some way meets or changes for the better with regard to H's interests.

(iii)   A Willing is not an undertaking to do A. The Now- v. Then-distinction is again relevant.

E: *Complain*

(i)   S wishes H to believe that S is not in favour of H's having performed an act A, as being against the interests of S.

(ii)   Clearly presupposed is that H did A.[38] In that A is against the interests of S, and H is held by S to be responsible for A, a speaker in making a Complain may be held to be not in favour of H – *ie* H's social standing with S is in jeopardy.

(iii)   It may well be feasible to sub-categorise Complains using terms such as 'criticize', 'accuse', and possibly others, but for our purposes this does not seem to be necessary. There is some indeterminancy between Complains and Requests in the case that A is a reversible act, as a Complain may be said to conversationally imply a Request that the Complainable be removed ('You're standing on my foot'). It is not necessary however to sub-categorise Complains according to whether or not the Complainable is reversible, as the potential discourse structure for these two sub-categories would not appear to differ. For example the removal of a Complainable does not necessarily Satisfy a preceding Proffered Complain.

F: *License*

(i)   S wishes H to believe that S is not against H's performing a future act A, as being in H's interests, and despite A's being, at least potentially, against S's interests.

(ii)   The issuing of a License implies that S believes H will not in fact do A unless such a Licence is given. The substance of A is such that an unlicensed execution of this act may be socially proscribed. A License is therefore a necessary but not a sufficient social antecedent to H's doing A.

(iii)   A License is intended to be neutral between 'invitations' and the giving of 'permission'. Given the complex of interests involved in Licensing, unclear cases may well arise, as a Suggest differs from a License only as concerns S's interests as affected by the future act A. Thus given an utterance of the form 'Take a seat', it is not easy to determine under which conditions the utterance would count as a License as opposed to a Suggest or indeed a

Request. The Now- and Then- distinction is relevant here once more.

G: *Resolve*

(i)   S wishes H to believe that S is in favour of S's performing a future act, as in the interests of S.

(ii)   Clearly, there will be implied a situation which makes A a necessary or potentially beneficial act for S.

(iii) The act A may be a negative course of action, and the Now-Then- distinction applies. Note that 'resolve' implies a determination to do A which the speaker does not necessarily have in making a Resolve.

H *Thanks*

(i)   S wishes H to believe that S is in favour of an act A, performed by H as in the interests of S.

(ii)   S, in Thanking may be held to believe that H did A knowingly, and that benefits to S consequent to A were known by H to be involved at the time of his doing A.

(iii) Thanks are clearly H-supportive, and the verbal means of performing this illocution are explicit.

I: *Apologise*

(i)   S wishes H to believe that S is not in favour of an act A performed by S as against the interests of H.

(ii)   S, in Apologising, may be held to regret that he did A, and to discredit himself socially for having done so.

(iii) Apologises are often used strategically, as in Disarming strategy ('I'm sorry, but that's my coffee'). In such cases, the act A may be a mental act on the part of S. Apologises are clearly H-supportive, such that the tokens used in performing this illocutionary act are highly conventionalised.

J: *Tell*

(i)   S wishes H to gain information[39] about himself and thus create or cement a social bond between himself and H.

(ii)   In performing a Tell, S may be held to assume that H may be interested to gain the acquaintance of or further familiarity with his person.

(iii) The information which S wishes H to gain is necessarily 'private' in the sense that S believes H cannot be expected to know whether or not it is true, nor indeed to do other than accept it as true, given that its source is the speaker. If therefore H does not accept the substance of a Tell as true, the ground can only be that H believes S is lying, not that S is 'ignorant' or 'misinformed'. Tells are distinguished from Claims, Opines, and Remarks (see below) largely as concerns the type of information that the speaker wishes to communicate. As a classification of types of information is very fuzzy edged, these category distinctions will in analysis not always be found to be sharp ones.[40] Various sub-categories of Tell might be set up in a more delicate description: one obvious sub-category would be that of Identification, in which the content of the Tell serves to assign the speaker to an appropriate membership category for the hearer. The ground for such a sub-category would be the social significance of this type of act, specifically the 'exchange' of names, for example.

K: *Claim*

(i)   S wishes H to believe that S believes that the information contained in the locution by means of which the Claim is made is true.

(ii)   In making a Claim, S may be held to believe that his doing so is in the interests of H. In making a Claim a speaker commits himself to believing what is entailed by the content of that Claim.

(iii) S believes that the truth value of his claim – the truth value of the information given in it – is a matter of knowledge, as opposed to experience or opinion[41] – roughly that its truth value may be established by scientific verificational procedures. No additional intentional states are involved in making a Claim, other than what has been specified above.[42] It is clear that a cline operates between Tells and Claims: the distinction is however not an arbitrary one. It is reflected for example in the distinction between 'introducing oneself' and 'giving one's name'.

L: *Opine*

(i)   As with the Claim above, S wishes H to believe that S believes that the information contained in the locution by means of which the Opine is made is true. An Opine differs from a Claim concerning the nature of the information transmitted. (See (iii) below).

(ii)   In producing an Opine a speaker is implicitly giving his hearer to believe that S believes the content of the Opine – the information contained therein – and/or the fact that S produces this Opine are potential matters of moment for H. In Opining a speaker may be held to commit himself to producing reasons for that Opine upon Request.

(iii) The content of an Opine differs from that of a Claim in that the state of affairs therein referred to may be said to be known experientially rather than scientifically. It is of course notoriously the case that speakers may differ as to how they interpret the fact/opinion distinction in a particular case. Note that an utterance such as 'I'm not sure really, but I think his wife died in 1970' is in all probability not an Opine, but a Claim, as the time of a person's death is a matter of fact, however tentatively a speaker may assert that fact to be the case: we need to distinguish between epistemic and deontic modality here. An Opine is further related to a Remark – see below.

M: *Remark*

(i)   S wishes H to know that there is some feature of the immediate conversational environment which has not escaped his attention, and which he believes is common to the current experience of both himself and H.

(ii)   S, in producing a Remark, may be held to draw H's attention to some feature of their immediate environment, and thus provide a neutral possible topic for talk.

(iii) In producing a Remark, S is neither Telling, Claiming, nor Opining – *ie* the content of a Remark is not information concerning S's person, nor is it information which S believes H may have a practical use for, nor is it a matter of causing H to know S's beliefs. The content of a Remark may however be a matter of 'opinion' as opposed to 'fact' – *ie* evaluative terms commonly occur in Remarks ('Lovely day, isn't it?'). An Opine and a Remark differ in their weighting however, and there is a difference concerning public and private domains. The topic of a Remark is 'public' in that S and H share the same immediate environment: any attitude S may display in this Remark is 'private' however in the sense that S can expect that H will tolerate S's attitude as beyond the scope of his own interests.[43] The content of an Opine, on the other hand, is a potential matter of moment for H: this is not the case with Remarks.

N: *Excuse*

(i) S wishes H to believe that S is not fully accountable for the fact that he performed a past action A, nor is he fully responsible for any consequences following that action.

(ii) To perform an Excuse is to presuppose that S did A, and that this may be deemed socially discreditable. S is therefore to be interpreted as making a plea as to his own standing as a social member in performing an Excuse.

(iii) An Excuse and Justify (see below) share some characteristics.

O: *Justify*

(i) S wishes H to know that S does not find a past action A, for which he is fully responsible, socially discreditable.

(ii) That S did A, and that this may be deemed socially discreditable is presupposed in the Justify. S is to be interpreted as making a claim as to his own social standing in producing a Justify.

(iii) There is a complementary relationship between Justifys and Excuses as concerns the answerability of the speaker, and whether or not there is, as it were, anything to answer.[44] However Excuses and Justifys are not mutually exclusive modes of illocutionary behaviour, and it may be expected that some utterances falling within this domain may be indeterminate between the one category or the other.

P: *Condone*

(i) S wishes H to believe that S does not hold H to be a socially discredited person, in that H did a past action A.

(ii) That H did A, and that this may be deemed socially discreditable, is presupposed in the Condone.

(iii) There is a link between Excusing, Justifying, and Condoning, discernible when the S and H roles are reversed. In English this is reflected in the use of the lexical item EXCUSE, such that it is possible to say both

> *I excused myself and left*   and
> *I excused him and he left.*

In the first instance it is likely that an Excuse (or Justify) is Proffered (in our terms), while in the second the behaviour referred to as excusatory is likely to have been a Condone (compare in German *Ich bitte um Entschuldigung* and *Ich entschuldige mich*).

Q: *Minimization*

(i)   S wishes H to believe that S is not against an action A performed by S, as not in the interests of S, but in the interests of H.

(ii)   That S did A, and that this may be seen as socially creditable, is presupposed in the Minimization.

(iii)   Thanks and Minimizations can be seen to be complementary. The act is a ritual one.

R: *Sympathise*

(i)   S wishes H to believe that S is not in favour of a non-future state of affairs A, as being against the interests of H, although S himself has no responsibility for bringing that state of affairs into being.

(ii)   In a Sympathise a speaker implicitly seeks to claim to share an emotional state known or assumed to be held by S with respect to the state of affairs A. S therefore in a Sympathise may be held to seek to establish a social bond between himself and his interlocutor.

(iii)   Sympathises are often ritualised: as with Thanks or Apologises indirectness is inappropriate, as a Sympathise is clearly H-supportive behaviour. A Sympathise can be seen as a special case of the Exclaim (see below), and is further similar to the Apologise, from which it is distinguished by S's non-involvement in the act or state of affairs A. (An utterance of the form 'I'm sorry' may be used as a Sympathise or as an Apologise.)

6.3.2 Discourse-internal illocutions

The illocutions specified so far are all capable of referring to a discourse-external event or state of affairs. In addition most if not all of them may be used with discourse-internal reference.

The question as to whether *all* illocutionary types are potentially discourse-internal is an empirical one. It is clearly in part determined by the delicacy of the categorisation of illocutionary acts. Thus while it will be made clear that Requests may be discourse-internal, Then-Requests are so defined that the requested act A is not part of the ongoing discourse. We need to distinguish here for example between a Request of the form

'Please be on time tomorrow'

and a Request of the form

'Promise me you'll be on time tomorrow'.

It is true that a Satisfying response will likely have the illocutionary force of a Willing in both cases, but the latter – a Request for a communicative act of a certain kind – may in theory be followed by a Willing concerning not the speaker's subsequent punctuality, but his making a 'promise' concerning his punctuality (cf note 4, p 77, and see discussion in 7.1 below).

In what follows we wish to define several further categories of illocution, which have an exclusively 'discourse-internal' function. A discourse-internal function may concern rituals necessary for commencing or terminating an Encounter, or may be reflected in the fact that the state of affairs referred to in the illocution is a discourse-internal event: thus both 'Greets' and 'Requests for a Repair' are discourse-internal illocutions. In some cases, a sub-category of a type of illocution introduced in 6.3.1 above is involved. A critical case is that of Requests, when that which is requested is a communicative act. It is necessary to have a distinct category here as a matter of delicacy of description, and also because of the problem of 'questions', to be discussed in 7.1 below. We have claimed above that for many of these discourse-internal illocutions, ritualised expressions may be used in the performing of them.

While it may be seen by inspection that many of the following illocutions have a predisposition to fulfil specific discourse functions – ie to fill certain slots in interactional structure: the Uptake slot is a case in point – the mapping of interactional function onto illocutionary act is never a one-to-one mapping. Thus while it might seem feasible in the case of highly ritualised expressions to term such expressions *interactional* acts, and bypass the question of illocutionary identification, this is not so. In fact it seems that even the most ritualised verbal expressions may be paralleled in discourse function by illocutions which explicitly do what we wish to claim is done in illocutionary terms by the ritualised formula. For example a minimal token such as *hm hm*, appearing in an Uptake slot in interactional structure has an illocutionary value which might be parallelled in an utterance such as 'got it', or even in certain contexts 'message received'. Similarly, an utterance of the form 'hello' may be an Exclaim (AE below) as well as a Greet (AB below): 'Good morning' may be used both to initiate and to terminate an encounter. Further, it is not the case that for example Greets occur exclusively at the beginning of an Encounter.

We may now give some further illocutionary acts, which are exclusively discourse-internal.

AA: *Request for a specific type of illocutionary act*

Under this head we include requests for the full range of illocutionary acts specified in 6.3.1 above. We do not have empirical evidence of all the resultant sub-categories from our data, but wish to put forward the hypothesis that any type of illocutionary act may be requested. It seems possible that a Request for a Request would in fact be characterisable as a Willing, but this is an issue on which we do not wish to be dogmatic.[45] It is not necessary to characterise these types of illocution once more, as a conjunction of the definition given for Requests (*p* 141 above), and that given for the illocution requested will suffice to define the Request for that type of illocution. The only additional remark to be made is that co-operative principles clearly make the withholding of Requested illocutionary acts marked anti-social behaviour when the Requested illocutionary act counts as a 'free good'.

AB: *Greet*
(i)   S wishes H to know that S has taken cognisance of H's presence
(ii)   In recognising H's presence via a Greet, S ratifies H's social standing with himself, and implies a readiness on his part for social interaction.
(iii)   It is intended that the Greet cover somewhat more ground than the everyday term 'greeting'. Further specification is therefore possible. Greets are highly ritualised.

AC: *Leavetake*
(i)   S wishes H to know that S has taken cognisance of H's impending non-presence
(ii)   In performing a Leavetake, S ratifies H's social standing with himself, and ritually implies a readiness on his part for future social interaction.
(iii)   Further sub-categorisation would seem to be possible. Leavetakes are highly ritualised.

AD: *Interruptor*
(i)   S wishes H to know that S wishes to address H at this point in time.
(ii)   An interruptor may be readily interpreted as a 'Request for a Hearing'. The implied ground for making such a Request is clearly that S has something he wishes to say or do involving H.
(iii)   Note that an utterance of the form 'I want to talk to you for a

moment' is not necessarily an instance of an Interruptor – if S already has H's attention and the turn at talk, it clearly cannot be. Further, Interruptor is here an *illocutionary* category: practically anything may be used in order to 'interrupt' a speaker: this has nothing to do with the illocutionary status of the utterance which is so placed that it 'interrupts'. A 'Summons' may be a sub-category of Interruptor.

AE: *Exclaim*

(i) S communicates via the Exclaim his emotional reaction to some event or state of affairs occurring or referred to in the immediate context of situation. The range of emotional reactions covered by the Exclaim includes doubt, regret, surprise, interest, dismay, and excludes what is covered by other illocutionary categories such as the Thank, Apologise, Sympathise.[46]

(ii) An Exclaim is often heard as implying a Go-On (See AG below) – *ie* in the case that a preceding communicative act is the occasion of the Exclaim, the recipient of that Exclaim may interpret it as an encouragement for him to continue with, expand, or otherwise elaborate that which was engaging him in the turn at talk during which the Exclaim occurred.[47]

(iii) We should more strictly include the Exclaim under 6.3.1 above, or restrict ourselves in the definition offered to the case in which a preceding illocutionary act is the occasion of the Exclaim, as it seems clear, though we have no relevant data, that an Exclaim may be occasioned by what had been up to that point a discourse-external event which is via the Exclaim brought into the discourse as a topic for talk ('Oh god, the bloody fire's gone out'). Exclaims commonly lack propositional content, the proximity of the state of affairs thereby reacted to rendering reference to it unnecessary or unlikely. Formulaic tokens are common, and non-verbal substitutes are further possible.

AF: *Accept*

(i) S communicates via the Accept that an immediately preceding communicative act A performed by H has been heard and interpreted, at least in part, by S.

(ii) S implies in the Accept that A is not unacceptable to him as a contribution to the ongoing discourse.

(iii) Accepts are often performed by conventionalised expressions. Note that the act is 'accepted' as it were at the locutionary level:

its illocutionary or interactional significance is not necessarily 'accepted'. The Accept acknowledges receipt. There is in fact some room for ambiguity in the tokens used in the performance of this act, as the same tokens may often be used to indicate a Satisfy of the preceding illocution (*yes*, *mm*, etc) *ie* show 'acceptance' of the content of a preceding communicative act. It seems plausible to suggest that any ambiguity here is strategic – *ie* built into norms of language use. Note that the Accept can be interpreted as a 'neutral' Exclaim, or, alternatively, the Exclaim can be seen as a non-neutral type of Accept.

AG: *Go-on*
(i)　S communicates via the Go-on that he is attending to H, and is in favour of H continuing to perform communicative acts in the immediate conversational context. The significance of the Go-on may be glossed as 'Please tell me more'.
(ii)　To perform a Go-on is implicitly to perform an Accept.
(iii)　There is some potential overlap with the Accept, as similar tokens may be used to realise both acts. Such tokens differ in the intonation however, such that we are not obliged to distinguish a Go-on from an Accept solely in terms of the placing of the utterance in question in the discourse.

AH: *Okay*
(i)　S communicates via the Okay that he is satisfied with a current outcome in the ongoing encounter.
(ii)　The Okay implies that for the speaker the matter of talk in the ongoing discourse is potentially closed. In that case that a reciprocal Okay is assumed on the part of a speaker, an Okay can mark the end of a phase of an encounter (*cf* Sinclair and Coulthard's 'Marker', 1975, *p* 40).
(iii)　The state of affairs which is Okayed is a negotiated outcome of preceding talk between S and H: to produce the utterance 'okay' in response to a Proffered Willing, Request, or Propose for example is not to produce a token of the illocutionary act Okay.

6.4 Realising communicative acts in conversational behaviour

The locutions by means of which illocutions as we have defined them in 6.3 above are performed have not been analysed in this study in detail, though we have suggested some pertinent observations in reviewing speech act theory, and have adopted a stricter notion of illocutionary action, as distinct from interactional action. Further we have shown that what might have been interpretable as a supportive move, or a Pre-Exchange Proffer can be interpreted as the move a speaker might have had it in mind to support or lead up to. Further we have claimed that for many illocutions called discourse-internal the verbal means of performing the illocution are highly conventional-ised. A more detailed analysis of the relation between locution and illocution will not be given here however.

We wish now to consider the surface texture of what is said, and point to some characteristics of conversational behaviour which need to be considered over and above the notions of interactional structure, conversational strategy, and illocutionary acts. The model set up relates the discourse structure of what is said and done to underlying interactional structures through the notion of conversational strategy, and the performance of a communicative act – *ie* an illocutionary act which is part of an ongoing conversation – is related to the actual substance of what is said and done in conversational encounters via various constraints and conversational procedures to be discussed in this section. We shall pay some attention to FUMBLING, Overlapping and Re-ordering, and Topic-Conflict and Incoherence.

6.4.1 Fumbling

In cataloguing some illocutionary acts which fill slots in interactional structure we have distinguished between discourse-external and discourse-internal illocutionary acts, and claimed that the latter especially may have highly conventionalised realisation tokens in which the illocutionary significance of the utterance cannot be derived from the semantic import (if any) of the verbal token. Here we consider a further aspect of conversational behaviour, namely the use of another class of standardised expressions or fixed formulae, for which reference to the semantic content of the uttered expression seems unhelpful. These expressions constitute in themselves neither interactional nor illocutionary acts[48], but are used in the performance of illocutionary acts – I proposed to call this class of expressions FUMBLES.[49]

As the name suggests, Fumbles are similar to false starts and other hesitation phenomena. They function to plug speaking-turn-internal conversational gaps –*ie* they are used by a speaker (in part) in order to gain time. Potential gapping is likely to occur in connection with

turn-changing, as it is often the case that a speaker needs time in order
to formulate his intentions with respect to what he has just heard (we
have earlier suggested that the interactional act of Uptake may have a
Fumbling function here). However speakers also require time in the
expression of what it is they have to say: in performing communicative
acts speakers hesitate, pause, 'cannot find the right word', and so on.
Fumbles are conventionalised ways of plugging such potential gaps,
such that in fact no gap is perceived by the interlocutor.

However Fumbles do more than this: it is not the case that any
evidence of hesitation (a filled, or, er, non-filled pause) is an instance
of Fumbling, as we wish to use the term. Different Fumbles
additionally serve different purposes in the performance of
illocutionary acts. Among the class of Fumbles we may characterise
the following: STARTERS, LET-ME-EXPLAINS,
UNDERSCORERS, CAJOLERS, and ASIDES.[50]

The Starter

The Starter is defined as a preliminary to a communicative act, such
that an instance in media res indicates that what follows substitutes for
what preceded ('the best thing we can do is well probably you er is . .'
(2B22)).

It does not itself communicate Acceptance (in the sense given on
p 157 above), and, though often followed by a silent stress and
appearing in turn-initial position, cannot be said to signal Uptake in
interactional structure, though it may well be seen as implying Uptake
in the light of the communicative act following. Interactionally it
simply signifies that the speaker has something to say. The most
commonly used Starter in the data analysed is of the form *well* (*well*,
well, *well*, *well now*, *oh well*). The token *now* was classified as a Starter
in sixteen instances, with varying intonational features.
'Noises' which may be graphically represented as *oh*, *uh*, *er*, *hmm*, etc.
might also be classified as Fumbles, in which case the most plausible
interpretation would be that on which they are considered Starters in
many instances. It seemed preferable however not to consider such
tokens as Starters, largely because such hesitation phenomena may
occur inside an utterance constituting a single communicative act,
without signalling a re-start. (Some of the listed tokens may be used as
communicative acts in fact, having an Accept or Exclaim illocutionary
force.)

The Let-me-explain

The Let-me-Explain may be said to communicate the fact that I'm trying to communicate. It is speaker-oriented. Let-me-Explains precede the performance of a communicative act. The most commonly-occurring token for this Fumble is *I mean*. *I dunno* may also be used as a Let-me-Explain, but an alternative analysis might see this token as an Aside. Note that an utterance of the form *I mean* or *I dunno* cannot be said to *mean* 'I mean' or 'I do not know' if it is to be accounted an instance of a Let-me-Explain.

The Underscorer

Underscorers are message-oriented devices, and as their name suggests draw special attention to a following, preceding, or ongoing communicative act. In the case that they have meaningful semantic content, they are metastatements about what the speaker is saying, has just said, or is about to say. Note however that in the case where it would appear that the Underscorer has significant semantic content, this is largely illusory. Given an utterance of the form 'He's not, I tell you', it cannot easily be claimed that in telling H that he is telling H that P, S can be said to be doing more than telling H that P. Common tokens for the Underscorer include *(I'll) tell you what*, *the thing is*, *it's just that*, *(the) point is*, *I can tell you*, *don't you worry about that*. *Really*, *actually*, and *in fact* are also used as Underscorers. It is however of course not the case that any instance of the use of these tokens constitutes an instance of an Underscorer.

The Cajoler

While the Underscorer is a message-oriented Fumble, and the Let-me-Explain is speaker-oriented, Cajolers are hearer-oriented. The Cajoler is used by a speaker as an appeal for understanding, *ie* through the Cajoler the speaker seeks to make his illocution more palatable to H. He seeks to increase the likelihood that the communicative act being performed will be acceptable to the hearer. Cajolers may occur in pre-, post-, or mid-position. By far the commonest tokens are *you know* and *you see*. We should again note that in using these expressions a speaker is not 'asserting' or Claiming that the hearer 'knows' or 'sees' that P — on the contrary, were this the case, cajoling would not be necessary. Other tokens include *please*, *don't forget that*, *you must admit*, *let's face it*, *just think*, *don't you see that*, and *do you know*.

The Aside[51]

The Aside can be said not to belong to the structure of the ongoing discourse in which it occurs. It serves a gap-filling function however

in that in verbalising the Aside, a speaker indirectly informs his hearer
as to what is concerning him, and thus indirectly communicates his
non-availability for talk. An Aside therefore fills a conversational gap.
It occurs when a speaker verbalises his involvement with some
necessary activity (including reflection) which causes him (temporar-
ily) to be a non-active participant in the ongoing conversation. Asides
may take the form of self-addressed communicative acts.[52] The
instances in the corpus investigated are limited in number: two
examples are capitalised in [6.35] below:

[6.35] (i) X: would you like to put a record on
             Y: yeah ∧ could do what you fancy
             X: erm (clicks tongue) LET'S SEE WHAT HAVE WE
                 GOT ∧
             Y: wouldn't mind listening to some Zaffa . . .

                                                              (1c21)

        (ii) X: . . .do you want one of these (proffering cigarettes,
                  having taken one himself)
              Y: erm ∧ well ∧ I was just smoking ∧ OH COME ON WHY
                  NOT (takes cigarette)
              X: (lights cigarettes) there you go

                                                              (4c12)

I shall pay little attention to Fumbles in the analyses to be presented
in 6.5 below, as the major purpose of this study is to characterise
discourse structure. An investigation of the distribution and relative
frequency of different types of Fumble, and of different tokens for
each type, remains a task for the future.

6.4.2 Overlapping and re-ordering

While Sacks, Schegloff, and Jefferson (1974) observe that turn-taking
rules follow the general principle that one speaker speaks at one time,
it is a matter of common experience and empirical observation that
there is considerable room for play in following such a general
conversational norm. If we posit some general conversational maxim
of the kind

    'Let your partner finish what he has to say before taking a turn at
    speaking!'

we must also consider an equally pervasive maxim of the kind:

    'Plug any conversational gaps!'

together with a maxim derivable from the general H-Support maxim
we have posited, which might take the form:
  'When you can support your interlocutor during his turn at speech,
  do so!'
The critical issues concerning these maxims are what it means to
'finish' what one has to say, what constitutes a conversational gap, as
opposed to a conversational pause[53], and when one can legitimately
support one's interlocutor without interrupting his turn at talk.
Anticipation is normative in the practice of assuming a turn at talk —*ie*
overlapping does not constitute interruption in the vast majority of
instances. On the contrary, it is normative and usual to commence
speaking when one has interpreted one's interlocutor's illocutionary
point. The phenomenon of licensed overlap has been amply
illustrated in most of the data cited so far; some further illustrations
may however be given here:

[6.36] (Situation 1B: X has just told Y that she has another
        engagement for the evening she had arranged to baby-sit)
        Y: oh well that's a nuisance
        X: yes [I
        Y: wh]en did you find out
        X: it was yesterday
        Y: (clicks tongue) it's a pity you [couldn't let me know
            yesterday
        X: and it's the first time I c]ould let you know
        Y: uhm oh dear
                                                              (1B21)

We have already cited this extract in illustrating anticipatory
strategy. The utterances 'when did you find out', and 'it's a pity you
couldn't let me know yesterday' may both be said to count in discourse
structure. However the content of X's first spoken contribution to this
extract, consisting of the Uptaker *yes* and the incomplete utterance
beginning *I* does not. In general, interspersed Communicative acts of
Uptake do not constitute turns at talk strictly speaking, as while a
communicative act is thereby performed, no interactional *move*
occurs, as Uptake has to be followed by a head interactional act before
a move in interactional structure is made. This does not of course
mean that a token or illocution which may be used to signal Uptake
may not occur *as* a head act in move structure, and thus count as a turn
at talk in the resultant discourse structure.

Supportive work can result in the phenomenon of BLENDING in which a move by a speaker A is taken over and completed by a speaker B:

[6.37]　(Situation 2B: X and Y have just witnessed a traffic accident, and are deciding how best to assist)

  Y:　now ∧ we've gotta help him ∧ whatever happens now he's probably badly injured there's a good [chance it's

  X:　it was a wo]man wasn't it I thor – I could have sworn it was a woman

  Y:　a woman ∧ well I don't know I mean I wasn't ∧ I was too busy trying to keep the car on the road ∧ but [whether it's a woman or a man you know he

  X:　well it doesn't matter anyway does it]

                                                       (2B21)

A further instance occurs later in the same version of the same situation:

[6.38]　(Situation 2B as above)

  Y:　they must have a phone I should think I hope they've got a phone ∧ I mean ∧ the best thing we can do is well probably you is [er

  X:　well] perhaps I could run down there and ∧ knock them up and see if they've [got a telephone and ask them there

  Y:　yeah ∧ yeah ∧ you ∧ that's] that's right yeah

                                                       (2B22)

What is being evidenced here is that a cline operates between licensed overlapping – the case in which a hearer assumes the turn at talk despite the continuing verbalisation of the speaker, as he has got the illocutionary point – and strategic anticipation – the case in which a move is responded to before it has been made. In the following extract there is no physical overlap between the first and the second turns at speech, while between the second and the third there is: it is clear however that in both cases the ongoing locutionary act of the speaker is incomplete, and that the second speaker assumes a turn at speech having interpreted the illocutionary point of that incomplete locutionary act. The phenomenon of overlap therefore links with general anticipatory strategy, though it does not follow that overlap necessarily occurs when anticipatory strategy operates.

[6.39] (Situation 3A: X and Y are arguing as to whether X has picked seven baskets, as he claims, or six, as the tally-sheet records)

   Y: ...and you do lose sen – track of time and er ∧ as I say it was raining this morning so I think you may∧

   X: no I'm I'm sure I did seven honestly ∧ you ∧ for instance this this girl above er Elizabeth Gosforth ∧ she's done two four ∧ she's done si – six ∧ it's a bit unusual isn't it for a Thursday ∧ cos she's done four and four and two before [are you sure you didn't

   Y: (clears throat) well I did] now I had a word with Elisabeth yesterday actually erm cos...

                                                  (3A14)

A theoretical problem is nonetheless clearly presented by the phenomenon of overlap: namely, whether in the case that an utterance is completely masked by an ongoing turn at talk by the other speaker that utterance can be said to count at all in the discourse structure. In the following extract, we will claim that X's utterances 'thank you very much', and 'oh that's lovely' count as communicative acts, but do not constitute turns at talk in discourse structure, filling Uptaker slots in discourse structure. Y's 'oh not a bit' however can be said to count in discourse structure, being a Minimization following a Thanks, even though the sequential ordering is disturbed – ie some Re-ordering may be seen to be taking place.

[6.40] (Situation 4A: X is taking leave of her landlady Y, having recently finished her university studies)

   Y: well it's been lovely having you Caroline you've been a super student I hope I get another one as nice and quiet and [peaceful

   X: thank you very much]

   Y: as you've been ∧ I've made you a little lunch here (picks up packet and proffers it) is that okay for the car [I know you've got

   X: oh that's lovely] (accepting lunch packet)

> Y: quite a journey
> X: oh you shouldn't have done really [I shall miss
> Y: oh not a bit]
> X: being here you know...

$$(4A11)$$

In the following extract however Y begins to substitute an alternative to his initial Proffer, having interpreted X's hesitation (here a potential gap in the discourse) as initiating a Pre-Responding Exchange, and therefore in his substitution re-presenting his original Request for a Claim (or maybe a Tell) in a more specific form, thereby attempting to Satisfy the subordinate Exchange Proffer. X however takes over the role of speaker and Satisfies the original Proffer. The subordinate Pre-Responding Exchange does not therefore count in the resultant discourse structure: there is no outcome in that Y does not succeed in specifying his original Proffer more precisely before Y in fact responds to it:

[6.41] (Situation 3A)
> Y: who ∧ was checking the tally this morning
> X: er
> Y: was it
> X: er I think it was your wife actually

$$(3A13)$$

In terms of identifying discourse structure, the theoretical problem as to whether or not a masked utterance can be said to count in the ongoing conversation is not critical in the analysis of the data used in this study. Firstly, the evidence clearly suggests that participants in ongoing conversations have the ability to speak and listen simultaneously: this ability is highly developed and constantly in operation. Clearly however the more predictable the masked response which appears to be adequately interpreted while the interpreter retains his turn at talk, the more likely that an interpretation will be made, and that it will be appropriate in that no subsequent repair work is necessary. If the masked utterance is non-predictable (it is a matter of common experience that hearers often hear what they wish to hear), either the speaker will re-present the masked utterance when the channel is clear, or it will be responded to, or it will be ignored. In the latter case we may indeed say that the utterance did not count in the ongoing discourse. We have further already pointed out that our notion of anticipatory strategy is sufficiently powerful to provide an alternative analysis in the case that a completely masked and in itself incomplete utterance is appropriately responded to. In terms of discourse structure this alternative analysis results in bracketing an *anticipated* element of discourse structure, as opposed to presenting without bracketing the same element of discourse structure, when that element occurs as a masked utterance or utterance fragment in the observed behaviour of the conversationalists. Instances in which these two alternative analyses both offer themselves will occur, but such uncertainty does not seem a serious weakness of the analytic system here proposed. Very possibly a more detailed analysis of non-verbal behaviour in ongoing conversations might help to choose between the two alternative analytic interpretations.

We conclude this section with a brief further note on the possibility of re-ordering communicative acts in conversational behaviour. What results from a re-ordering of communicative acts is that in a turn at talk a speaker makes more than one Proffer, for example, without the latter substituting for the former, and thus without self-correcting. Further the sequenced Proffers do not evidence subordinate linkage one to another such that *one* may be considered the head move. That such 'multi-headed' moves may evidence additive strategy also has already been suggested (*p* 130 above), but a potential difference was also there noted between Multi-head moves and re-ordered sequences. The case in which several goods are ordered sequentially or in a block in a service encounter has already been referred to. In academic discussion, and other contexts in which the operation of turn-taking is mediated and controlled through an official chairperson, it is common for an individual speaker to Proffer for example several 'questions', which may be taken up in turn.[54]

The few examples of re-ordering encountered in the corpus investigated concern only exchanges occurring in the Ave and Vale Phases of an Encounter: such exchanges are of course often ritualised. For example consider the concluding utterances following:

[6.42] (Situation 1B: X and Y have just negotiated a solution to the problem arising from X's inability to keep a baby-sitting appointment made with Y)

    X: fine okay see you next week

    Y: yes okay then bye bye

                                                 (1B22)

We have here a case in which two Proffers are made in one turn at talk, and both are Satisfied in the following turn at talk: both speakers produce Okays and Leavetakes.

Opening exchanges are of course often highly ritualised. The definition we propose for a Greet illocution simply claims that a speaker communicates thereby his awareness that the addressee is present as a potential interactant. Proffered Greets are Satisfied by their reciprocation – *ie* in the case that A communicates to B his awareness of B's presence, and B then communicates to A his awareness of A's presence, we are justified in seeing a happy outcome as resulting. A Greet on its own constitutes a minimal Proffer with which to initiate an Encounter. Some variations on the part of both initiating and responding members will be illustrated here. Several of these evidence the phenomenon of Re-Ordering. A specification of the situational background does not seem warranted for this set of data.

[6.43] (Enter X, carrying basket)
    X: well ∧ afternoon Jím here's the last básket
    Y: òh hello Tóny er oh nò it's er [Pèter
    X: Pèter]
    Y: Pèter yeàh
                                             (3A11)

The Remark 'here's the last basket' should in fact here be seen as a Satisfy to an implicit Proffer, the outcome being the handing over of the basket in question. This communicative act follows however a Proffered Greet, and the Greet is Satisfied by a reciprocating Greet, after some self-correction necessitating a firming Post-Exchange. Re-Ordering is clearly occurring. In the following a second re-ordered Proffer following a Proffered Greet 'gets lost' so to speak, in that only the proffered Greet is responded to, and Satisfied.

[6.44] (X enters, carrying basket, which Y takes from him)
    Y: oh hello Pèter how àre you
    X: hellò Mr Knox
    Y: are you er ∧ are you going òff now . . .
                                             (3A21)

(Note incidentally that the above gives some evidence for the claim concerning the Satisfy status of 'here's the last basket' in [6.43]). The utterance 'how are you' is of course highly ritualised – in the terms we have developed it would be a Request for a Tell, but there are grounds for setting up a distinct illocutionary category for this and similar locutions. In German 'wie geht's?' may be Satisfied by a 'danke'. The ritualisation is not so overtly marked in possible conversational responses in English, but it can be argued that it is only a matter of degree which distinguishes the status of such utterances in the two language communities. In the following two extracts, it is the Proffered Greet which is not overtly responded to, a second re-ordered Proffer following the Proffered Greet forming the focus of the responder's communicative act:

[6.45] (i) (X enters Y's surgery, Y looks up)
             Y: good afternoon Miss Hammersmith back again?
             X: yes (sits)
             Y: how's your tonsils then

                                                                (3B21)

        (ii) (Y enters, and during the initial exchange sits)
             Y: hello Vicky where's Simon
             X: oh he's out at the moment

                                                                (1C11)

We have claimed that a Satisfy may be assumed in a ritual exchange, and it could be claimed that this is what is happening here. However the Greeting ritual is so conventionalised that Greets Satisfying Proffered Greets occur, even though the Proffered Greet is followed in the same turn at talk by some other communicative act:

[6.46] (i) (Y approaches X from behind)
             Y: hello there Steve I thought I'd [find you in
             X: hello John]
             Y: find you in here ∧ how are you then
                                                                (4C11)

        (ii) (Enter Y, bearing a cup of tea)
             Y: ah good morning Jerry your cup of tea
             X: hello Mrs Summers [er I
             Y: d'you]
             X: don't want any tea thank you
                                                                (5A11)

Note in the last extract that Y's false start ('d'you') does not count in the discourse such that strict re-ordering is to be observed here in that X responds to the Proffered Greet and then reacts to Y's offering him the cup of tea. Further the Remark 'your cup of tea' is not *Proffered* such that Y's Remark is a Contra to it – he is 'contraing' the physical 'offering' of a cup of tea, not the communicative act from Y. Y's Remark is a Satisfy of an implicit Proffer, and it is the Execution of the outcome that X is concerned with. This complication does not alter the fact that we have a clear case of re-ordering on our hands here. The empirically-based claim that Satisfys to ritual Proffers may be assumed or simply omitted[55] does not in itself therefore account for the phenomenon of re-ordering, though in the data analysed such re-ordering occurs only in ritualised exchanges located in the Ave and Vale phases of an Encounter.

6.4.3 Topic-conflict and incoherence

The notion of discourse structure clearly assumes that in an ongoing conversation the interactants are in fact interacting. Amongst other things this presupposes that each conversant to some extent at least listens to what the other says, and reacts in the light of his belief as to what was said and done. However we have to face the fact that apparently sane and mature humans at times produce verbal acts consecutively and/or simultaneously in each other's presence without paying any attention whatever to what the other party is saying or doing. This, happily, does not arise in the data collected and used in this study. It would however surely be unrealistic to claim that there is no such thing as incoherent discourse. We may of course define discourse such that it is true as a matter of definition that all discourse is coherent, but in doing so we shall apparently introduce circularity into the notion of discourse structure, as we shall simply rule out of court any empirically observed verbal behaviour which does not exhibit structure, by claiming that it is not a discourse. In theory this is a serious weakness, even though we may wish to claim that in practice incoherent talk is readily recognisable as such. Consider the following oft-cited snippets of talk:

[6.47] (i)   – What is your name?
            – Well, let's say you might have thought you had something from before, but you haven't got it any more
            – I'm going to call you Dean

(from Labov 1971)

(ii)   LINUS: Do you want to play with me Violet?
        VIOLET: You're younger than me (Shuts door)
        LINUS: (puzzled) She didn't answer my question
                                        (cited in Coulthard 1977)

It would appear that there are no grounds for terming (i) above incoherent, and (ii) coherent, other than an intuitive sense of what is and what is not coherent. There must be a sense in which (i) above *is* 'coherent'; the fact that we (I assume) share the counsellor's interpretative problems in (i) above, while we can afford to laugh at Linus' interpretative problems in (ii) is a reflection of the researcher's standing and assumptions as a social member: it is only in this sense a reflection of the nature of what is happening here in these cited pieces of talk. Thus an alleged 'incoherent' discourse may be no more than a discourse which *I* cannot interpret as coherent, where 'I' am a discourse analyst, not a discourse participant.[56]

We may perhaps at this stage of research content ourselves with the observation that there is enough data whose status is not in dispute as 'coherent' discourse, and leave to one side problems raised by data such as that in [6.47] (i) above.[57] We shall have to recognise however that in conversational behaviour not every verbal or other act counts as a communicative act – *ie* has interactional significance.

In attempting to *argue* and *account for* instances in which a verbal or non-verbal act may be said not to count, we seek to avoid the circular position of simply discounting that which does not fit into the structural schema developed.

Here we wish to develop some empirically-based, albeit informal, notions as to what may be said to constitute a licensed change of topic in an ongoing conversation – the case in which 'incoherence' is nonetheless generally accepted by conversing members as coherent – *ie* socially licensed communicative behaviour. Firstly we may note that just as there is nothing incoherent about [6.47] (ii) above, nor is there any incoherence in a (fabricated) sequence such as

– Can you lend me ten quid?
– Read any good books lately?

in which the Proffered Request is clearly rejected. We wish to suggest however that in ongoing conversations there are licit types of topic-switching which lead to interspersed exchanges which have no systematic relation to the ongoing exchange at the point of topic change.[58] To characterise precisely what may be the substance of a legitimized insertion is not easy, but the physical needs, whether real or imagined, of either party is a clear case. Thus food, drink, cigarettes, and other creature comforts are potential topics of talk which may be raised while some other topic is still being negotiated. The following is an example:

[6.48] (Situation 3A)
    Y: well Iris is usually ∧ Iris is more competent than any of us
         ∧sit [sit down sit down er
    X: oh I'm sure she is] thanks (sits)
    Y: Peter sit down
                                                       (3A13)

There is clearly an overlap here, and Re-Ordering is evident also. There is a sense in which the business of Peter's getting seated does not belong to the structure of this conversational extract, and also a sense in which the Exchange negotiating an outcome on this topic does not interrupt the ongoing conversational behaviour. (The notion of co-existent discourse worlds is suggested as a mechanism for describing such inserted exchanges in 7.3 below.)

Generalising from such familiar cases of topic-change, we suggest that at times tension may be seen in ongoing conversation between reacting to a person's physical, mental, or emotional state, and reacting to what that person is saying or doing in the ongoing discourse. Norms of social etiquette seem quite complex here: when is it more 'polite' to ignore the fact that one's interlocutor has split something on his person, and when is it more polite to render effusive assistance?[59]

There may of course be a causal link between an ongoing topic of conversation and an interposed business concerning the creature comforts of a participant, as when the offering of a drink or of some other palliative may be interpreted as an expression of sympathy, as in the following extract:

[6.49] (Situation 1C: X and Y share a flat: Y returns home to find X in)
    Y: hello Vicky where's Simon
    X: oh he's out at the moment how's it been going anyway
    Y: oh okay bit bit grotty today
    X: why
    Y: well had that blooming ∧ political theory lecture and it's
         always∧∨
    X: well look ∧ sit down for a while ∧ relax
                                                     (1C11)

We may say here that X's last Proffer here results from the outcome
of the preceding Exchange, but the link is not of a type we have
accounted for in suggesting types of exchange linkage. A
'World-Shift' may be said to have taken place – see 7.3 below.

Factors of the immediate situation may also give rise to interspersed
exchanges which are not felt by speakers to be interruptions to the
ongoing conversation. In the following a party is in progress, and X
'offers' to get Y a drink after making contact. It is the social occasion
which causes this Proffer to come about: it is not intrinsic to the
interactional structure of the Encounter, but as the Encounter takes
place inside the social occasion and belongs to it, the Proffer of a
Willing here is incorporated into the discourse structure of the
ongoing conversation:

[6.50] (Situation 1D: X approaches Y at a party following the first day
        of a Summer School)
        X: hello
        Y: ah hello
        X: did you enjoy the ∧ introduction
        Y: ah it's allright I suppose think of better ways of spending
            the summer
        X: ah er sorry er would you like a drink
        Y: yes yes . . .

                                                                (1D21)

A potential conflict of topic can arise for a speaker who is faced with
a situation which itself presents a pressing topic for talk, while at the
same time a conversationalist makes social claims by his presence and
physical, mental, or emotional state, such that *he* constitutes a
pressing potential topic for talk. It might indeed be possible to
characterise such CRISIS situations in terms of the constant switching
of topic which may occur. The clearest instance in the corpus used is
situation 2A, in which Y, X's landlady, hears an explosion in his
room, and upon investigating finds the room damaged and her lodger
somewhat dazed. Informally we might suggest that Y is torn between
her concern for X, and her concern for her house, and the possibility
of similar accidents occurring. The resultant discourse shows a degree
of apparent 'incoherence' as a result of this topic conflict. The
following extract illustrates the point being made:

[6.51] (Situation 2A)

Y: no I must explain to you ʌ I was going to tell you but you
were out all day and ʌ when you passed me on [the stairs
X: I could have] been injured there Mrs [Walker
Y: but you] only had time to say good night to me I was about
to explain ʌ I'm very sorry are you allright
X: yes I'm perfectly okay now
Y: and don't think I'm only concerned for the gas because
also I'm concerned for you I mean [you are my lodger I
X: well I understand that now]
Y: have the responsibility

                                                          (2A11/2)

The tension here may be determined by the complexity of the
situation – *ie* there are several matters of concern presented by the
situation, and X and Y may weight these differently. Consequently,
there may be the appearance of a 'conflict of interests' in the ongoing
talk.

6.5. Illustrative analyses

The descriptive machinery developed in the foregoing sections of this
chapter is based on two central distinctions. On the one hand we have
the distinction between interactional and illocutionary work, and
claim that both kinds of functionality are present in the notion of
communication. On the other hand we have distinguished between
categorised acts, moves, and exchanges and the procedures used in
performing them: we may gloss this distinction as that between deep
and surface. In terms of interactional structure the central claim is
that speakers use anticipatory conversational strategies, both in the
interests of face, and towards the attainment of conversational goals.
Similarly, we suggest that in the performance of illocutionary acts, a
principle of tact may be seen to operate, affecting both the degree of
explicitness with which an illocutionary act is performed, and the use
of certain discourse lubricants we have termed Fumbles.

In seeking to display the developed descriptive machinery in
operation, we shall necessarily be selective, having anticipated to
some extent in the listed illocutions given in 6.3 above our purposes
here. However, any additions needed in that illocutionary inventory
would, it is hypothesised, concern ritual illocutionary acts,

specifically found in the Ave or Vale phase of a conversation. In the Encounters analysed here, we attempt to consider and characterise *all* the perceived behavioural tokens which may be said to belong to these conversational episodes. It is not easy however to display full analyses in one schema, given the relative complexity of the analytic model, and the not inconsiderable length of the transcribed conversations. In what follows therefore we shall concentrate on the central notion of discourse structure: phenomena of the types discussed under 6.4 above will not be analysed or referred to: Fumbles for example will be ignored.

6.5.1 Structural display conventions
It is convenient to summarise here the terms and graphic conventions proposed in order to capture the notion of discourse structure.

A: Discourse structure: interactional units
An *Encounter* is made up of *Phases*, in turn made up of *Exchanges*, made up of *Moves*, made up of *Acts*.
Phases: Ave, Vale, Business (. . . . . .)
Exchanges: Head, Pre-Head, Post-Head, Pre-Responding
Exchange Links: Chaining, Reciprocity, Execution
Moves: Proffer (PR), Satisfy (SAT), Contra (CON), Counter (CTR), Prime (PM), Re-Proffer (Re-PR)
Strategic Supportive Moves: Grounder, Expander, Disarmer
Acts: Uptake, Head, Appealer

B: Discourse Structure: Interactional Sequences
At the level of the Phase and Exchange, the structural potential is built into the definitions of the Exchanges and Moves of which a Phase and Exchange respectively may be composed.
ENCOUNTER
  (Ave) Business (Vale)

This is a minimal Encounter structure: no graphic representation is proposed at this level of analysis.
PHASE:
A Phase is composed of one or more Head Exchanges, linked by Chaining, Reciprocation, or Execution. A Head Exchange may be linked to different subordinate Exchanges. Subordinate Exchanges may also be linked by Chaining or by Execution, but not by reciprocation. The following graphic conventions will be used: in

these illustrative interactional structures, simple PR-SAT Exchange
structures will be assumed.

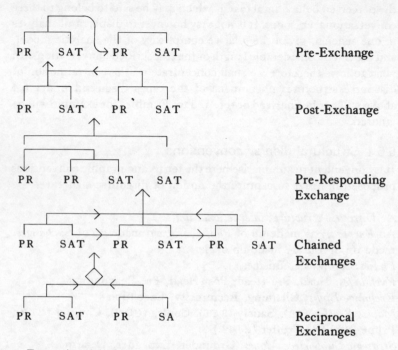

Executional linkage will be labelled as such: the Execution of a
previous outcome may consist of one act, or may have a complex
structure:

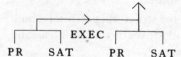

EXCHANGE

An Exchange consists of a permissible sequence of Moves. A Proffer
always initiates an Exchange, though a Prime may precede that
initiating Proffer. An Exchange is not terminated other than by a
Satisfy. The occurrence of a Satisfy does not necessarily terminate the
Exchange however – if the Satisfy produces 'local' outcome, a
Re-Proffer may sequentially follow the Satisfy, together with other
possible Moves. The Exchange sequences here presented do not
exhaust the possibilities of Exchange structure, but illustrate
potential move combinations:

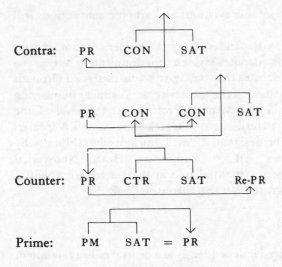

Contra: PR CON SAT

PR CON CON SAT

Counter: PR CTR SAT Re-PR

Prime: PM SAT = PR

MOVE

Moves have the following simple structure:

(Uptake) Head (Appealer)

6.5.2 Three annotated analyses

The display problems are considerable. In the interests of comprehension we shall adopt a top-to-bottom display procedure such that the observed units of conversational behaviour will appear as continuous text, save that each unit will be given a new line. Alongside each unit of conversational behaviour, its illocutionary and interactional status will be given, and discourse structures will be built up on the basis of these identifications. This means that the graphic conventions which have been reviewed in 6.5.1 above will now be used in a top-to-bottom format, instead of a left-to-right format. In operating this transformation, we read left as top, right as bottom. Thus a sequence which hitherto has been presented as

PR CON SAT

will now appear as follows:

PR ←

CON ←

SAT

The following further abbreviations and graphic conventions will also be followed:

GR = Grounder, EX = Expander, DA = Disarmer. A number after such an abbreviation denotes which communicative act is so supported: thus GR5 denotes that the move so characterised Grounds the act to be found on line 5 of the transcription. A similar numbering procedure will be followed with Re-Proffers. At the level of the interactional Act, H = Head, UPT = Uptake and APP = Appealer: Multiple Heads will be designated 'MH', and joined graphically by double-headed arrows. SH = Supportive Head. Non-verbal behaviour which plays a structural role in the conversation will at times simply be designated NV. Sp. denotes speaker.

Analysis 1 (*pp* 173–4)

SITUATION 2D

X and Y have just arrived independently at a central railway station in Birmingham, and are both consulting a displayed street map of that city. Y is following the index with her finger: she stops at Broad Street, and proceeds to locate with her finger the appropriate square on the map.

NOTES TO ANALYSIS 1

(i)   That the Exchange in lines 1 and 2 is not graphically linked to the following communicative activity does not mitigate the clear fact that the outcome of this initial Exchange is a discourse-internal one – both speakers communicate their availability for talk.

(ii) The sequence of communicative acts on lines 13–18 may require some elucidation. The point at issue is whether or not the utterance on line 14 counts as a communicative act at that point in time (note that it overlaps the utterance on line 13). The analysis proposed claims that it does so count, and that the utterance on line 15 initiates a Post-Exchange. On the most obvious alternative analysis, 15 would be seen as initiating a Pre-Responding Exchange, and a Satisfy to the Proffer in line 13 would then be *assumed* by Y. The chosen analysis would appear justified in the light of the oddness of the following fabricated sequence:

Y: are you on that course doing . .
X: you mean the three-day course

Int. Move in Exchange Structure	Int. Act	Illocutionary Act	Sp.	Observed Communicative Act	Line
PR	H	Interrupt	X:	excuse me	1
SAT	H	NV Attend	Y:	(looks up)	2
PR	H	Req Tell	X:	you don't happen to be going to Broad St do you	3
SAT	H	Tell	Y:	yes I am actually I am [I'm er	4
PR	H	Req Tell	X:	erm you're] not going to the New Salford Technical College	5
SAT	H	Tell	Y:	yes yes	6
PR	H	Req Tell		why [are you	7
SAT	H	Tell	X:	yes] I am	8
EXP8	SH	Tell		I have to be there at eleven o['clock	9
(PR)	H	Req Tell			
SAT	H	Tell	Y:	so do I]	10
EXP9	SH	Claim	X:	and it's ten-thirty now	11
	UPT	Exclaim	Y:	oh gosh	12
PR	H	Req Tell		are you on that course [doing	13
SAT	H	Tell	X:	yes I]	14
PR	H	Req Tell		three day course	15
SAT	H	Tell	Y:	yes ∧ yes	16
	UPT	Exclaim		oh gosh ∧ how funny ∧	17
GR21	SH	Claim		well I've just found it here ∧	18

A
V
E

Int. Move in Exchange Stucture	Int. Act	Illocutionary Act	Sp.	Observed Communicative Act	Line
PR	H	Propose	X:	perhaps we could go along together	19
SAT	H	Propose	Y:	yes	20
PR	H	Propose		I wonder do you think we ought to get a taxi cos	21
GR21	SH	Claim		it's getting on a bit isn't it	22
PR	H	Req Claim	X:	how far is it from here then	23
SAT	H	Claim	Y:	well we're here (points) [erm	24
—		Accept	X:	oh yes]	25
EXP24	SH	Claim	Y:	I suppose we could walk along ∧ wherever this is ∧ I don't know∧	26
(CON)	H	Propose			
CON	MH	Resolve		I think I'm going to get a taxi	27
CON	MH	Suggest		do you want [to go halves	28
	UPT	Accept	X:	yes	29
GR31	SH	Tell/Claim		I'm not very] good on directions	30
SAT	H	Propose		yes we [could do	31
			Y:	yes]	32
			X:	call a taxi	33
PR	H	Propose	Y:	yes	34
GR34	SH	Opine/Claim		I think that would be quickest	35
GR35	SH	Opine/Claim		cos I really think time's getting on ∧	36
(SAT)	H	Propose			
PR	MH	Okay		okay	37
PR	MH	Propose		shall we go and get a taxi then	38
SAT	H	Propose	X:	yes that's a good idea	39
PR	H	Okay	Y:	right	40
(SAT)	H	Okay			

(At this point X and Y move off towards exit)

Y: yes that's right
X: no I'm not actually

Further the utterance in line 15 appears to have a checking function: it does not make sense to say that X is 'informing' or 'telling' Y that the course in question is a three-day one. We have plenty of evidence from our corpus that the masking of an utterance does not necessarily mean that it does not count in the ongoing discourse: this seems to be such a case. Note that on the proposed analysis the Exclaim in line 17 is reacting to the *reciprocal* outcome of the previous discourse, and not simply to the content of Y's immediately preceding move.

(iii)   The utterance 'I don't know' which occurs turn-internally in line 26 is here interpreted as an Aside – *ie* a type of Fumble. We are therefore claiming that any hesitation phenomenon could carry the same functional load interactionally. It seems intuitively plausible to suggest however that this utterance may be signalling self-correction here (see 7.3 below for a more adequate interpretation of Asides).

(iv)   The analysis proposed for lines 24 to 28 well illustrates the phenomenon of anticipation. What is suggested by this analysis is that the Pre-Responding Exchange initiation on line 23 is interpreted by Y as implying some counter-Propose to that in line 21. This would be a Contra in discourse structure. In line 26 Y offers information relevant to the substance of such a Contra, but then in lines 27 and 28 Contras this assumed Contra, and in doing so re-presents the current substance of her original Proffer in line 21. That a Resolve plus a Suggest may be seen as together constituting a Propose has already been suggested (*p* 142 above). Lines 27 and 28 are therefore interpreted as constituting a Multiple Head of one interactional Move.

Analysis 2 (*pp* 176–8)

SITUATION 3D
X returns to the seating position in a university library where she has been working to discover that her place has been occupied during her short absence by Y, that her books and working materials have been moved to one side, and that there is no available alternative place.

Int. Move in Exchange Structure	Int. Act	Illocutionary Act	Sp.	Observed Communicative Act	Line
PR	H	Interruptor	X:	excuse me	1
(SAT)	H	Attend		(looks up)	
PR	H	Req Tell		I I don't know you do I	2
SAT	H	Tell	Y:	I don't think so no	3
DA5	SH	Apologise	X:	well er ∧ I'm terribly sorry but er∧	4
PR	MH	Complain		I'm afraid you're in my seat ∧	5
PR	MH	Complain		you've moved [my books	6
	UPT	Exclaim	Y:	oh dear]	7
			X:	and papers	
PR	MH	Complain		you must have realised somebody was here	8
—	UPT	Exclaim	Y:	oh that's er	9
CNT	MH	Excuse		well I looked around there wasn't anybody else any any other space and er	10
	SH	Apologise	X:	[well I'm awfully sorry	11
			Y:	I waited a little] while and nobody came	12
CNT	MH	Apologise		I'm sorry if I've taken your place	13
CNT	MH	Excuse		but there doesn't seem to be ∧ anywhere else and	14
CNT	MH	Excuse		I I thought perhaps you'd gone away for a long time	15
GR10	SH	Claim		people do and er	16
GR18	SH	Claim	X:	well honestly I left my books here and my bag	17
CON	MH	Complain		surely you could see it was my place	18
RE-PR5	MH	Complain		I'm [awfully busy	19

Int. Move in Exchange Structure	Int. Act	Illocutionary Act	Sp.	Observed Communicative Act	Line
PR	MH	Complain	X	(Structural summary of	
CNT	MH	Excuse/Apol.	Y	previous talk)	
CON	MH	Complain	X		
RE-PR	MH	Complain	X		
CON	H	Excuse	Y:	I did wait] a little while to see if anybody was coming back ∧ if you'd just been to the ladies or something but it ∧ time went on I thought you must have gone out	20
(SAT)	H				
CON	H	Willing		but er okay I'll move I [don't want to	21
DA31	SH	Apologise	X:	well I'm] terribly sorry about this but	23
DA31	SH	Apologise		you know I know we're supposed to speak quietly in here but	24
GR31	SH	Tell/Claim		I simply must get on	25
GR25	SH	Tell/Claim		I've got all this work to do	26
GR25	SH	Remark		and er it's Friday afternoon ∧	27
GR25	SH	Tell/Claim		I haven't worked well all morning	28
—	UPT	Sympathise	Y:	mm I know	29
RE-PR25 (=GR31)	SH	Tell/Claim	X:	you know I just have to get on	30
SAT	H	Req-Now		so if you[wouldn't mind getting out	31
EXECUTION		NV	Y:	(has already started collecting her papers etc)	32

Int. Move in Exchange Structure	Int. Act	Illocutionary Act	Sp.	Observed Communicative Act	Line
PR ←	MH	Complain	X	(Structural summary of	
CON	H	Willing	Y	previous talk)	
SAT	H	Req-Now	X		
→ EXECUTION		NV	Y		
GR35	SH	Tell/Claim	Y:	well I've got er I've] got to read this article	33
GR35	SH	Tell/Claim		I've got to get my essay finished too	34
PR	H	Req License		erm could I possibly∧ share your desk ∧	35
PR	H	Req Opine	X:	(has now assumed her place) well do you think you can find another chair	36
GR36	SH	Claim		I mean [you can't share my chair	37
SAT	H	Claim	Y:	well I think I'll find another chair]	38
SAT	H	License	X:	okay okay	39
PR	H	Willing		I'll move over∧	40
SAT	H	Req-Now	Y:	well that would be very kind	41
GR41	SH	Claim		I won't get in your way then	42
PR	H	Okay	X:	right hm hm (moves over)∧	43
PR	H	Req Okay	Y:	okay∧	44
(SAT)	H	Okay			
SAT	H	Okay		right	45
PR	MH	Thanks		well thanks very much	46
PR	MH	Resolve		I'll go and look for another chair	47
SAT	H	Minimization	X:	not a bit (Y departs)	48

NOTES TO ANALYSIS 2

(i)   Note the occurrence in this data of a large number of Multiple-Heads – *ie* instances in which more than one illocutionary act of a specific or related type fills one slot in interactional structure. This appears to be common in negotiations initiated by a Complaining illocution. It seems reasonable to suggest this is so because a complainable is by definition an anti-social act, calling therefore for much face-work, and further because it is not transparent what will Satisfy a Proffered Complain. The complainee therefore profusely Counters, in the hope that one or more of his moves will be effective as a Contra –*ie* will elicit a Satisfy annulling the Complain.

(ii)   The utterance in line 19 ('I'm awfully busy') is worthy of comment. The analysis proposed leads to a certain untidiness in the resultant discourse structure, but this is not of course a sufficient ground for proposing an alternative analysis. Note that the utterance does not support the Counter realised in lines 10 and 12–16, as the matter of substance under negotiation here – the culpability of Y in taking X's place – is not affected by the degree to which X is busy. The most obvious interpretation is that the utterance could function as a Ground for a Request of the form 'Please let me have my seat back', which Request we may say is conversationally implied by the original Complaint on line 5, as the complainable here is reversible – see *p* 143 above. Further, as a Grounding Move may function as the Head move it could ground, the utterance is here interpreted as a re-Proffer of the Complaint in line 5.

(iii)   We observe in this Encounter two instances in which an Uptaker occurs alone, and is therefore accorded no status in interactional structure. The Exclaim in line 7 and the Sympathise in line 29 do not in themselves constitute interactional Moves. Note further that X attempts unsuccessfully to gain the turn at talk on line 11 by producing an Apologise, which, while it would most likely be interpreted as a Disarming Move could also function itself to re-present the Proffered Complain in line 5 which is the current topic of negotiation. Y however retains the turn at talk, and does not take cognisance of X's behaviour on line 11: this utterance therefore does not count as valid in interactional structure.

Analysis 3 (*pp* 181–3)

SITUATION 3B
Y is a patient of doctor X, by whom she was recently treated for tonsillitis. She returns to see the doctor during surgery hours.

NOTES TO ANALYSIS 3
(i)   The second Exchange in this Encounter (lines 3–5) is a legitimately interpolated Exchange (*cf* the offering of cigarettes, etc): in the context of the ongoing discourse itself however the initiating Proffer ('Please take a seat') might be classified as an 'Invite into Territory' (compare 'Come in' and similar locutions). Note that the analysis given is a simplification: the non-verbal act of sitting is in fact the Execution of a Willing or Resolve which would properly speaking be the Satisfying Move. Clearly the act of sitting itself implies a willingness to do so.
(ii)   The locution in line 5 ('Tonsillitis cleared up okay now') functions as a Prime in discourse structure: it is characterised here as a Request for a Claim or Tell as an illocution. It can be argued with some justification however that the nature of the communicative behaviour requested by this Prime cannot be so precisely specified. In fact in the given analysis, the Complain in line 10 is interpreted as belonging to the Multiple Head move which Satisfies this Prime, but it seems clear that the Prime is not to be characterised as a Request for a Complain in illocutionary terms. The point here is that *in this situation*, the doctor's locution on line 5, and similar locutions however specific in content, will be interpreted as meaning something like 'What's wrong' or 'What seems to be the trouble'. A possible alternative analysis to that given would see line 6 as Satisfying the Prime, and the Moves on lines 7 and 10 as Expanding the Satisfy (=Proffer) in line 6. This complicates the notion of a Prime however, though little of theoretical substance hangs on the question as to which of these two analyses is to be preferred.
(iii) Note that the analysis claims that following line 21 Y *assumes* her Counter to the Complain is 'accepted' by X – an anticipated Satisfy appears in the discourse structure at this point. Having assumed this Satisfy, Y proceeds to the issue of compensatory offering – *ie* remedying the complainable. This is a clear strategic tactic, and people such as doctors are in a strong social position to utilise it.

Int. Move in Exchange Structure	Int. Act	Illocutionary Act	Sp.	Observed Communicative Act	Line
PR	H	Greet	Y:	good afternoon Miss Hammersmith∧	1
(SAT)	H				
PR	H	License-Now		please take a seat	2
	UPT	Thanks	X:	thank you	3
SAT	—	NV		(sits)	4
PM	H	Req Tell/Claim	Y:	tonsillitis cleared up okay now	5
	UPT	Claim	X:	well the tonsillitis has cleared up okay	6
SAT=					
PR	MH	Claim		but unfortunately I've got a rash	7
PR	H	Exclaim	Y;	a rash	8
SAT	H	Claim	X:	yeah∧	9
PR	MH	Complain		I think it's from the antibiotics you gave me	10
EX7	SH	Tell		and it's very itchy	11
EX7	SH	Tell		it's all on me face and me hands and me arms	12
EX7	SH	Tell		it's very itchy	13
GR10	SH	Complain		and I think∧ well∧ you told me to take double the dosage that the leaflet given with the medicine∧ prescribes_M	14
EX14	SH	Complain		you told me four spoonfuls and it should only really be two	15
CNT	MH	Claim	Y:	well of course it's obvious you've got an allergy to this sort of thing	16
GR16	SH	Justify		because I looked at your case individually and I decided you needed double the dosage∧	17
GR17/20	SH	Justify		because you know when they say you should only have a certain amount it's really a general∧ rule to everybody	18
GR17/20	SH	Justify		and as everybody is different	19
RE-PR17	SH	Justify		I decided that you should have this∧ double dosage	20
CNT (=16)	MH	Claim		but it seems you've developed an allergy to this	21
(SAT)	H	Claim			

Int. Move In Exchange Structure	Int. Act	Illocutionary Act	Sp.	Observed Communicative Act	Line
PR	H	Complain	X	(Structural summary of	
CNT	H	Claim	Y	previous talk)	
(SAT)	H	Claim	X		
CON	H	Willing	Y:	so we'll have to try and do something about the allergy and get your rash cleared up first won't we	22
SAT	H	Request	X:	well can you ∧ can you prescribe anything för the allergy	23
EX23	SH	Req Tell/Claim		I mean will it go away	24
EXECUTION GR23	SH	Opine/Claim		I mean it's ∧ quite nåsty to loŏk at	25
PR	H	Req Tell	Y:	does it itch at all	26
SAT	H	Tell	X:	yes it it itches quite a lot	27
PR	H	Req Tell	Y:	do you get scabs forming on it [or anything	28
SAT	H	Tell	X:	no]	29
	UPT	Go-on	Y:	mm mm	30
EX29	SH	Tell	X:	just very itchy	31
	UPT	Go-on	Y:	mm	32
EX29	SH	Tell	X:	well it's sore with scratching	33
	UPT	Accept	Y:	hum hum ∧	34
PR	H	Req Tell		it's just on your face and hands is it	35
SAT	H	Tell	X:	and my arms	36
	UPT	Accept	Y:	and your arms	37
PR	H	Req Tell		is it on any other place of the body	38
SAT	H	Tell	X:	well it's spreading yeah	39
	UPT	Accept	Y:	hm hm (begins writing)	40
EX39	SH	Tell	X:	all over	41
PR	H	Req Tell	Y:	and is it painful at all	42
SAT	H	Tell	X:	well only ∧ well if I scratch it ∧ yes it becomes very painful	43

Int. Move in Exchange Structure	Int. Act	Illocutionary Act	Sp.	Observed Communicative Act	Line
CON	H	Willing	Y	(Structural summary of	
SAT	H	Request	X	previous talk)	
PR	H	Req Tell	Y		
SAT	H	Tell	X		
PR	H	Req Tell	Y		
SAT	H	Tell	X		
PR	H	Req Tell	Y	is there anything coming out of it at all	44
SAT	H	Tell	X	no	45
PR	H	Willing	Y	liquid or anything ∧ well I think I can prescribe some ointment for you ᴍ give you a prescription to go along to the chemist which should clear it up in a couple of days (places prescription on table)	46 / 47
	UPT	Accept	X	hm hm	48
SAT	H	NV		(picks up and inspects prescription)	49
PR	H	Willing/ Propose	Y	and then perhaps we could do some tests on you to see why you've reacted in this way to the antibiotic which I've given you	50
SAT	H	Req/Propose	X	allright	51
PR	H	Thanks		thank you	52
(SAT)					
PR	H	Okay	Y	okay	53
SAT	H	Okay	X	fine (X rises to leave surgery)	54

The left margin reads vertically: E X E C U T I O N

(iv)   The structure of the Execution of the outcome of the Exchange on lines 22–3 is itself of considerable complexity. The 'question-answer' sequences (lines 26–45) are a chained sequence of Pre-Exchanges leading to the Proffering of the *prescription*. The verbal Proffer on line 46 is a supportive accompaniment to the non-verbal Proffering of the item itself (compare 'Here's your coffee'). This analysis is supported by the obvious fact that the patient's leaving with the prescription is the most significant outcome of the total Encounter.

Notes

1 A more detailed account of the data source, its original purpose, and the collection procedures used is available in Edmondson et al 1979.
2 The 'pre-history' given to the subject assuming role X in situation 1C (X wants, Y do P, [–social distance], [+ familiar]) reads for example as follows:
    'Background Information
    You, Sheila Wells, aged 20, have been unemployed since you completed a diploma in Industrial Design and Draughtsmanship two months ago. You share a room with your boyfriend Simon in a large flat in Battersea. You are both going to a party this evening given by a friend of Simon's whom you have not met. Simon promised to take along some good records to dance to, a rather rash promise, as he himself does not have any. He had banked on asking Colin Tate, a friend of both of you who has a room in the same flat, if he could borrow some of his. Simon has asked *you* to ask Colin, as he thinks Colin is less likely to say no to you. Colin has an extensive record collection, but you are aware that he is extremely careful about handling them.
    It is six o'clock and you are alone in the flat drinking a beer. You are not expecting Simon to be in until about eight, but have promised him that you will ask Colin about the records. The door opens and Colin comes in from the university where he studies Political Science . . . .'
3 On problems of data-collection when the conversationalists are aware that they are being observed, see for example Dick 1974; Cicourel 1974; Lomax et al 1977; Churchill 1978.
4 See here for example Fodor 1964; Carden 1976; Labov 1978, *pp* 345–58.
5 Note here the following (Goffman 1971, *p* 151): '. . . although it is convenient to speak of statements and replies (as I shall), and although verbal utterances are often employed, it is not communication *in the narrow sense of the term* that is at the heart of what is occurring. Stands are being taken, moves are being made, displays are being provided, alignments are being established.'(my italics)
6 On reciprocation, see Won-Doornink 1979 for a recent study.
7 When data is cited from the corpus used, the two speakers will be designated X and Y: this means that in a cited piece of data 'X' signifies an individual whose situational role in the given situation is consistent with the interactional role 'X' as this was indicated in the 'interactional bases' given on *p* 75 above.
8 Sinclair and Coulthard's terms 'Initiation' and 'Response' are similar. We prefer to coin two new terms, as the notion of a 'response' is too broad: there is a real sense in which any move produces or elicits a 'response'. Further, what would count as a 'Response' in S&C's system would not necessarily count as a Satisfy here.

9 Goffman uses the term 'primer' in a different, but not unrelated sense (1971, *pp* 189 et seq.). Compare also Klammer's 'responding moves which are at the same time a stimulus to the following move' (Klammer 1973, *p* 34), and the notion of the mediating response in learning psychology.

10 See however 7.1 below, where this claim is somewhat qualified.

11 We are not yet in a position to characterise the last element in this extract, which is in fact a Proffer initiating a Pre-Responding Exchange (see *pp* 105–8 below).

12 A theoretical problem here concerns the case in which a Satisfy is followed by an illocution one might gloss as a 'request for repetition', or something such. In the schema developed here such a move would initiate a Post-Exchange, not a Pre-Responding Exchange. It could be argued however that what is at issue is not the *outcome* of the previous exchange, but the content of the preceding move. In such a case we would argue that the 'satisfy' does not count as such in interactional structure until its nature as such has been communicated. The problem is theoretical in that no such problematical instances are to be found in the corpus used.

13 See 6.2 below.

14 The 'grammaticality' of native-speaker utterances is a topic outside the scope of this investigation: it may be recorded however that the above is not a typing error, nor is an error of transcription involved.

15 This is not to say that a chained exchange may not be Primed. The shopkeeper's 'anything else?' may clearly prime a chained exchange in the case informally considered here.

16 There is of course some regrettable hedging here, given that the specification of a type of illocution may be as broad or narrow as one's analytic purposes decide – see 6.3 below.

17 The social duty of reciprocation (or at least 'acknowledgement' – *cf* Uptake) may of course be explicitly set aside, especially perhaps with letters of condolence or sympathy. See for example letters to Bertrand Russell from Jane E. Harrison (June 1911), vol 1 *p* 214: Albert Einstein (14 October 1931), vol 2, *p* 205: M. F. Ashley-Montague (31 March 1940), vol 2, *p* 228: Augustus John (15 Feb 1961), vol 3, *p* 146, reprinted in the *Autobiography*.

18 *cf* Candlin et al 1976, who observe that doctor-patient interviews normally occur within a 'Greet-Leavetake' frame.

19 *cf* Weiser 1975, *pp* 649–50: 'If a speaker intends U to accomplish P by means of the addressee's recognition that the speaker intends U to accomplish P, I will call U a *communicative device* for accomplishing P. If a speaker intends U to accomplish P by some other means, I will call U a *conversational strategy* for accomplishing P.' (italics as in original; U = utterance, P = purpose). The problem with a definition of this kind is that the intentions of a speaker are not open to inspection, except as evidenced in the 'communicative devices' or 'conversational strategies' he may be said to be using.

20 These utterances will likely count as Contras or Counters in being potential *Grounders* of Contras or Counters (see *p* 129 below).

21 Thus in the case that one telephones, and asks to speak to, Professor X, a secretary's query as to one's identity, *preceding* the information that Professor X is not in, tends to be somewhat deflatory.

22 The move in question here is likely to be a Counter, rather than a Contra, in that while we feel intuitively that 'acceptance' of the content of this move by X may cause him to amend his claim that he has picked seven baskets, if X Contras this claim (which he in fact does), a following Satisfy from the farmer in no way commits the farmer to 'accepting' that X has picked seven – he may and does go on to produce further Counters.

23 Members often feel obliged to use Grounders. Consider the following data extract:

Y: we've gotta do something ∧ you knŏw don't wanna go down to the pub tonĭght and say well look sórry Mike you knŏw you can't cóme ∧ got to try and give him some sort of explanàtion . . .   (2c12)

24 Compare Labov and Fanshel's claim that 'refusals' to requests 'may lead to a break in social relations', if the 'refusal' is not grounded (in their terms 'unaccounted') (Labov & Fanshel 1977, p 168).

25 It has been suggested that even advanced learners of a foreign language may fail to follow this social norm, unintentionally seeming 'abrupt' or 'impolite' – see eg Götz 1977; Edmondson et al 1979; House and Kasper, 1981.

26 Conversational co-operation – following the H-support rule – decrees both that a speaker make his 'meaning' clear to his hearer, and that a hearer successfully interpret the speaker's 'meaning'. Thus a Disarming Apology may precede both a request for a Repair, and the Satisfying Repair:
   – He's a real procrastinator
   – Sorry he's a what
   – Oh sorry a procrastinator
   he never makes up his mind   (fabricated)

27 cf Watzlawick on 'pre-empting' – Watzlawick 1978, pp 150–3.

28 The logical counterpart is the strategy sketched above (p 118) in which a speaker S seeks to oblige H to reveal his (S's) illocutionary point rather than explicitly make it himself. In formal debating it is a common procedure to anticipate and argue against the Opposition's arguments, before the Opposition spokesman has a turn at speaking.

29 On the use of Disarming Apologies, see Edmondson 1981.

30 Widdowson's example – Can you fly to Edinburgh tomorrow?
                        – B.E.A. pilots are on strike
(Widdowson 1973, p 72) illustrates the common interpretative procedure whereby a Ground is understood as communicating that which it could serve to ground. See also data in [6.17], p 116 above.

31 We have no occasion to develop an apparatus for handling such phenomena given the data used, but instances certainly occur. On re-ordering see 6.4.2 below.

32 The power relation holding between X and Y would appear to be a relevant factor concerning the extent to which Satisfys may be assumed: what is conventionally referred to as a 'command' may for example be interpreted as a 'Request' whose Satisfaction is so to speak implicit in its Proffering.

33 We allow of the possibility that more than one illocutionary act fill the Head slot in the structure of an interactional move, as detailed in 6.2.3 above.

34 Consider here Candlin et al's (1976) sub-categorisation of different types of 'informative', 'directive', or 'elicitatory' functions. Candlin et al distinguish for example between the ELICIT, the INTERROGATE, the QUESTION, the ADMIN-ASK, and the MED-ASK in terms of the type of information so requested. Circularity results, but this degree of delicacy is warranted by the pedagogic goals of the research.

35 When a category has been defined, the name will be used thereafter with initial capitalisation: when that term is used in a pre-theoretical sense it will be given in quotation marks, as has hitherto been the practice.

36 It is probably necessary to distinguish here between the case of companionable joint action and that of co-operative joint action (ie [You do P] + [I do P] versus [You + I] do P). This distinction is clearly highly relevant to potential outcomes of an exchange containing a Propose: for example while S may possibly go to a cinema alone, it may not be possible for S to lift a heavy table alone. The distinction is however ignored here.

37 cf here Wunderlich 1977.

38 For a very useful discussion see Fillmore 1971.

39 'Information' is here taken to be the substance of a proposition explicitly or implicitly expressed in a locutionary act, and which the speaker may be held to claim to be true.

40 This sounds once more like a fairly devastating caveat, but appears to reflect the conversational facts, as a hearer is presented with them. In other words, it is essentially the hearer who decides in the last resort what the illocutionary value of a preceding illocutionary act is. In interpretation therefore we may follow a 'hearer-know-best' principle. Thus if I say 'I've got a bad cold' my friends are unlikely to contradict me, but my doctor may.

41 This is clearly a subjective distinction: it may be claimed however that there is a general consensus among speakers over a wide range of cases, and that the distinction is felt to be a real one, despite unclear cases.

42 This is clearly a necessary limitation, as otherwise many instances of Complains, Thanks, and other illocutions would also be Claims.

43 To anticipate somewhat, the central point here is that Remarks are often so trivial in content that a hearer cannot not 'agree' with them: if challenged with a non-co-operative response such as 'So what?', a speaker proffering a Remark has essentially nothing further to say. In fact few Remark occur in our corpus, possibly because a conversational goal was specified beforehand for at least one interactant. Compare here Labov and Fanshel 1977, p 63n.

44 See Fillmore 1971; Rehbein 1972.

45 A ground for in fact being dogmatic here would be that potentially infinite recursion is avoided. However maybe on occasion I might ask you to ask me to ask you to ask me to say hello to someone. But this is pure speculation.

46 The Exclaim is here set up as something of a catch-all expressive illocutionary category: the issue of delicacy is raised here once more.

47 The wording is intended to leave open the question as to whether to utter an Exclaim is necessarily to assume a turn at talk in terms of discourse structure – ie whether an Exclaim when occurring alone necessarily counts as a discourse move.

48 The case of the ASIDE (see pp 155–6) is a special one: several of the general remarks made about the class of Fumbles do not apply to Asides, which are nonetheless included here. cf n52 below.

49 In Edmondson 1977 I used the term GAMBIT to cover both what are here termed Fumbles and utterance tokens appearing as Uptakers, together with some of what I here characterise as discourse-internal illocutions. It seems likely that any such class of phenomena can only be delimited at all sharply inside the framework of a model of discourse analysis. The criticism applies as much to Edmondson 1977 as it does to for example Keller and Warner 1976; Keller 1979.

50 Here again the required delicacy of description may influence the degree to which sub-categories are developed. However, we suggest the gross categories here cover the main observed types of Fumbles. cf House and Kasper (1981) for a much more refined schema, which embraces however phenomena other than Fumbles as I wish to define that set of phenomena here.

51 The term is taken over from Sinclair and Coulthard 1975, p 44.

52 We have more to say on the Aside in discussing further development of the model in 7.3 below. It is conceded that the inclusion of the Aside as a class of Fumble does not in itself capture what is going on when such expressions are used.

53 Gaps are felt as such, pauses imply Satisfaction, in the sense in which we have used the term – ie it is assumed by at least one speaker that the conversing parties have reached a point of 'understanding' or 'agreement': 'Since I knew exactly what he meant, it would have been insulting to comment that Mozart didn't draw (he did, actually). There was a long, nodding pause of agreement and understanding'. . . 'There was a long, pregnant pause. But we both knew what the man had meant . . .' (Extracts from an account of an interview with Michael Ffolkes by Bill Grundy, *Punch* 20–26 July, 1977).

54 It is of passing interest that a common case of the 'block' order in a shopping
transaction might be that in which a child submits a *written* list of goods, indirectly
Requested by a parent, and further, that a lecturer who is Proffered several
illocutionary acts in one turn at speech is often seen to *take notes* during the
questioner's turn at talk. This would suggest that there are limitations on the extent
to which re-ordering can be indulged in everyday communication, in part
determined by such things as memory-span.

55 A predictable case in which this occurs is given below:
(Y knocks repeatedly at X's door)
X: ha hi hello er are you er
Y: erm [I live
X: for the party]
Y: below you and do you realise you're making a hell of a noise   (5D21)

56 With written discourse this seems most obviously true with respect to literary
works. The poetry of T. S. Eliot, to take a simple example, has now become
'coherent' in a sense in which it never was when it first appeared on the literary
scene. On some features of the allegedly incoherent discourse produced by some
schizophrenic speakers, see Rochester and Martin 1979.

57 The notion of a set of possible discourse worlds may be relevant here – see 7.3 below.

58 Coulthard uses the term 'topic conflict' in reporting on Sacks' 1968 lecture notes
(Coulthard 1977, *pp* 78–9). The perspective however is that of the individual
speakers, between whom the conflict arises. By 'topic conflict' I refer to observed
conversational behaviour in which in terms of discourse structure a topic change
may be said to occur – a topic may be 'inserted' in ongoing talk without disrupting
that talk, or topics may even alternate in exchange sequences.

59 A relevant anecdote is given by Rupert Crawshaw-Williams (*Russell Remembered*,
London: O.U.P. 1970, *p* 38):
'Today when we were having tea, there was a heavy thunderstorm. For some reason
Elisabeth went to open the sittingroom door, immediately above which was fixed a
telephone junction box. At the same instant this junction box was struck (or at any
rate attacked in some way or other) by lightning. There was a piercing and
high-pitched bang, and blue flames appeared around Elisabeth's feet. Since she was
clearly quite unharmed, Bertie and I resumed our conversation. Elisabeth, still in
the grip of her remarkable experience, became restive at our lack of excitement.
"Goodness," she eventually interrupted, "you two are going on as though nothing
had *happened*." "Oh," said Bertie, removing his pipe and observing her over the top
of his spectacles, "I see; I think I know what's wrong. How's this: OOh . . you
might have been *killed*; what a *narrow* escape. And my! How brave you were! What
consummate courage! Anybody else would have . . ." "Thank you," said Elisabeth.
"That was *exactly* what I needed."'

Chapter 7:

Perspectives

In discussing the model which has been presented in Chapter 6, I shall both point to clear limitations and suggest some ways in which the model may be further developed. In 7.1, under the rubric 'Some unanswered questions' I shall mention some areas in which further research is necessary to further clarify some issues raised by the work presented in Chapter 6. I shall also briefly consider here how far and in what ways the analytic model presented may be explicitly formulated — *ie* how we may approach the issue of writing a generative grammar of discourse. The peculiar nature of 'questions' is also raised in this section. In 7.2 we return to the relationship between discourse and text, and begin to explore the relationship between spoken and written discourse. Finally the model is given further descriptive power via the notion of a set of discourse worlds in 7.3.

7.1 Some unanswered questions

The analytic model presented is clearly in need of refinement and empirical validation in many points of detail. Further the range of conversational data covered is relatively small. We should remember also that the data used in this study was simulated. The claim that this data is valid for the purposes of setting up a model of discourse structure requires empirical validation with non-fabricated data. Some selected areas from this complex are discussed under separate heads in what follows.

The structure of an encounter
The structure of an Encounter in terms of Phases has been paid only

cursory attention in what has preceded. It is likely for example that different types of Phases are to be characterised in terms of different Exchange complexes. I do not however feel justified in attempting to be more precise at this level of analysis: the following few observations are offered merely as observations worthy of investigation.

An analysis of the structure of the Ave Phases of the Encounters used as data in this study suggests that a more precise characterisation of this Phase of talk would require a fuller illocutionary inventory than has been given. Further it is clear that the notion of 'phatic' talk is not to be equated with the Opening Phase of a conversation. Phatic talk might be characterised by discourse-internal outcomes, a relatively high frequency of formulaic expressions, and a relatively high density of reciprocal Exchanges in which Tells often feature. Such talk does not occur exclusively at the beginning of an Encounter however. Firstly the exchange of social ritual (particularly fellow-membership categorisation rituals) can *follow* a considerable period of talk in which outcomes of immediate concern to both parties occur. Secondly, after transacting a Business – perhaps one involving much difficult face-work – speakers can and do turn or revert to phatic talk, as if to ratify their social standing with each other. Indeed in the case that the social role relationship between speakers is unequal, a phatic episode following a Business may be seen as a reciprocal ritual. (Crudely, for example, I tell my student how bad his essay was, and then ask him about the prospects of the College football team, of which he is the captain – cf the serving of drinks after the Board Meeting.)

It is also intuitively clear that the Business Phase of a conversation may contain more than one Business Exchange. It might be necessary in fact to introduce a further rank in interactional structure between the Exchange and the Phase, which one might wish to call Transaction. These are issues requiring further empirical investigation.

Towards a generative grammar of discourse

Insofar as the interactional structures detailed in 6.1 above present a discourse as *product*, as opposed to *process*, it should be possible to formulate a set of 'discourse formation rules', which would recursively enumerate an unbounded number of interactional structures. Both system-networks and re-write rule-systems could generate such structures. Given that elements of structure are in part defined as change-of-state procedures, however, specifically at the rank of the Exchange, such a re-write system would need to be context-sensitive. Further a re-write convention of the kind $A \longrightarrow B_{o-n}$ C would be necessary to avoid unwanted hierarchical structure. Indeed, it would seem that one condition of rule-application would concern the number of instances (from o-n) a particular symbol is chosen. If this number is even, further specific rules might apply, while different rule-options would apply if this number were odd. A case in which this would hold would concern the number of consecutive Contras occurring between a Counter and a Satisfy. In general the structural potential of the Counter would lead to complexity in a re-write rule system. Either a sequence starting with a Counter would be treated as an embedded sequence, requiring then a distinction in non-terminal vocabulary between for example a Head Exchange and a 'sub-Exchange', or a distinction in terminal vocabulary would be necessary, two symbols being required for a 'Satisfy', according as it functions with respect to a preceding Counter, or with respect to some other Move. If such a set of discourse formation rules were formulated, outcomes and their hierarchical ordering could be defined in the light of the structural configurations allowed by the rule-system.

However, a *discourse* structure – *ie* an interactional structure in which the interactional acts have substance as illocutionary or other (non-verbal) acts – is both product and process; the individual illocution is selected as appropriate at one point in time in a specific context of situation, its value in the ongoing discourse being a matter of negotiation between the interacting parties. Thus given a set of re-write rules which generate interactional structures, and the terminal elements of which are interactional acts, an illocutionary inventory from which individual illocutions would be selected as possible realisations of the interactional acts would require for each type of illocutionary act

(i)   a specification of the type of Exchange and type of Exchange sequence it may appear in (this is necessary in that for example it appears a Complain cannot appear as a Proffer in a Proffer-Satisfy Exchange structure),

(ii)   a specification of the range of interactional acts the illocution may realise,

(iii)   a specification of the co-occurrence restrictions relative to other selected or potential illocutions in the same interactional configuration.

Such specifications on illocutionary acts would seem to be complex, but some parallels to Chomskyan categorisation rules, sub-categorisation rules, and selectional restrictions are evident.

A further complex issue concerns the business of turn-taking. We have claimed that following a Satisfy either speaker may initiate a following Exchange, be it tied to the preceding Exchange terminating in that Satisfy or not.[1] It follows that if turn-taking were to be assigned to the output of a generative rule-system at the level of the interactional Move, restrictions would need to be formulated in terms of which illocutions were possible options for speaker A, and which for speaker B. Thus for example in the case that the outcome of a Request-Willing sequence is a matter for further negotiation or specification in a Post-Exchange, a Proffered Willing concerning that outcome can (presumably) only be made by the requestee. However in a reciprocal Exchange following a Request-Willing sequence, a Proffered Willing would (presumably) be made by the requester. Compare here

   – I'll do it next week
   – I'll do it next week   (fabricated)

If such a generative system were feasible it would then require supplementation by a complex of further rule-systems, in which the strategic possibilities open to any speaker at any point of play would have to be made explicit, and whole complex issue of deriving illocutionary force from locutionary acts would require explication, optional and obligatory cohesion devices would need to be given, and intonational options and patterns would need to be assigned – it seems likely in fact that this could not be done independently of the other requirements given here.

There is of course an element of idealism, if not perversity in attempting to set up in this way a generative discourse system, independently of situational constraints. In other words, generating discourse in a vacuum seems purposeless. The notion of an operant world is a minimal pre-requisite.[2] Two potentially fruitful approaches may be mentioned here. Given a situation of a specific type, and known facts about the two (or more) conversationalists (crudely, information of the type supplied to the subjects used in this study), it would be quite feasible to detail in rule-format the behavioural options open to both (or all) participants (compare Hasan 1977 and the notions of a 'structural formula' and of a 'contextual configuration'). Alternatively, given an *outcome* of a contextualised conversation, it would be quite feasible using the model developed in this book to set up in explicit format various ways of achieving this outcome in conversational discourse. These seem to be realistic and immediate research goals.

The notion of a conversational outcome

The notion of the 'tied-pair' is reflected in the proposed model in the simplest Exchange structure – Proffer Satisfy. In many cases, given a specific illocutionary value for the Proffer, what illocution or illocutions may be said to Satisfy that Proffer can be derived from the definitions given in 6.3 above, in that Satisfaction may be equated with 'agreement', and 'agreement' may be said to show itself in the expression of the same attitude towards the same state of affairs. Thus if we take Willings and Requests, we find them defined as follows:

> WILLING: S wishes H to believe that S is not against his (S's) performing a future act A, as in the interests of H.
> REQUEST: S wishes H to believe that S is in favour of H's performing a future act A, as in the interests of S.

A 'happy outcome' can be seen to have been arrived at in the case that a Willing follows a Request, or a Request a Willing, assuming that the act A referred to in both locutions is the same.

Similar is the case of Suggests and Resolves. It seems indeed counter-intuitive to claim, as we have done, that a Resolve may be Satisfied by a Suggest, precisely because our non-technical notion of making a 'Suggestion' is bound up with the notion that the content of the 'Suggestion' be new information in the operant context of discourse. However it is noticeable that in 'agreeing with' or 'supporting' a 'resolve' made by an interlocutor, one may well use locutionary forms which in other contexts would serve equally well to put forward the content of the 'resolve' as a preceding 'Suggestion'. Consider the following (fabricated) examples:

> NEW: – I would do P̣
> – why don't you do P̌
> – I think it would be a good iděa if you did P̣
> – I would suggest you do P̀
>
> OLD: – yes, Ỉ would
> – hm, why not

– yes I think that's a good idea
– yes, that's what I would suggest

Note that in the case of both Willing-Request and Resolve-Suggest sequences there is a possibility that a following third illocution will occur, in which the content of the Willing or Resolve will be repeated. Such illocutions are to be interpreted as initiating Post-Exchanges, firming an outcome which is already occurrent. Thus in a (fabricated) sequence such as the following:

AA: shall I open the window
B: do that thing
A: okay

an outcome in the form of let us say an undertaking has already been arrived at after the second utterance, the Request. The sequence of the second and third moves does not constitute an Exchange therefore in this sequence.

There are however at least two respects in which the notion of an Exchange outcome is more complex than is suggested above. Firstly there are illocutions which cannot be (immediately) Satisfied, as the perlocutionary intent of the speaker Proffering the illocution cannot be said to be interpretable from the nature of the illocution itself. The case of the Complain is one such. An Apologise is so defined that if it follows or indeed precedes a Complain, and if the same act A is addressed in both illocutions, then both S and H may be said to have the same attitude towards that act A. However this 'agreement' does not in itself guarantee a happy outcome. That this is so is bound up with the social law of retribution (see discussion in Edmondson 1979c).

Secondly, we need to investigate rather more closely the notion of a happy outcome when different types of Request are Proffered. With a Request-Now for a non-verbal act, it is clear that the Execution of the Requested act may itself Satisfy the Proffer, and indeed an illocution counting as a Willing so to do Satisfies such a Proffered Request only to the extent that the substance of the illocution is brought into being – ie executed (see discussion pp 37–8 above). While it makes sense to talk of the execution of the Request as implying a willingness so to do in some cases – and indeed a less crude notation than that found in our transcriptions might in fact reveal some paralinguistic signal conveying a Willing in such cases – this is not so with some 'questions'. Thus if a locution in the form Can you open the window is to be interpreted as a Request that the hearer open the window, a nod of the head may be said to communicate a Willing. However if the locution is to be interpreted as a Request for a Tell, or a Request for a Claim, a nod of the head will not in the unmarked case communicate a Willing – *ie* a readiness on the part of the performer to perform an act of Telling or Claiming. In fact of course, other things being equal, the nod of the head is likely to be interpreted as *constituting* an act of Telling or Claiming. In other words, as Lyons points out:

> 'If the addressee says *No* in response to a question of the form *Is the door open*? he is answering the question. But if he says *No* in response to what is clearly a mand, such as *Open the door*, he is refusing to do what he is being commanded or requested to do.'[3]

Note that the distinction between Requests for verbal acts and Requests for non-verbal acts will not resolve the difficulty here. One might seek to argue that the latter is Satisfied by a Willing locution, which may be implied by the execution of the Requested act, while the former is simply Satisfied by the Execution of the Requested act. This would work for the case in which a Request for a non-verbal act is performed via a Query-locution, but not for the case in which a verbal act is Requested via some locution other than a Query. Thus 'Tell me your name', or 'I want to know the time please' may be responded to by Willing illocutions, to be followed, we may assume, by Executions ('Okay, my name's Fred actually'/'Sure, erm, it's half past three'). What is clearly critical here is not the nature of the act requested, but the locutionary form of the requesting illocution. We are faced here with the peculiar nature of 'questions'.

The term 'question' has been avoided as a technical term in this study, but for the purposes of brief discussion here we shall understand a question to be a query-locution used to perform an illocutionary act of Requesting a Claim, Tell, or other illocution with a minimum of indirectness (this somewhat unsatisfactory qualificatory clause is necessary as *Will you tell me the time please* is not to be considered a 'question' for our purposes here). The peculiar nature of questions then is that it is highly unusual for such illocutions to be followed by an illocution expressing willingness to perform the Requested act.[4] It follows from this peculiarity of course that questions may function as Primes in discourse structure, and the peculiar nature of the Prime as a conversation-specific interactional move follows from the peculiar nature of questions as communicative acts.[5]

Further we should note that the 'answer' to a question is itself the outcome of the Exchange it brings to a point of possible closure, constituting as it does the Execution of the Requested act. This may be seen as consistent with the claim that in conversation many assertive locutions, functioning as Telling, Opining, and other illocutions, may be plausibly interpreted as 'answering' an 'assumed' question, rather than being interpreted as some type of Proffered illocution requiring some form of Satisfaction. It is in this sense that one may agree with Lyons that 'asking and telling are two distinguishable subtypes of saying' (Lyons 1977b, *p* 278). Lyons further refers to interrogativisation as the 'grammaticalisation of doubt': rather might one suggest that interrogativisation is a grammatical reflection of the interactional purposes of the language system. Asking and telling are two complementary interactional units reflected in the grammatical system.

To point to the peculiar nature of questions in this way does not resolve our original difficulty concerning what may Satisfy a Proffered Request for a communicative act. The restrictions operating on the occurrence of Willings following and Satisfying such Requests would need to be specified in any grammar of discourse. It would appear from the above discussion that this cannot be done other than by reference to the locutionary act performed in the realisation of the Request. The problem of questions remains unanswered.

7.2 Spoken and written discourse

The following is an extract from the transcription of situation 3B1, analysed on pages 181–3 above, and constitutes one turn at talk:

[7.1] 'Well it's obvious you've got an allergy to this sort of thing because I looked at your case individually and I decided that you needed double the dosage ∧ because you know when they say that you should only have a certain amount it's really a general ∧ rule to everybody and as everybody's different I decided you should have this ∧ double dosage but it seems that you've developed an allergy to this so we'll have to try to do something about the allergy and get your rash cleared up first won't we'

We recall that this conversational segment follows a Complain on the part of the patient that the doctor is responsible for the rash the patient has developed, in having prescribed double the recommended dosage of an antibiotic. The analysis given in 6.5 above essentially claims that this spate of talk is structured via anticipatory strategy on the basis of a dialogic discourse structure, a fabricated version of which might appear as follows:

[7.2] Y: well of course it's obvious you've got an allergy to this sort of thing
       X: what do you mean, it's obvious
       Y: well I looked at your case individually and I decided you needed double the dosage
       X: but it says on the leaflet only two spoonfuls
       Y: well when they say that you should only have a certain amount it's really a general rule to everybody
       X: but if it's a rule for everybody, how come you prescribed four spoonfuls for me
       Y: well everybody is different you see that's why I decided you should have this double dosage
       X: oh I see
       Y: yes so as I say it seems you've developed an allergy to this
       X: hmm well what do we do now
       Y: well we'll have to do something about the allergy and get your rash cleared up first won't we

                                                                 (fabricated)

A dialogue such as that above may be said to underpin the original data in [7.1] above, and this is shown in the analysis provided for that data.

If we now fabricate a *written* report of the content of the above episode from the doctor's perspective, we might write as follows:

[7.3] It was clear that the patient was allergic to the prescribed antibiotic, and that no blame attached to myself for her condition. The recommended dosages given by druggists offer only the most general guidance, and I had examined this patient most thoroughly before deciding that her condition warranted the dosage I prescribed. I determined therefore to prescribe for the complaint, and to investigate the nature of the allergy.

                                                                 (fabricated)

Several things may be noted here. Firstly, the Claim that the patient's allergic condition shows that no blame attaches to the doctor

is demonstrated in [7.1] above by the placing of the discourse segment
inside the total conversation: in [7.3] however this relevance is
explicitly stated in the written account. Secondly we notice that in
[7.3] the placing of the second sentence itself suffices to make its
content an 'explanation' or justification of the Claim made in the first.
That this relation holds in [7.1] derives from the structural identity
between [7.1] and [7.2]. The suggestion is therefore that a similar
structural relation holds between [7.1], [7.2], and [7.3] – the nature of
the tie between the first two sentences in [7.3] derives from the
structural link evidenced by Pre-Responding Exchanges of the type
evidenced in [7.2]. Thirdly, we notice that the repetition of the Claim
with which [7.1] opens later in this extract ('but it seems you've
developed an allergy to this so . .') has been omitted from the version
of this event given in [7.3]. We could of course reinstate it:

[7.4] '. . deciding that her condition warranted the dosage I
         prescribed. So it was clear that the complaint was caused by an
         allergy. I determined therefore. .'
                                                                    (fabricated)

However this re-instatement seems intuitively unnecessary. The
result is 'clumsy', 'overworked', and 'unnatural'. This is not the effect
given by the second mention of this Claim in [7.1] above however.[6] In
fact to omit it may be said to detract from the original:

[7.5] '. .and as everybody's different I decided you should have this
         double dosage but erm we'll have to try to do something about
         the allergy and get your rash cleared up first won't we. .'
                                                                    (fabricated)

The reason we might tentatively suggest is simply that [7.3] is a
written discourse, while [7.1] is a transcribed segment of a spoken
discourse. Because of factors of memory-span and interpretative load,
and given the sequential realisation in real time of a conversational
episode, the Claim with which [7.1] begins is sufficiently removed
from the immediate focus of attention of the hearer to bear repetition:
this does not hold true of the written version of this episode in [7.3].

We note in fact that [7.1] above has the classic structure of a lengthy
expository text: it has a beginning, a middle, and an end. A Claim is
presented, argued for, and repeated in a summing up which leads
directly to a conclusion. A tentative conclusion here is that a central
feature of the notion of textual or rhetorical structure, of

compositional planning, derives indirectly from the necessity in spontaneous talk of presenting the Head of one's interactional move sufficiently close to the end of the speaking turn in which the move is executed to allow the hearer to interpret the discourse function of that head communicative head – *ie* to interpret the internal structure of the head and supportive moves of which that turn at speech may be composed.

What these three observations, derived from a fairly superficial investigation of [7.1] above, suggest is that the coherence of a written 'text' ultimately derives from the notion of coherence in spoken discourse. The model presented in Chapter 6 begins to suggest ways in which this relation between spoken and written discourse may be made explicit. This becomes possible by reference to empirically-established discourse structure rules, and the powerful notion of anticipatory strategy. It was argued in Chapter 2 that in many textlinguistic studies an attempt is made to discover the nature of textual structure without reference to the nature of discourse, and then further to seek to interpret spoken discourse in terms of textual structural concepts. The opposite procedure is here proposed as appropriate.

The central idea is not of course new. It is suggested as a 'concluding remark' in Coulthard (1977, *p* 181), and a similar notion is explored in Gray (1977)[7]. Gray develops three types of 'inter-sentential relations', namely 'descriptive' (continue and contrast), 'explanatory' (conclude and support), and 'rhetorical' (question and answer) – (Gray 1977, *pp* 190–209). Gray further claims that 'implied dialog' is the 'generating force' in text production, and that 'a writer is obliged to decide after each assertion what question to acknowledge and what questions to ignore or defer' (*p* 213). There is here a danger of course in thinking that the insertion of a 'question' after each 'assertion' in a text, such that the next occurrent 'assertion' answers that interposed question in some sense accounts for or clarifies the structure of the 'text', but Gray's approach here is clearly compatible with that taken in this study. In short, Gray analyses 'text' as spoken discourse.

The nature of 'questions' has already been raised in 7.1 above in connection with the notion of a conversational outcome. What was suggested there and illustrated in the analyses proposed in 6.5 above is that it makes sense to talk as Gray does of an 'assertion' as an 'answer that contains its question' (Gray 1977, *p* 4). In the full Encounters analysed in 6.5 above there is only one clear instance of a locution which might be deemed 'assertive' in illocutionary force which fills a Proffer slot in interactional structure (a Claim realises a Proffer slot in a Pre-Exchange in analysis 3, line 7, *p* 181). Here one does not wish to claim that Tells, Claims, Opines, and Remarks are *always* elicited, nor that the three short conversations analysed in full can in any sense be said to be indicative of the frequency of distribution of different types of illocution, or of the function these may have in discourse structure. It seems however on the basis of the corpus used that a Tell for example is not normally Proffered, but produced in response to an occurrent or assumed Proffered Request for a Tell, which it therefore Satisfied. In speech act theory this is reflected in the felicity condition said to hold for an 'informative' speech act, namely that S believe the content of the 'informative' act be unknown to H. In other words, an 'assertive' act in discourse is pointless unless the speaker believes there is a 'doubt' or 'interest' which that act removes or satisfies. One might claim extending the argument here that expository texts clearly presuppose a 'request' or 'doubt' they are designed to Satisfy, and that this is sometimes reflected in the titles of works of reference (*Who's Who*, *What's on in London*, *Which*, *How to Succeed in Business without really Trying*). Such titles do not of course constitute Requests for Communicative acts, but indicate which Requests for Communicative acts the book or magazine in question attempts to Satisfy.

In written discourse however it is not *simply* a matter of Satisfying anticipated moves. The notion of anticipation in both spoken and written discourse embraces the case in which the substance of a possible hearer move – a Counter for example – is incorporated into the substance of the speaker's turn at talk, or into his textual exposition. Thus expressions such as 'Of course I admit that P, but . .' or 'One might suppose here that P, but . .' may be understood as signalling that what follows is an anticipated H-move, which the speaker will himself go on to Satisfy, Counter, Contra, or otherwise respond to.

Further, as briefly noted above, a written discourse is not normally constrained by time in the way that a spoken discourse is: written discourse is commonly edited, revised, and generally polished before being exposed to a reader. A considerable element in this pre-publication work is concerned with providing previews and reviews designed to assist the reader in discovering the coherence of the whole. Sinclair (1980) distinguishes relevantly here between 'prospective' and 'retrospective' directionality (the first sentence appearing in Chapter 3 of Sinclair and Coulthard 1975 reads as follows: 'This has been a difficult chapter to write as we are catering for two audiences.')

The remarks and suggestions above are to be seen as indicating possible directions in which further research into the relation between spoken and written discourse might be pursued. The model developed in Chapter 6 may be seen as a tentative first step towards such research.

7.3 Discourse worlds[8]

In seeking to extend the descriptive power of the model, I wish to add to it the notion of a DISCOURSE WORLD, such that a communicative act is to be defined as an interactional act A manifest in an illocutionary act I, via a locutionary act L, in a world W. A discourse world is to be understood as an application of the notion of a possible world derived from logical semantics to the pragmatic interpretation of conversational behaviour. A discourse world is then a function from interactional act to communicative act: the locutionary act acquires an illocutionary value by reference to an operant discourse world.

Consider a (fabricated) sequence such as the following:

[7.6] − John, can you give me an example of a Sidestep?
       − Sorry, I'm not very good at dreaming up linguistic examples

One possible continuation might be of the form 'Never mind', giving a Proffer-Contra-Satisfy structure to the resultant Exchange. An alternative continuation might be of the form 'Thanks very much', which would have to be interpreted as (roughly) a Proffer-Satisfy, Proffer-(Satisfy) structure, the second Exchange being a Post-Exchange. The former 'discourse reading' is surely more normative, and the reason is that one operant discourse world is maintained in this exchange, while if the responding utterance is to be interpreted as a Satisfy, it is necessary to interpret the locutionary act as having a (potential) illocutionary force only by reference to some world other than the operant one at this point of time in the interaction.

However the relevance of the notion of a discourse world is not restricted to such contrived cases, nor is it always a case of *alternative* interpretations of communicative acts, relative to different discourse world. Consider the case of teacher-pupil interaction in the foreign language classroom.[9] What is going on in the following (fabricated) sequence?

[7.7]   TEACHER: John, ask me what time it is
            JOHN: What time is it?
            TEACHER: It's half-past three. Good, another one . .

John's utterance counts as two different communicative acts in two
different discourse worlds. On the one hand John is executing the
content of the teacher's request; on the other hand in doing so, John is
making a request of the teacher – *ie* he is asking the teacher the time.
The teacher's utterance 'It's half-past three' is a response to the
Request for the time, while the following utterance 'Good' is a
response to the Satisfy of the teacher Request. Note we cannot say
here that the opening teacher move in [7.7] is a Prime, as among other
things we shall be at a loss as to how to analyse the teacher evaluation
that may follow ('Good' might be replaced by 'well done', 'say it more
clearly', 'your intonation was wrong', and so on). In the world of
classroom discourse, in which John's utterance Satisfies the teacher
Request, its illocutionary status is that of what I have called a 'Saying'
– *ie* it has none. In the discourse world in which John's utterance does
have the illocutionary value of a Request for the time, it has the
interactional value of a Proffer. Because of his institutionalised social
role as pedagogue, the teacher has a potential for bringing discourse
worlds into being. The teacher's initial utterance in [7.7] signals a
world-shift, analogous in status to a verb like DREAM in semantics.[10]

The notion of world-shift allows us to interpret one utterance as
functioning as more than one communicative act. World-shift is
involved in the case that one locution is simultaneously addressed to
more than one hearer, the recipients having different positional roles
such that the communicative act performed via the locution may be
differently characterised with respect to the different recipients.
Candlin et al (1976) give the example of a doctor-utterance having one
'function' for the patient-hearer, and another for the nurse-hearer.
Note that in this situation both hearers are addressed, and that the
doctor may be assumed to intend that his locutionary act be
differently interpreted by the respective participants.

Consider also the Fumble termed the Aside in the analytic
apparatus developed in this study. A more adequate treatment is
possible via the notion of discourse worlds and the notion of
world-switching.

In one of the situations used to obtain data for this study, a student
takes a form to one of his teachers and asks him to fill in certain
sections of it.[11] This the teacher does. While so engaged, he verbalises:

[7.8] Y: yeah ∧ uhm ∧ so I have to erm ∧ assess your capabilities I see
            ∧erm ₘ well we'll put your name in here ₘ school of ens – uh
            Norwich County Council ₘ uhm ∧ has studied for ∧ four
            years uh ∧ erm ∧ well now I I know that you're very capable
            you know in French language so ∧ I'll just er have a look
            through these and try and assess which ∧ I think would be
            more suitable . . . (omission) . . . it it's gonna be you know
            very good experience ∧ classroom can only really ∧ you know
            take you so far with the theory but I think this this is a very
            good idea instead er indeed ∧ erm ∧ yeah well I think we can
            safely say ∧ you're at least Ḇ standard anyway uh
       X: well certainly not perfect
       Y: no no but ∧ if you're going to er study at university I'm sure
            this is gonna ∧ put you in very good stead ∧ yes erm ∧ right
            (He continues filling form) (mutter) well ∧ (hands over
            paper) that's that
                                                                                    (1A22)

We can see here, without going into a detailed analysis, that Y, the
teacher, is operating in two discourse worlds, often simultaneously.
He is in a real sense interacting with the form which he is filling in, in
that it Proffers Requests for different Tells, Claims, and Opines
which the teacher attempts to Satisfy. He verbalises his responses to
the form's Requests in the form of Willing illocutions ('I'll just have a
look at these and try and assess which . .') as though these Requests
came from the student. He does this as these printed Requests on the
form are subordinate to the Request to fill in the form which was
originally Proffered by the student. In doing so he also fills a
conversational gap in his ongoing interaction with the student,
indirectly telling the student what he is about. In verbalising his
Satisfies ('Norwich County Council') he indirectly Tells the student
the content of his Satisfies, though he is Asiding here in terms of the
discourse world he shares with the student.

The notion of a set of possible discourse-worlds is necessary for
such data, and allows of insightful, if complex, analysis. The status of
some of the teacher's locutions is admittedly not clear – it is not always
obvious which locutions are as it were self-addressed, and which are
directly or indirectly student-addressed. However, firstly intonation
will possibly be found to be discriminating here – requiring a much
more delicate analysis than that provided in the transcription in [7.8] –

and secondly we may surely claim that this uncertainty reflects the social reality of such a situation: one can well imagine that in such a situation the student might himself feel uncertain as to whether some comment or response from himself is licensed or not.

The notion of co-existing discourse-worlds and of world-shift are then to be added to the descriptive apparatus developed in Chapter 6, in order to increase the descriptive power of the model. It is clear that what results is a model of some complexity: it remains to be established by further research how far the complexity of the model proposed here is adequate for the description of the phenomenon it seeks to elucidate – the simple business of people talking to one another.

Notes

1 Some qualifications to this generalisation have been exhaustively specified, namely the case of Satisfies following Counters, which do not bring the ongoing Exchange to a point of possible closure, and the case of Proffers following Satisfies which terminate Pre-Exchanges, which are made by the speaker initiating the Pre-Exchange only.

2 As in Artificial Intelligence, where highly restricted worlds are constructed inside which a particular programme is designed to function (eg Weizenbaum 1966; Winograd 1977; Woods 1977). Much work on answering systems inside Artificial Intelligence has considerable relevance to the concerns of discourse analysis. In systems in which the programme assumes a 'responding' role some problems concerning impure input have been tackled, such that programmes can (in our terms) initiate Repair or other Pre-Responding Exchanges. Thus a programme can ask which block is meant in the case that a given instruction is ambiguous in reference, can point out that a selected square in noughts-and-crosses is already taken, and so on. In Weizenbaum's programme, Eliza is capable of handling almost any conversational contingency, as the conversational initiative is always kept by Eliza, who initiates a Pre-Responding or Post-Exchange regardless of the communication serving as input (see the data cited by Longuet-Higgins 1972, p 257). Eliza we may say cleverly uses a particular conversational strategy to cover up the fact that her knowledge is practically nil. In the terms used by Longuet-Higgins, the programme makes up in 'tactics' what it lacks in 'semantics'.

3 Lyons 1977a, p 754. Lyons uses this observation as an argument against the notion that yes-no questions are a subclass of mands. However here Lyons conflates locutionary and illocutionary force: if the addressee says 'No' in response to what is in context equally clearly a mand, having the form Can you open the door, he is both 'answering the question' and 'refusing to do what he is being commanded or requested to do'.

4 The qualification 'highly unusual' may be necessary in that although no such instances occur in our corpus it seems reasonable that a speaker, when in a situation such that the Execution of the Requested verbal act can only occur after a short time-lapse, may produce a Willing, as in the following (fabricated) example:
   – what's the time please
   – (fumbles in pocket for watch) erm I'll tell you in a minute yes it's half-past three.
One has also heard a lecturer answering a question of the type 'Why did you say in your lecture that P' by commencing 'Well I'll tell you why I said that . .'

5 It should be noted that in the framework developed in Chapter 6, 'questions' are not strictly speaking a category of communicative act, nor indeed of illocutionary act.

6 The argument here is based purely on intuitive appeal. The conclusion the argument is designed to support however is, one hopes, attested by the bulk of the analyses proposed in this study, and by the argumentation supporting the analytic model developed.

7 Widdowson and Sinclair explore this notion in relation to the teaching of the spoken language and the teaching of the written language (Widdowson 1980; Sinclair 1980).

8 See Ballmer 1972 for a similar use of this term.

9 What follows on this topic is explored in greater detail in Edmondson 1978b, 1978c.

10 This type of behaviour is not restricted to classroom settings. Compare many jokes and other verbal plays (Sounding would be one such: we recall that the insult ceases to be ritual when the recipient interprets the speaker as asserting that its content is true).

11 The relevant section of the form has the following format:
'...... (name) has studied French for ... years at ...... (name of school). I would assess his competence in speaking French as ... (Insert A–F: see key below).'
The original is in French, and somewhat more elaborately worded.

Bibliography

ABERCROMBIE, D. (1968) 'Paralanguage', *British Journal of Disorders of Communication*, 3, 55–9 (Reprinted in Laver and Hutcheson 1972, 64–70)

ALLEN, D. E. and GUY, R. F. (1974) *Conversational Analysis: the Sociology of Talk*. The Hague: Mouton

ALLEN, J. (1977) 'Synthesis of Speech from Unrestricted Text', in Zampolli, 1977, 1–30

APEL, K. O. ed (1976) *Sprachpragmatik und Philosophie*. Frankfurt: Suhrkamp

ARDENER, E. ed (1971) *Social Anthropology and Language*. London: Tavistock

ARGYLE, M. and KENDON, A. (1967) 'The Experimental Analysis of Social Performance', in Berkowitz, 1967, 55–98

AUSTIN, J. L. (1963) 'Performative-Constative', in Caton, 1963, 22–54

AUSTIN, J. L. (1976) (2nd edition) *How to do Things with Words*. London: Oxford University Press

BALLMER, T. T. (1972) 'Einführung und Kontrolle von Diskurswelten', in Wunderlich, 1972b, 183–206

BARKER, C. (1975) 'This is just a first approximation, but. . .', *Chicago Linguistic Society*, 11, 37–47

BENJAMIN, G. R. (1977) 'Tone of voice in Japanese conversation', *Language in Society*, 6, 1–13

BERKOWITZ, L. ed (1967) *Advances in Experimental Social Psychology*. New York: Academic Press

BEVER, T. G., KATZ, J. J. and LANGENDOEN, D. T. eds (1977) *An Integrated Theory of Linguistic Ability*. Hassock: Harvester Press

BRAZIL, D. C. (1975) *Discourse Intonation*. Discourse Analysis Monographs 1, English Language Research: Birmingham

BRAZIL, D. C. (1978) *Discourse Intonation II*. Discourse Analysis Monographs 2, English Language Research: Birmingham

BREUER, D. (1974) *Einführung in die pragmatische Texttheorie*. München: Fink

CAMPBELL, R. and WALES, R. (1970) 'The Study of Language Acquisition', in Lyons, 1970, 242–60

CANDLIN, C. N., LEATHER, J. H. and BRUTON, C. J. (1976) 'Doctors in Casualty: Applying Communicative Competence to Components of Specialist Course Design', *IRAL*, 14, 245–72

CARDEN, G. (1976) 'Syntactic and Semantic Data: replication results', *Language in Society*, 5, 99–104

CATON, C. E. ed (1963) *Philosophy and Ordinary Language*. London: University of Illinois Press

CHATMAN, S. ed (1971) *Literary Style: A Symposium*. London: Oxford University Press

CHERRY, C. (1968) (2nd edition) *On Human Communication*. Cambridge, Mass: M.I.T. Press

CHERRY, C. ed (1974) *Pragmatic Aspects of Human Communication*. Dordrecht: Reibel

CHRIST, H. and PIEPHO, H-E. eds (1977) *Kongreßdokumentation der 7. Arbeitstagung der Fremdsprachendidaktiker*. Limburg: Frankonius

CHURCHILL, L. (1978) *Questioning Strategies in Sociolinguistics*. Rowley, Mass: Newbury House

CICOUREL, A. V. (1974) 'Interviewing and Memory', in Cherry, 1974, 51–82

COHEN, L. J. (1964) 'Do illocutionary forces exist?', *Philosophical Quarterly*, 14 (Repr. in Fann 1969, 420–44)

COLE, P. and MORGAN, J. L. eds (1975) *Syntax and Semantics, vol 3: Speech Acts*. New York: Academic Press

CORDER, S. P. and ROULET, E. eds (1973) *Theoretical Linguistic Models in Applied Linguistics*. Brussels: AIMAV/Paris: Didier

CORDER, S. P. and ROULET, E. eds (1975) *Some Implications of Linguistic Theory for Applied Linguistics*. Brussels: AIMAV/Paris: Didier

COULMAS, E. ed. (1981) *Conversational Routine*. The Hague: Mouton

COULTHARD, M. (1977) *An Introduction to Discourse Analysis*. London: Longman

COULTHARD, M. and BRAZIL, D. (1979) *Exchange Structure*. Discourse Analysis Monographs 5, English Language Research: Birmingham

DANEŠ, F. (1970a) 'One Instance of Prague School Methodology: Functional Analysis of Utterance and Text', in Garvin 1970, 132–46

DANEŠ, F. (1970b) 'Zur linguistischen Analyse der Textstruktur', *Folia Linguistica*, 4, 72–8

DASCAL, M. and MARGALIT, A. (1974) 'A new "Revolution" in Linguistics? – "Text-Grammars" v. "Sentence-Grammars"', *Theoretical Linguistics*, 1, 195–213

DICK, D. (1974) 'Experiments with Everyday Conversation', in Cherry, 1974, 27–50

DIJK, T. A. van (1972) *Some Aspects of Text Grammars*. The Hague: Mouton

DIJK, T. A. van (1973) 'Text Grammar and Text Logic', in Petöfi and Rieser, 1973, 17–78

DIJK, T. A. van (1977a) 'Pragmatic Connectives', *Interlanguage Studies Bulletin, Utrecht*, 77–93

DIJK, T. A. van (1977b) *Text and Context*. London: Longman

DINGWALL, W. O. ed (1978) (2nd edition) *A Survey of Linguistic Science*. Stamford, Conn: Greylock

DIXON, R. M. W. (1963) *Linguistic Science and Logic*. The Hague: Mouton

DOLEŽEL, L. (1971) 'Towards a Structural Theory of Content in Prose Fiction', in Chatman, 1971, 95–110

DOWNES, W. (1977) 'The imperative and pragmatics', *Journal of Linguistics*, 13, 77–97

DRESSLER, W. (1972) *Einführung in die Textlinguistik*. Tübingen: Niemeyer

DRESSLER, W. ed (1977) *Current Trends in Textlinguistics*. Berlin: de Gruyter

DUNCAN, S. D. (1972) 'Some Signals and Rules for Taking Speaking Turns in Conversations', *Journal of Personality and Social Psychology*, 23, 283–92

DUNCAN, S. D. (1973) 'Towards a grammar for dyadic conversation', *Semiotica* 9, 29–46

DUNCAN, S. and NIEDEREHE, G. (1974) 'On signalling that its your turn to speak', in *Journal of Experimental Social Psychology*, 10, 234–47

EDMONDSON, W. J. (1977) 'Gambits in Foreign Language Teaching', in Christ and Piepho, 1977, 45–8

EDMONDSON, W. J. (1978a) 'A note on "Pragmatic Connectives"', *Interlanguage Studies Bulletin, Utrecht*, 100–06

EDMONDSON, W. J. (1978b) 'Worlds within Worlds – problems in the description of teacher-learner interaction in the foreign language classroom', Paper read at 5th AILA Congress, Montreal, 1978

EDMONDSON, W. J. (1978c) 'Context and Stress – the "Old" and the "New" in Foreign Language Teaching', *Anglistik und Englischunterricht*, 6, 63–73

EDMONDSON, W. J. (1979a) 'Harris on performatives', *Journal of Linguistics*, 15, 331–4

EDMONDSON, W. J. (1979b) 'Funktionen von Fragen im Fremdsprachenunterricht', in Heuer et al, 1979, 206–09

EDMONDSON, W. J. (1979c) 'Illocutionary Verbs, Illocutionary Acts, and Conversational Behaviour', in Eikmeyer and Rieser, forthcoming

EDMONDSON, W. J. (1981) 'On Saying You're Sorry', in Coulmas, 1981, 273–88

EDMONDSON, W. J., HOUSE, J. KASPER G. and McKEOWN, J., (1977) *A Pedagogic Grammar of the English Verb*. Tübingen: Narr

EDMONDSON, W. J., HOUSE, J., KASPER, G. and McKEOWN, J. (1979) *Sprachliche Interaktion in lernzielrelevanten Situationen*. LAUT Series B, paper 51, Linguistic Agency: University of Trier

EHLICH, K. and REHBEIN, J. (1972) 'Zur Konstitution pragmatischer Einheiten in einer Institution: Das Speiserestaurant', in Wunderlich, 1972b, 209–54

EHRICH, V. and FINKE, P. eds (1975) *Beiträge zur Grammatik und Pragmatik*. Kronberg: Scriptor

EHRICH, V. and SAILE, G. (1972) 'Über nicht-direkte Sprechakte', in Wunderlich, 1972b, 255–87

EIKMEYER, H-J and RIESER, H. eds (forthcoming) *Worlds, Words and Contexts*. Berlin: der Gruyter

ENKVIST, N. E. (1973) *Linguistic Stylistics*. The Hague: Mouton

FABIAN, B. (ed) (1971) *Ein anglistischer Grundkurs*. Frankfurt: Athenäum

FANN, K. T. ed (1969) *Symposium on J. L. Austin*. London: Routledge & Kegan Paul

FILLMORE, C. J. (1971) 'Verbs of Judging: an Exercise in Semantic Description', in Fillmore and Langendoen, 1971, 273–89

FILLMORE, C. J. (1977) 'Scenes-and-frames semantics', in Zampolli, 1977, 55–79

FILLMORE, C. J. and LANGENDOEN, D. T. eds (1971) *Studies in Linguistic Semantics*, New York: Holt, Rinehart & Winston

FIRTH, J. R. (1964) *The Tongues of Men* and *Speech* (First published 1937 and 1930 respectively), London: Oxford UP

FISHMAN, J. A. ed (1971) *Advances in the Sociology of Language, volume 1*, The Hague: Mouton

FODOR, J. A. (1964) 'On knowing what we would say', *Philosophical Review*, LXXIII, 198–212

FRANCK, D. (1975) 'Zur Analyse indirekter Sprechakte', in Ehrich and Finke, 1975, 219–31

GARFINKEL, H. and SACKS, H. (1970) 'On Formal Structures of Practical Actions', in McKinney and Tiryakian, 1970, 337–66

GARVEY, C. (1975) 'Requests and Responses in Children's Speech', *Journal of Child Language*, 2, 41–64

GARVIN, P. L. ed (1970) *Method and Theory in Linguistics*. The Hague: Mouton

GOFFMAN, E. (1955) 'On face-work: an analysis of ritual elements in social interaction', *Psychiatry*, 18, 213–31 (Repr. in Laver and Hutcheson, 1972, 319–46)

GOFFMAN, E. (1971) *Relations in Public*. Harmondsworth: Penguin

GOFFMAN, E. (1976) 'Replies and Responses', *Language in Society*, 5, 257–313

GORDON, D. and LAKOFF, G. (1975) 'Conversational Postulates', in Cole and Morgan, 1975, 83–106

GÖTZ, D. (1977) 'Analyse einer in der Fremdsprache (Englisch) durchgeführten Konversation', in Hunsfeld, 1977, 71–81

GRAY, B. (1977) *The Grammatical Foundations of Rhetoric*. The Hague: Mouton

GRICE, P. (1975) 'Logic and Conversation', in Cole and Morgan, 1975, 41–58

GÜLICH, E. and RAIBLE, W. eds (1972) *Textsorten*. Frankfurt: Athenäum

GUMPERZ, J. J. and HYMES, D. eds (1972) *Directions in Sociolinguistics*. New York: Holt, Rinehart & Winston

GUNTER, R. (1974) *Sentences in Dialog*, Columbia, S. C: Hornbeam

GUTKNECHT, C. ed (1977) *Grundbegriffe und Hauptströmungen der Linguistik*, Hamburg: Hoffman & Campe

HABERMAS, J. (1972) 'Vorbereitende Bemerkungen zu einer Theorie der kommunikativen Kompetenz', in Holzer and Steinbecher, 1972, 208–36

HALLIDAY, M. A. K. (1973) *Explorations in the Functions of Language*. London: Arnold

HALLIDAY, M. A. K. and HASAN, R. (1976) *Cohesion in English*. London: Longman

HARRIS, R. (1978) 'The descriptive interpretation of performative utterances', *Journal of Linguistics*, 14, 309–310

HARRIS, Z. S. (1952) 'Discourse Analysis', *Language*, 28, 1–30

HARTMANN, P. (1971) 'Text als linguistisches Objekt', in Stempel, 1971, 9–29

HARTMANN, P. (1974) 'Zur Anthropologischen Fundierung der Sprache', in Schmidt, 1974, 11–20

HASAN, R. (1977) 'Text in the Systemic-Functional Model', in Dressler, 1977, 228–46

HAYDEN, D. E. and ALWORTH, E. P. eds (1965) *Classics in Semantics*. New York: Philosophical Library

HEAL, J. (1974) 'Explicit Performative Utterances and Statements', *Philosophical Quarterly*, 24, 106–121

HENDRICKS, W. O. (1973) 'Methodology of Narrative Structural Analysis', *Semiotica*, 7, 163–85

HEUER, H., KLEINEIDAM, H., OBENDIEK, E. and SAUER, H. eds (1979) *Dortmunder Diskussionen zur Fremdsprachendidaktik*. Dortmund: Lensing

HOLZER, H. and STEINBACHER, K. eds (1972) *Sprache und Gesellschaft*. Hamburg: Hoffman & Campe

HOUSE, J. and KASPER, G. (1981) 'Politeness Markers in English and German', in Coulmas, 1981, 157–185

HUNSFELD, H. ed (1977) *Neue Perspektiven der Fremdsprachendidaktik*. Kronberg: Scriptor

HYMES, D. (1971) 'Sociolinguistics and the Ethnography of Speaking', in Ardener, 1971, 47–93

HYMES, D. (1972) 'On Communicative Competence', in Pride and Holmes, 1972, 269–93

IKEGAMI, Y. (1976) 'A Localist Hypothesis and the Structure of Text', in Nickel, 1976, vol 1, 339–48

JACOBS, R. A. and ROSENBAUM, P. S. eds (1970) *Readings in English Transformational Grammar*. Waltham, Mass: Ginn

JEFFERSON, G. (1972) 'Side Sequences', in Sudnow, 1972, 294–338

KALLMEYER, W., KLEIN, W., MEYER-HERMANN, R., NETZER K. and SIEBERT, H. J. (1974) *Lektürekolleg zur Textlinguistik, Band 1*. Frankfurt: Athenäum

KALLMEYER, W. and SCHÜTZE, F. (1976) 'Konversationsanalyse', *Studium Linguistik*, 1, 1–28

KATZ, J. J. (1977) *Propositional Structure and Illocutionary Force*. New York: Thomas Crowell

KELLER, E. (1979) 'Gambits: Conversational Strategy Signals', *Journal of Pragmatics*, 3, 219–38

KELLER, E. and WARNER, S. T. (1976) *Gambits 1*. Ottawa: Supply & Services, Canada

KEMPSON, R. M. (1973) Review of Fillmore and Langendoen, 1971, *Journal of Linguistics*, 9, 120–40

KIEFER, F. (1977) Review of Petöfi and Rieser, 1973, *Journal of Pragmatics*, 1, 177–92

KLAMMER, T. P. (1973) 'Foundations for a Theory of Dialogue Structure', *Poetics*, 9, 27–64

KLEIN, W. (1977) 'Wegauskünfte', Mimeo: Max-Planck-Institut, Nijmegen (to appear in *Zeitschrift für Literaturwissenschaft und Linguistik*)

KOCH, W. A. (1965) 'Preliminary Sketch of a Semantic Type of Discourse Analysis', *Linguistics*, 12, 5–30

KOCH, W. A. (1971) 'Textlinguistik', in Fabian, 1971, 212–35

KRZESZOWSKI, R. P. (1975) 'Is it possible and necessary to write text grammars?', in Corder and Roulet, 1975, 33–45

KUMMER, W. (1972) 'Aspects of a Theory of Argumentation', in Gülich and Raible, 1972, 25–58

LABOV, W. (1971) 'The Study of Language in its Social Context', in Fishman, 1971, 152–216

LABOV, W. (1972) 'Rules for Ritual Insults', in Sudnow, 1972, 120–69

LABOV, W. (1978) 'Sociolinguistics', in Dingwall, 1978, 339–72

LABOV, W. and FANSHEL, D. (1977) *Therapeutic Discourse*. New York: Academic Press

LANGENDOEN, D. T. (1968) *The London School of Linguistics*. Cambridge, Mass: M.I.T. Press

LAVER, J. and HUTCHESON, S. eds (1972) *Communication in Face to Face Interaction*. Harmondsworth: Penguin

LEECH, G. N. (1971) *Meaning and the English Verb*. London: Longman

LEECH, G. N. (1976) 'Metalanguage, Pragmatics, and Performatives', in Rameh, 1976, 81–98

LEECH, G. N. (1977a) *Language and Tact*. Paper no. 46, Linguistic Agency: University of Trier

LEECH, G. N. (1977b) Review of Sadock, 1974, and of Cole and Morgan, 1975, *Journal of Linguistics*, 13, 133–45

LEECH, G. N. and SVARTVIK, J. (1975) *A Communicative Grammar of English*. London: Longman

LOMAX, A. et al (1977) 'A Stylistic Analysis of Speaking', *Language in Society*, 6, 15–36

LONGUET-HIGGINS, H. C. (1972) 'The Algorithmic Description of Natural Language', *Proceedings of the Royal Society*, London, 1972, 255–76

LYONS, J. ed (1970) *New Horizons in Linguistics*. Harmondsworth: Penguin

LYONS, J. (1977a) *Semantics 2*, Cambridge: Cambridge UP

LYONS, J. (1977b) 'Statements, Questions, and Commands', in Zampolli, 1977, 255–80

MALINOWSKI, B. (1923) 'The Problem of Meaning in Primitive Languages', Supplement 1 in Ogden, C. K. and Richards, I. A. *The Meaning of Meaning*, London: Routledge & Kegan Paul, 1923

MARSHALL, J. C. (1970) 'The Biology of Communication in Man and Animals', in Lyons, 1970, 229–41

McKINNEY, J. C. and TIRYAKIAN E. A. (1970) *Theoretical Sociology*. New York: Appleton-Century-Crofts

MERRITT, M. (1976) 'On questions following questions in service encounters', *Language in Society*, 5, 315–57

MEYER-HERMANN, R. (1976) 'Direkter und indirekter Sprechakt', *Deutsche Sprache*, 4, 1–19

MORRIS, C. W. (1964) *Signification and Significance*. Cambridge: Cambridge UP

NICKEL, G. ed (1976) *Proceedings of the Fourth International Congress of Applied Linguistics*, vols. 1–3. Stuttgart: Hochschul-Verlag

PETÖFI, J. S. (1973) 'Towards an Empirically Motivated Grammatical Theory of Verbal Texts', in Petöfi and Rieser, 1973, 205–73

PETÖFI, J. S. (1976) 'Formal Pragmatics and a Partial Theory of Texts', in Schmidt, 1976, 105–121

PETÖFI, J. S. and RIESER, H. eds (1973) *Studies in Text Grammar*. Dordrecht: Reibel

PIKE, K. L. (1967) (2nd edition) *Language in relation to a Unified Theory of the Structure of Human Behaviour*. The Hague: Mouton

POYATOS, F. (1976) 'Verbal and Nonverbal Expression in Interaction', in Nickel, 1976, vol 1, 87–97

PRIDE, J. B. and HOLMES, J. eds (1972) *Sociolinguistics*. Harmondsworth: Penguin

RAMEH, C. ed (1976) *Semantics: Theory and Application*. Washington: Georgetown UP

REHBEIN, J. (1972) 'Entschuldigungen und Rechtfertigungen', in Wunderlich, 1972b, 288–317

REHBEIN, J. (1977) *Komplexes Handeln*, Stuttgart: Metzler

REHBEIN, J. (1979) *Fragesequenzen: Elizitieren im Fremdsprachenunterricht*. Mimeo: Bochum

REHBEIN, J. and EHLICH, K. (1975) (2nd version) *Begründen*, 'KidS' Working paper 1. Mimeo: Düsseldorf/Bochum

REHBEIN, J. and EHLICH, K. (1976) 'On Effective Reasoning', in Nickel, 1976, vol 1, 313–38

ROCHESTER, S. and MARTIN, J. R. (1979) *Crazy Talk*. London: Plenum

ROSS, J. R. (1970) 'On Declarative Sentences', in Jacobs and Rosenbaum, 1970, 222–72

ROSS, J. R. (1975) 'Where to do Things with Words', in Cole and Morgan, 1975, 233–56

ROULET, E. (1977) 'Approche des actes de langage directs et indirects en francais: l'offre et la promesse', Mimeo: Université de Neuchâtel

RUSSELL, B. (1940) *An Inquiry into Meaning and Truth*. London: George, Allen & Unwin

SACKS, H. (1972) 'On the analysability of stories by children', in Gumperz and Hymes, 1972, 325–46

SACKS, H., SCHEGLOFF, E. A. and JEFFERSON, G. (1974) 'A Simplest Systematics for the Organisation of Turn-taking for Conversations', *Language*, 50, 696–735

SADOCK, J. M. (1974) *Towards a Linguistic Theory of Speech Acts*. New York: Academic Press

SANDULESCU, C. G. (1976) 'Theory and Practice in Analysing Discourse', in Nickel, 1976, vol 1 349–65

SCHEGLOFF, E. A. (1972a) 'Sequencing in Conversational Openings', in Gumperz and Hymes, 1972, 346–80

SCHEGLOFF, E. A. (1972b) 'Notes on a Conversational Practice: Formulating Place', in Sudnow, 1972, 75–119

SCHEGLOFF, E. A. (1977) 'On Some Questions and Ambiguities in Conversation', in Dressler, 1977, 81–102

SCHEGLOFF, E. A., JEFFERSON, G., and SACKS, H. (1977) 'The Preference for Self-Correction in the Organisation of Repair in Conversation', *Language*, 53, 361–82

SCHEGLOFF, E. A. and SACKS, H. (1973) 'Opening up Closings', *Semiotica*, VIII, 289–328

SCHEGLOV, YU. K. and ZHOLKOVSKII, A. K. (1975) 'Towards a Theme-(Expression Devices) -Text Model of Literary Structure', *Russian Poetics in Translation*, 1, 3–50

SCHMIDT, S. J. (1973) *Texttheorie*, München: Fink

SCHMIDT, S. J. ed (1974) *Pragmatik* 1, München: Fink

SCHMIDT, S. J. (1975) 'Zur Linguistik der sprachlichen Kommunikation', in *Linguistische Probleme der Textanalyse*, Schriften des Instituts für Deutsche Sprache 35, Düsseldorf: Schwann, 20–35

SCHMIDT, S. J. ed (1976) *Pragmatik/Pragmatics* 2, München: Fink

SEARLE, J. R. (1969) *Speech Acts*. Cambridge: Cambridge UP

SEARLE, J. R. (1975) 'Indirect Speech Acts', in Cole and Morgan, 1975, 59–82

SEARLE, J. R. (1976) 'A Classification of Illocutionary Acts', *Language in Society*, 5, 1–23

SINCLAIR, J. McH. (1980) 'Some Implications of Discourse Analysis for ESP Methodology', *Journal of Applied Linguistics*, 1, 253–61

SINCLAIR, J. McH. and COULTHARD, R. M. (1975) *Towards an Analysis of Discourse*. London: Oxford University Press

STEINBERG, D. D. and JAKOBOVITS, L. A. eds (1971) *Semantics*. London: Cambridge UP

STEMPEL, W-D. ed (1971) *Beiträge zur Textlinguistik*. München: Fink

SUDNOW, D. ed (1972) *Studies in Social Interaction*. New York: Free Press

TWER, S. (1972) 'Tactics for Determining Persons' Resources for Depicting, Contriving, and Describing Behavioural Episodes', in Sudnow, 1972, 339–66

WATZLAWICK, P. (1978) *The Language of Change*. New York: Basic Books

WATZLAWICK, P., BEAVIN, J. H. and JACKSON, D. D. (1967) *Pragmatics of Human Communication*. New York: Norton

WEISER, A. (1975) 'How to not answer a question: Purposive Devices in Conversational Strategy', *Chicago Linguistic Society*, 11, 649–60

WEIZENBAUM, J. (1966) 'Eliza, a computer program for the study of natural language communication between man and machine', *Communications of the Assoc. of Computing Machinery*, 9, 36–45

WIDDOWSON, H. G. (1973) 'Directions in the Teaching of Discourse', in Corder and Roulet, 1973, 65–76

WIDDOWSON, H. G. (1977) 'Approaches to Discourse', in Gutknecht, 1977, 236–60

WIDDOWSON, H. G. (1980) 'Conceptual and Communicative Functions in Discourse', *Journal of Applied Linguistics*, 1, 234–43

WIGGINS, D. (1971a) 'On sentence-sense, word-sense, and difference of word-sense', in Steinberg and Jakobovits, 1971, 14–34

WIGGINS, D. (1971b) 'A reply to Mr Alston', in Steinberg and Jakobovits, 1971, 48–52

WINOGRAD, T. (1977) 'Five Lectures on Artificial Intelligence', in Zampolli, 1977, 399–520

WON-DOORNINK, M. J. (1979) 'On Getting to Know You: The Association between the Stage of a Relationship and Reciprocity of Self-Disclosure', *Journal of Experimental Social Psychology*, 15, 229–41

WOODS, W. A. (1977) 'Lunar Rocks in Natural English: Explorations in Natural Language Questions Answering', in Zampolli, 1977, 521–69

WRIGHT, G. H. von (1963) *Norm and Action*. London: Routledge & Kegan Paul

WUNDERLICH, D. (1972a) 'Zur Konventionalität von Sprechhandlungen', in Wunderlich, 1972b, 11–59

WUNDERLICH, D. ed (1972b) *Linguistische Pragmatik*. Frankfurt: Athenäum

WUNDERLICH, D. (1974) *Grundlagen der Linguistik*. Reinbek: Rowohlt

WUNDERLICH, D. (1976) 'Sprachtheorie und Diskursanalyse', in Apel, 1976, 463–88

WUNDERLICH, D. (1977) 'Assertions, Conditional Speech Acts, and Practical Inferences', *Journal of Pragmatics*, 1, 13–46

WUNDERLICH, D. (1978) 'Wie analysiert man Gespräche? Beispiel Wegauskünfte', *Linguistische Berichte*, 58, 41–76

ZAMPOLLI, A. ed (1977) *Linguistic Structure Processing*. Amsterdam: North-Holland

Index

Capitalisation denotes that the term is a technical one. In such cases, reference is often only made to where that term is defined. References are to *pages* throughout.